William Mullins
Fall, 2019

"In recent years, intense research has been directed at Christological and trinitarian themes with exciting and insightful results. *Jesus in Trinitarian Perspective* is on the cutting edge of this research because it is the only volume to approach these themes in a multidisciplinary perspective. Faithful to Scripture and Chalcedon yet creative and fresh, Sanders and Issler have given the church a theologically rich and devotionally practical guide to the person and work of Christ. Pastors and informed laypeople will profit greatly from this book. Moreover, it would be my first choice as a text in Christology."

J. P. Moreland (Ph.D., University of Southern California), Distinguished Professor of Philosophy, Biola University, and author of Philosophical Foundations for a Christian Worldview *(2003) and* Kingdom Triangle *(2007)*

"The study of Jesus Christ is obviously important to all Christians. However, it is not obvious that he must be understood in light of the Trinity. We must reflect upon Jesus' life and ministry in relationship to God, the Father, if we are rightly to appreciate and apply what Scripture says about him. Likewise, we need to consider the person and work of the Holy Spirit throughout Jesus' life. *Jesus in Trinitarian Perspective* helps Christians to understand and appreciate the importance of the Trinity in considering Jesus—the life he lived, the salvation he provided, and the role model for how we should live and minister. The book provides clear-cut axioms for investigating the dynamics and significance of Jesus' relationship to the Father and the Holy Spirit. Christians will benefit greatly from the variety of ways *Jesus in Trinitarian Perspective* explores who Jesus is, especially in light of who he is in relationship to God the Father and the Holy Spirit.

Don Thorsen (Ph.D., Drew), Professor of Theology, Haggard Graduate School of Theology, Azusa Pacific University, and author of An Invitation to Theology: Exploring the Full Christian Tradition

JESUS

IN

TRINITARIAN

PERSPECTIVE

AN INTERMEDIATE CHRISTOLOGY

JESUS
IN
TRINITARIAN
PERSPECTIVE

Foreword

FRED SANDERS
& KLAUS ISSLER

FOREWORD BY GERALD BRAY

ACADEMIC

NASHVILLE, TENNESSEE

We dedicate this book to

John Landers

upon his retirement as

Academic Acquisitions and Project Editor

For his commitment to the body of Christ

through his ministry at

Broadman & Holman Publishers

(1992–2007)

and

For his gracious personal involvement in

bringing this book to publication

CONTENTS

Foreword—Gerald Bray   ix

Chapter 1   Introduction to Christology
                   Chalcedonian Categories for the Gospel Narrative   1
                   Fred Sanders

Part 1

The Person of Christ

Chapter 2   *The Eternal Son of God in the Social Trinity*   44
                   J. Scott Horrell

Chapter 3   *The One Person Who Is Jesus Christ*
                   The Patristic Perspective   80
                   Donald Fairbairn

Chapter 4   *One Person, Two Natures*
                   Two Metaphysical Models of the Incarnation   114
                   Garrett J. DeWeese

Part 2

The Work of Christ

Chapter 5   *Christ's Atonement*
                   A Work of the Trinity   156
                   Bruce A. Ware

Chapter 6   *Jesus' Example*
                   Prototype of the Dependent, Spirit-Filled Life   189
                   Klaus Issler

Axioms for Christological Study   226
Abbreviations   229
Contributors   231
Name Index   233
Subject Index   237
Scripture Index   240

FOREWORD

No subject is more central to the Christian faith than the doctrine of Christ, which is set in the context of the doctrine of the Trinity. Whether these are two doctrines or one is hard to say; certainly, one could not exist without the other. In the early centuries of the Christian church, theologians and controversialists battled out the parameters required to express this teaching adequately. In the words of the Quicunque vult (Athanasian Creed): "For like as we are compelled by the Christian verity to acknowledge every Person by himself to be God and Lord; So are we forbidden by the Catholic religion to say; There are three Gods or three Lords." The "Christian verity" is the New Testament, which reveals the divinity of Father, Son and Holy Spirit. The "Catholic religion" is the entire Bible, which insists that there is only one God. The result of this double affirmation is the doctrine of the Trinity, which reconciles the New Testament revelation with the whole of Scripture.

The Fathers of the church were never in any doubt about this. They borrowed the language of ancient philosophy and law in order to express their beliefs, but the Bible was always their guide. Formulations that proved inadequate to express its teaching were either rejected or modified until they did. The great achievement of the first four centuries of Christian history was to find a framework capable of accommodating both the divinity of Christ and the oneness of God. Later generations were able to build on this achievement to develop the great theme of atonement and to tie the person and work of the Holy Spirit into the overall picture. Not everyone came on board with every aspect of this development, and there are still some historical divisions that have been stubbornly resistant to all attempts to overcome them. The non-Chalcedonian churches of the East have never accepted the "one person in two natures" formula for expressing the divinity of Christ, nor have the Eastern churches been able to affirm the double procession of the Holy Spirit, that is to say, his procession from the Son as well as from the Father. But Protestant Christians at least are united on these matters, which continue to play an essential part in the construction of our theology.

The contributors to this volume have not been afraid to revisit ancient debates, nor have they hesitated to tease out their implications for our own beliefs and proclamation. They are to be congratulated for their courage and admired for both their learning and their discernment. In this book they speak to the central issues of our faith, and in doing so, they stir us up to greater devotion. "The Word became flesh and dwelt among us," and it was in that flesh that we have seen the glory of God revealed. May he grant us the grace to persevere in our search for greater understanding, and bless both the authors who teach and the readers who learn more about the One who came in the flesh for our salvation.

Gerald Bray
Anglican Professor of Divinity at
Beeson Divinity School of Samford University Birmingham,
Alabama

1

INTRODUCTION TO CHRISTOLOGY
Chalcedonian Categories for the Gospel Narrative

Fred Sanders

Chapter Summary

Christology begins as an intellectual attempt to account for the mystery of salvation that every Christian experiences, but it is a task that demands the labors of biblical, historical, philosophical, systematic, and practical theologians. We are living in an age when contemporary theologians have begun appropriating the conceptual wealth of the great tradition of Christian doctrine, and Christian philosophers are turning their attention to examining the doctrinal content of Christian truth claims. This situation makes possible an interdisciplinary investigation of a new kind. The fourth ecumenical council, Chalcedon (451), is widely accepted as a standard of orthodox thought on Christology, and this chapter briefly explains the logic of Chalcedon. However, Chalcedon raises questions that are answered by the next ecumenical council, Constantinople II (553). This post-Chalcedonian Christology, representing a clarification of Cyrillian insights that were implied but not directly stated at Chalcedon, yields an anhypostatic-enhypostatic Christology. More importantly, it puts the two-natures categories of Chalcedon back into motion by affirming identity between the second person of the Trinity and the person who is the subject of the incarnation, providing the conceptual

1

categories evangelicals need to tell the story of their personal savior the way they need to. He is one of the Trinity, and he died on the cross.

Axioms for Christological Study

1. Christology is an interdisciplinary theological project requiring insight from biblical, historical, philosophical, practical, and systematic theologians.
2. To think rightly about the Trinity, the incarnation, or the atonement, the theologian must think about them all at once, in relation to each other.
3. The good news of Jesus the Savior presupposes the long story of the eternal Son of God's entering into human history, and the doctrinal categories provided by Chalcedon are a helpful conceptual resource for making sense of it.

KEY TERMS

ecumenical council	philosophical theology	historical theology
patristics	biblical theology	practical theology
systematic theology	constructive theology	theanthropic person
hypostatic union	Chalcedonian Definition	person
nature	Cyrillian	Cyril of Alexandria
anathema	dyophysites/diphysitism/ two-nature	anhypostatic/ enhypostatic Christology
Heresies	Arianism Nestorianism	Apollinarianism Eutychian monophysitism
Greek terms	*homoousios* *taxis*	*hypostasis*

C hristology is one of the most difficult doctrines in all of theology, perhaps second only to the doctrine of the Trinity. Since the goal of this book is to explore the theological project of Christology accessibly and at an introductory level, what sense does it make to combine one difficult doctrine with another? Putting Christology into trinitarian perspective sounds like multiplying complexity times complexity, or explaining one unclear thing by another thing even more unclear: *obscurum per obscurius*! For the sake of analytic clarity, it would seem more promising to isolate the doctrine of Christ as strictly as possible from all other considerations and make sense of it on its own terms first. But the thesis of this book, and the conviction of each author, is that the intellectual work of Christology is best undertaken in the context of the doctrine of the Trinity.

Even at the introductory level, trinitarian resources best equip the student of theology to grasp Christian teaching on the incarnation, person, and work of Christ. We could say many things about Jesus and the salvation available through him, but the logic built in to the central Christian truths requires us to confess what the fifth ecumenical council said in the year 553: "that our lord Jesus Christ, who was crucified in his human flesh, is truly God and the Lord of glory and one of the members of the holy Trinity."[1] To say the truth about Jesus, we must keep him in trinitarian perspective and say, with this ancient council, that one of the Trinity died on the cross.

Recognizing Jesus as one of the Trinity is a conceptual breakthrough that throws light on all the great central beliefs of Christianity. The six chapters of this book explore the implications of Jesus' identity as one of the Trinity, tracing the long arc from God's eternal being to humanity's redemption. We begin (insofar as is humanly possible, and strictly on the basis of God's self-revelation) above all worlds in the homeland of the Trinity, with a richly elaborated doctrine of the eternal Trinity as an interpersonal fellowship of structured relations among the perfectly coequal Father, Son, and Holy Spirit (Horrell, chap. 2). From that height we trace the act of infinite condescension in which the preexistent eternal Son of

---

[1] Tanner, "Constantinople II, 553," in *NL*, 118, quoting from Anathema 10. The word *members* is not represented in the Greek text and should not be thought of as a technical term, but was added by the translator to make a smoother English reading.

God becomes the incarnate Son of God by taking on a full human nature. The resulting doctrine of the person of Christ is elaborated with guidance from the church fathers (Fairbairn, chap. 3), and its terms are clarified, disciplined, and disambiguated by analytic philosophy (DeWeese, chap. 4). Because the incarnation took place "for us and for our salvation," as the Nicene Creed states, we complete the trajectory by attending to the way the incarnate Logos accomplished our redemption in his death and resurrection (Ware, chap. 5), and how, as the Son, he is the example of a truly human life of faith, radical dependence on God, and being filled with the Holy Spirit (Issler, chap. 6).

In this introductory chapter, I will do four things. First, I will explain why it takes an interdisciplinary team of authors—three systematicians, a historical theologian, a philosophical theologian, and a practical theologian—to put Jesus into trinitarian perspective and make the case that one of the Trinity died on the cross. Second, I will summarize the classic ground rules laid down in the logic of the fourth ecumenical council's Chalcedonian Definition of 451 for thinking biblically about Jesus: that he is one person in two unmixed, unconfused, undivided natures. Third, I will argue that contemporary Evangelical theology can and should take one step beyond Chalcedon, embracing as well the guidance of the fifth ecumenical council (Constantinople II, 553), which took the decisive step of placing Christology in its proper trinitarian context. Finally, I will summarize the five remaining chapters and give an overview of the way they relate to one another and to the total project of placing Christology in trinitarian perspective.

Saying Everything at Once

A preliminary question may already be forming in the minds of some readers: Why take on such a difficult task as this? Could such an extended theological project possibly be of any assistance for Christians in living faithfully and carrying out the work committed to the church in our time? Or is a detailed book on Christology in trinitarian perspective merely an academic exercise with no bearing on Christians outside the confines of scholarship? Could an argument covering so much doctrinal territory be relevant to the gospel?

Once upon a time, the people most committed to the gospel were the people most inclined to serious theological thought. The deepest doctrines of Christianity, the ones that are not on the surface of the Scriptures but lie waiting in its depths, were quarried through disciplined theological meditation and patient discernment. It was not academics or aesthetes with too much time on their hands who did this work, but busy pastors, suffering martyrs, and bishops overseeing the evangelization of entire cities. As they preached and taught and suffered for the gospel, they worked out the deep logic of the revelation of the Trinity, the incarnation, and redemption. The more seriously they took the life-changing power of the good news, the more concentration they devoted to the details of sound doctrine.

In modern times, things have been different: we take for granted that there must be an absolute divide between vital Christian experience on the one hand and careful doctrinal theology on the other. To us, action and reflection seem mutually exclusive, especially when it comes to Christian faith. The last thing we would expect to find is gospel and theology flowing from the same passionate commitment. But in the long sweep of Christian history, that is how it has usually been, from the church fathers and the scholastics through the Reformers and Puritans. All of them recognized that simple, saving faith could and should be elaborated into the Trinitarianism of Nicaea and the incarnational theology of Chalcedon. It took the crafty liberal theologians of the nineteenth century to popularize the argument that central Christian doctrines were, in Adolf Harnack's words, "a work of the Greek spirit on the soil of the gospel"[2] and a betrayal of the simplicity of Jesus' message. At that time, conservative theologians disagreed. One of the great ironies of modern theological history is that the heirs of those conservatives who opposed high liberalism have become the chief bearers of the Harnackian bias against doctrine. Whenever we assume that the best way to embrace the simple gospel is to eschew the difficulties of doctrine, Evangelicals are unconsciously adopting the position of their historic opponents and standing in contradiction to their own best interests. In doing so, they take themselves out of the very stream of power that made their movement

---

[2] Adolf von Harnack, *History of Dogma* (Boston: Little, Brown, 1907), 1:20.

possible in the first place: the gospel stream of doctrine and devotion that flows from the church fathers to the first fundamentalists. J. I. Packer once defined Evangelicalism as "fidelity to the doctrinal content of the gospel,"[3] counseling Evangelicals not to bypass the "doctrinal content" in the rush to get to a gospel. Fidelity to the gospel requires us to recognize doctrinal content, and those who would preach the gospel must make use of the tools of theology.

Christology is the doctrinal locus where Christianity has the greatest need for theological precision. To be wrong here is to be wrong everywhere. It also happens to be the place where the greatest thinkers in the history of the church have expended the most effort most productively, and have left their achievements as a heritage to contemporary theologians.

Consider the confession "Jesus died for me." Anyone who believes this simple sentence has entered the sphere of Christian faith and has learned the one thing that God is concerned to teach his human creatures in order to bring them into his school for all further lessons. "Jesus died for me" is knowledge that can be grasped by anyone. It is not a truth restricted to the leading intellects of an age, or to scholars with enough leisure time to include theology among their academic pursuits. It is truth that proves itself by its ability to "come to the unlearned, the young, the busy, and the afflicted, as a fact which is to arrest them, penetrate them, and to support and animate them in their passage through life."[4] Yet, because Christian faith does not exhaust itself at the level of simplicity, there are depths in this confession that invite further search and inquiry. The prepositional phrase "for me" is loaded with possible meanings, and the verb *died* is not normally the carrier of good news outside of this strange sentence. And perhaps most important, who is this Jesus, the subject to whom this strangely "good" death happens? This is the crucial question, because only when one knows who Jesus really is can one establish the meaning of *died* and "for me."

By asking these questions, evangelical faith seeks theological understanding, and the project of Christology in trinitarian perspective is an example of that "faith seeking understanding." Christian theology should

---

[3] J. I. Packer, *Fundamentalism and the Word of God* (Grand Rapids: Eerdmans, 1984), 38.
[4] John Henry Newman, *An Essay in Aid of a Grammar of Assent* (1870; repr., Notre Dame: University of Notre Dame Press, 1976), 112–13.

always start out from the gospel story (Jesus died for me) and explore the staggering theological claims that Christians are committing themselves to when they say such things. In particular, this book takes seriously the Christian claim that the person called Jesus is a person who is God, and belongs in the Trinity as the eternal second person. He is "the Son" from the formula "the Father, the Son, and the Holy Spirit" (Matt 28:20), and he is precisely the same one who went to the cross, undergoing and overcoming death for our salvation. The Christian church has confessed this truth since the early centuries, and finally stated it in classical form at the second council of Constantinople with the slogan, "one of the Trinity suffered in the flesh," which might be better paraphrased for modern ears as "one of the Trinity died on the cross." Though the doctrine is biblical, has deep roots in Christian history, and commends itself as reasonable and practical, it has been denied by a variety of modern theologies.[5] Refuting those denials would be a worthwhile task, but the goal of the present book is more constructive, seeking to clarify the doctrine itself for the benefit of those who desire to know what they are believing when they believe.

Something remarkable happens during the passage from simple belief in the gospel to complex theological understanding. When simple faith's straightforward statements are elaborated in fully developed theological systems, theologians are compelled to hold together a vast number of details without losing hold of their original unity. You could say that the one idea of the gospel becomes inwardly complex, and whole regions of doctrine become apparent within it. The assertion that one of the Trinity died on the cross unfolds itself as a series of interconnected claims about the doctrine of the triune God, the preexistence of Christ, the incarnation, the death of Christ, and redemption. Which of these things should be said first, since all of them remain linked together as closely as they were in the simple expression that Jesus died for me? Pity Christian theologians: they have to say everything at once, but they cannot. This tension is probably felt by scholars in a wide variety of nontheological fields, as they try to articulate the details of their subject in light of the whole field, and the whole field in light of all its details. This tension is present in each

---

[5] The most blatant and therefore instructive example remains John Hick, ed., *The Myth of God Incarnate* (Louisville: Westminster/John Knox, 1977).

of the subtopics of theology, such as the doctrine of humanity, where the central idea is a twofold statement: humanity is in God's image and also radically fallen. But even if a theologian leaves aside all the details and only tries to say the one main thing that makes Christian faith what it is, the one main thing includes within itself the three gigantic doctrines of atonement, incarnation, and Trinity.

Though the body of Christian truth is made up of a great many doctrines, perhaps hundreds of them, there are only three great mysteries at the very heart of Christianity: the atonement, the incarnation, and the Trinity. All the lesser doctrines depend on these great central truths, derive their significance from them, and spell out their implications. Each of these three mysteries is a mystery of unity, bringing together things which seem, in themselves, to be unlikely candidates for unification. The Christian doctrine of atonement describes reconciliation between the holy God and fallen man. The Christian doctrine of the incarnation confesses that the complete divine nature and perfect human nature are united in the person of Jesus Christ. The Christian doctrine of the Trinity affirms that the one God exists eternally as three persons: Father, Son, and Holy Spirit.

Furthermore, atonement, incarnation, and Trinity are directly related to one another in a particular way. The good news of salvation is that Jesus Christ accomplished the reconciliation of God and man through his indissoluble life, death, and resurrection (the atonement). To have accomplished such a feat, Jesus Christ must be someone who belongs equally to the divine and human sides, so that his work is grounded in his person. The logic of the gospel compels us to say that to be the Savior, Jesus must be God and man (the incarnation). Once we have seen the divinity of Jesus, it is merely a matter of intellectual consistency to acknowledge that in some way Jesus must be part of the very definition of what it is to be God. The implication, necessary but still surprising, is that the one God includes God the Son who brought salvation, God the Father who sent salvation by sending the Son, and God the Holy Spirit who brings salvation into human experience (the Trinity). The doctrine of the Trinity is the revision of the Old Testament understanding of God made necessary by the gospel revelation of the incarnate Son—though revision in this case cannot mean alteration or even correction, so much as elaboration or expansion. The doctrine of the Trinity grows out of the stunning fact that the Bible, after emphasizing throughout the Old Testament that there is only one God, now in the New Testament reveals that Jesus Christ the incarnate Son is that very God. Thus, to follow the order of discovery, up from our experience of salvation to its presuppositions, atonement requires incarnation, requires Trinity. Or to follow the order of being, down from the most essential presuppositions to their effects, Trinity makes possible incarnation, which makes possible atonement. The whole trip is necessary if one of the Trinity died on the cross.

This book affirms that central theme, and it is the largeness of that center that accounts for the scope of the book. It also accounts for the inclusion of chapters by scholars from a range of theological disciplines. The field of theology is necessarily divided into distinct subdisciplines, if for no other reason than the division of academic labor.[6] Any seminary catalogue shows the traditional way of dividing the field, whether in terms of courses offered or of faculty hired: biblical studies, history, philosophy, systematic theology, and a range of practical or applied disciplines. Each of these, of course, is also subdivided into more manageable fields: biblical studies, for example, into the fields of Hebrew and Greek language study, historical and cultural backgrounds, exegesis, the field called "biblical theology" with its own New Testament and Old Testament distinctions, and so on. While it is always possible for academic specialization to devolve into artificial and overly narrow compartmentalization, there is also a legitimate need for scholars to focus on a manageable subfield, developing expertise in that field's methodologies and mastering its literature. Specialization runs the risk of over-specialization only when a discipline's narrowed focus prevents its practitioners from being able to address certain topics. Reality is bigger than our conventional academic subdivisions, and certain truths loom so large that they span multiple disciplines and require collaborative effort for their investigation. Christology in trinitarian perspective is such a truth, and it calls for systematic, historical, philosophical, and practical study.

---

[6] The most useful history of the development of these subdisciplines is still Edward Farley's *Theologia: The Fragmentation and Unity of Theological Education* (Minneapolis: Fortress, 1983).

9

Accordingly, the authors in this volume are each free to operate according to the standards of their own disciplines and have chosen their subtopics with a view to doing their best work on the part of the task where their discipline is most helpful. One of the benefits of this approach is that the range of dialogue partners is extended, as authors make reference to the literature in their own field of specialty: J. Scott Horrell's presentation of social trinitarianism provides a torrent of footnotes to trinitarian theology in the last few decades; Donald Fairbairn's account of Cyrillian Christology cites patristic primary texts and the latest work in historical theology; Garrett J. DeWeese's proposal for a metaphysical model of the incarnation is developed in conversation with contemporary analytic philosophers of religion; Bruce A. Ware chooses to cite large passages of Scripture in his presentation of the person and work of Christ; and Klaus Issler, in addition to interacting with biblical scholarship, is also conversant with the literature of spiritual formation and child development. In each case, the extensive footnotes function as introductions to the respective theological disciplines of the authors.

While the various theological disciplines are peers, each operating with their own independent and valid methodologies, there is also a kind of normative order to them which is dictated by the one object which they study in common. Because Christianity is based on scriptural revelation, the biblical disciplines have a decisive priority when engaging the content of the faith. As Scripture is absolutely primary, the disciplines that engage it directly are at the front of the line: exegesis and biblical theology. As contemporary thinkers undertake the task of interpreting Scripture, historical theology steps next into line, for these texts and concepts have a history of effects in the interval between their time and ours. Christian theology is a long conversation with Scripture, and historical theology attends to the earlier voices in the conversation. Philosophical theology, understood modestly as the discipline that ensures terms are being used clearly, unambiguously, and consistently, is involved all along the way, but it becomes especially prominent after the biblical and historical scholars have given their account of what Scripture says and what the Christian tradition has thought it says. A more robust kind of philosophical theology does not just clarify terms but also has metaphysical and epistemological commitments that it seeks to coordinate with the revealed truth of Scripture. This kind of philosophical theology shares space (and sometimes disputes turf) with the discipline of systematic theology, whose task is to synthesize exegetical, biblical, and historical theology in order to restate it in contemporary terms. Biblical and historical theologies can limit their projects to careful descriptive work in a historical past tense, but at the level of systematic theology, truth claims must be phrased in the present tense. Last in line, logically speaking, are a host of practical disciplines such as ethics, homiletics, counseling, Christian education, spiritual formation, and apologetics. These fields begin their work in a receptive mode, taking theological truth and applying it to current events, the life of the church, and actual people.

This schematic account of the order of the theological disciplines is a sketch that could probably start a real faculty brawl at most good schools of theology. While it is not quite fair to the boundaries of any of the disciplines, it serves as a good first statement of the chain of command among the disciplines. I say "first statement" because as soon as all the fields are present and accounted for, the disciplines, which are downstream, so to speak, begin to exert pressure on the disciplines which are upstream. Just because homiletics is toward the end of the line, for example, does not mean that it is merely passive in its reception of Christian thought. If a doctrine comes down the line which in the final analysis is simply unpreachable, it is a good sign that something has gone wrong upstream. A theology that gives rise to a spirituality, which nobody can live out, is a highly suspect theology, however good its biblical, traditional, and logical credentials may claim to be. We cannot switch our doctrines to whatever happens to work, but we can take dysfunction as an indicator that our previous conclusions need to be revisited. Such back-loops are in evidence everywhere in the theological disciplines. Indeed, the seed of the present book lay in a conversation between a philosophical theologian (DeWeese) and a practical theologian (Issler) as they puzzled over what the Christian tradition could possibly have meant when it declared at the sixth ecumenical council that Jesus Christ had two wills, one human and the other divine. The philosopher found that he could not simply do his job of clarifying these terms, because the clearer they became the less coherent they seemed. The practical theologian found himself unable to square the doctrine with another doctrine, the teaching that Christ is our example of a true human life. Together they decided they needed to move upstream and check their work, not simply accepting the traditional claim, but inquiring into its sources, criteria, and meaning. When they did, as is usually the case with such back-loops, they were asking new questions and finding new evidence which then reentered the normal flow.[7] Evidently it is just as important for theologians to dabble in each other's fields as it is for them to respect the boundary markers and dig deep in their own fields.

In Christology and trinitarian theology in particular, the disciplines are aligned in roughly the way described above. For example, consider the way the technical terminology functions. From biblical evidence it is clear that there are unities, dualities, and a triad that must be accounted for in telling the gospel story. The unities involved are, among others, the one God of Hebrew monotheism, and the one person who is our Lord Jesus Christ. The most important duality is the humanity of Christ on the one hand and his divinity on the other. The triad is Father, Son, and Holy Spirit. At the level of exegesis and also of biblical theology, there is a great deal of flexibility in how this one, two, and three are to be described, but any account of the gospel story which does not feature some sort of placeholder for this one, two, and three is simply not right. Scripture does not go much further than this, and the biblical disciplines have other work to do. At the level of historical theology, the descriptive options narrow quite sharply, and the Christian tradition specifies some terminology. What is one in God is his nature or essence or *ousia*; what is one in Jesus Christ is his person or hypostasis; what is two in Christ are his natures; what is three in God are persons, and so on. At this point, one sort of systematic or doctrinal theology could be quite satisfied with its ability to answer questions: God is three persons in one nature, and one of these persons took to himself a different nature, an assumed human nature. The result is one divine person, one of the three persons, with two natures, one of which is identical with the one nature of God. The whole account would function just as well no matter what terms are used, so

---

[7] They also discovered that the kind of dyotheletism they found unacceptable is not quite the kind of dyotheletism taught at the sixth council. For the full discussion, see pp. 125–35.

long as they are used consistently. If asked, "Does the incarnate Logos have one 'glorph,' or two?" the biblical theologian would simply point out that Scripture does not talk about glorphs directly. But the systematic theologian could respond by asking whether a glorph belongs to person or to nature. If glorph is person, Jesus has one; if glorph is nature, Jesus has two. The theologian would even be in a position to anathematize the heretical diglorphites, or condemn the error of the execrable monoglorphites. He could be right, without even knowing what he meant. Ask him what a glorph is, and he can reply: What Jesus had one or two of.

All of this is as silly as it sounds, and unworthy of the name theology. All the disciplines rise up in revolt against it: the historical theologian wants to know what the tradition meant by what it said; the philosophical theologian has a lively interest in it now; and the practical theologian is eager to apply it to life. Whatever the dispute was about (wills, glorphs, energies, a soul), theology would not stop at the level of moving ciphers around as if Christology were a conceptual game. In addition to its designated task of synthesizing the claims of the other theological disciplines and raising their questions in the present tense, systematic theology also accepts the task of monitoring, managing, and regulating the way the backloops and cross-checks function among the biblical, historical, philosophical, and practical disciplines. And in this sense, systematic theology is a field-encompassing field that needs to mind everybody else's business because it has no business of its own; all must be resolvable into biblical, historical, philosophical, or practical disciplines. The need for systematic theology is most apparent when Christian thinkers confront those central doctrines that loom so large that they sprawl across all the fields and require labor from each.

Chalcedonian Categories

We have seen that the simple, central gospel truths are inwardly complex and quite large in their scope. In order to frame an adequate Christology, we must also take the step of provisionally accepting the conceptual categories which the Christian theological tradition has developed. These categories are Chalcedonian, deriving from their classical statement at the fourth ecumenical council, held at the city of Chalcedon in 451. Here, if anywhere, a sensitive believer is aware of a felt transition from simple faith to conceptual severity. The difference between saying "Jesus is Lord" and saying "the two natures of Christ are hypostatically united without confusion, change, division, or separation" is striking. The transition, however, is not only necessary, but also tremendously helpful, fruitful, and nourishing for Christian faith and understanding.

Consider, for example, how Chalcedonian categories helped a Christian poet express himself. In one of his hymns, Charles Wesley wrote: "O Love divine, what has thou done! The immortal God hath died for me!" This is a bold thing to say, because it claims so much: "God ... died." The Bible itself says it that bluntly in a few places, such as Acts 20:28, "God purchased the church with his own blood."[8] This is how the voice of faith speaks when it confesses what God has done. This is a good Christian sentence. When theologians get hold of stark, paradoxical statements like "God died," they have an instinct to clarify what is being said. They do not want to remove the shock or the force (that would be very bad theology), but they do want to make sure that the true paradox rather than something else is being communicated. They want to rule out misunderstandings that either take away the shock, or substitute for it the fake shock of logical incoherence.

For example, it is possible to think "God died" means something like, "just as there is a human death for humans to die, there is apparently a divine death for God to die, and that is what happened at Calvary." But the analogy is nonsense. Death is a concept that only works inside of the context of a creation. You need finite, contingent existence to have its eclipse or dissolution in death. "Divine death" as the analogue of "human death" is probably not even a coherent idea. It seems to belong to the category of "neat tricks you can do with language," by combining any adjective with any noun: square circle, blue height, quiet toddler, cold heat, divine death. When you remove the chimera of a properly divine death, you can see that "God died" means that God experienced the only kind of death there is to experience, and that is creaturely death. How could that have happened? This is precisely where Chalcedonian categories come into

---

[8] My own translation, in agreement with KJV, NASV, ESV, and others. NRSV, NET, and others opt for "the blood of his own Son," taking the genitive construction as possessive rather than attributive.

play, and rather than stripping away the poetic power of Wesley's words, the incarnational theology of Chalcedon, so to speak, put the poetry into the poetry. According to the Chalcedonian explication of the incarnation, the Son of God took into personal union with himself a complete human nature, and thus existed as one theanthropic (divine and human) person. He did not cease to be God, but he took up human nature into hypostatic (personal) union with himself. He made that humanity his own, and in that appropriated humanity he appropriated real human death. He died the only death there is to die, our death.

It is worth noticing, by the way, that in stating the incarnation in this way we have implied one of its presuppositions, the doctrine of the Trinity. In the sentence "God died," the subject, "God," has to mean "the second person of the Trinity, God the Son." Each of the three persons is God, but they are distinct persons standing in interpersonal relationship to one another. The Son is not one third of God, or the Son part of God, or the nice version of God, but just God. God (the Father) so loved the world that he gave his only Son, and thus God (the Son, one of the Trinity) died on the cross. Chalcedon already provides us with Christology in trinitarian perspective, and makes no sense without presupposing the Trinity.

So with all the elaborate distinctions in place, the sentence "God died" can also be said in this longer form: "The eternal second person of the Trinity, God the Son, took into personal union with himself, without confusing it, changing it, dividing it or separating it from his eternal divine nature, a complete human nature through which he experienced death." It is no surprise that Charles Wesley did not set that longer sentence to music. On the other hand, there is no doubt that the longer sentence is precisely what he meant by the shorter one. To the suggestion that he could have meant anything else by it, Charles Wesley would have replied that, being an orthodox Christian and no heretic, he could not possibly have intended anything else.[9] Furthermore, there is no trickery and no sleight of hand in that expanded paraphrase of "God died." The longer

---

[9] Charles Wesley did occasionally try to put densely theological formulations into verse; for example, in an entire volume of hymns on the Trinity. For Wesley's doctrinal sophistication and orthodoxy, see the essays in *Charles Wesley: Poet and Theologian*, ed. S. T. Kimbrough Jr. (Nashville: Abingdon, 1992).

sentence is what the shorter sentence means, and both sentences are true precisely insofar as they mean each other.

Still, a temptation does lurk here. The temptation is to feel disappointed by the longer, Chalcedonian sentence, as if something has been taken away, dissolved into too many distinctions, or spun into insubstantial refinement. The danger lies in hearing the longer sentence as if it meant, "Half of a third of God had a bad weekend." But that is not what it means. It means that God died, and it means it in the only way that Christian theology can possibly mean it. The trick is to hear the longer sentence as meaning the same thing as the shorter sentence, and not to feel cheated by it. The trick is never to hear that third sentence ("half of a third of God . . .") echoing behind the others in your mind. Only the conceptual categories of Chalcedonianism, taken together with their proper trinitarian context, can banish such unworthy notions from Christian theology and doxology. This set of distinctions has always functioned within Christian thought to enable it to retain the power and precision of the longer and shorter sentences, the immediate utterance of the believing heart and the accuracy of the catechized understanding. God did not take the easy way out, or save us in a way that leaves him untouched by the depth of human suffering. We can be confident that the Almighty One went to the uttermost limits to accomplish our rescue. God died on the cross! Charles Wesley certainly knew the value of the incarnational and trinitarian conceptual framework, because when he sang "O Love divine, what has thou done! The immortal God hath died for me!" he immediately paraphrased it in terms of the second person of the Trinity's vicarious action on our behalf: "The Father's coeternal Son bore all my sins upon the tree."

The broad outlines of Christology's Chalcedonian categories are easy to discern, and anybody who speaks of Christ as one person in two natures is already operating according to these guidelines, broadly speaking. But it is worth taking a moment to rehearse the specific judgments rendered by these councils in the time of the undivided (or at least less divided) church. The ecumenical councils were gatherings of bishops from across the Christian world in the early centuries of the church. Most of them took place in Constantinople: three go by that name; three others happened in cities that were essentially suburbs of Constantinople on the Asian side of the Bosphorus (Nicaea and Chalcedon), leaving only the council of Ephesus on the west coast of Asia Minor (modern Turkey). They are fascinating historical events to study,[10] rich in geopolitical intrigue, forceful personalities, dense argumentation, and intellectual drama. The maneuvering and posturing that went on in some of them, on all sides apparently, is not always an edifying subject of study. No wonder the sixteenth-century Thirty-Nine Articles of Religion of the Church of England said of the ecumenical councils, "forasmuch as they be an assembly of men, whereof all be not governed with the Spirit and word of God, they may err and sometime have erred, even in things pertaining to God." Because of the all-too-human fallibility of the councils, the Anglican confession perfectly expresses the authority that can be conceded to the councils: "Things ordained by them as necessary to salvation have neither strength nor authority, unless it may be declared that they be taken out of Holy Scripture." Seven councils are normally considered ecumenical councils of the undivided church, running from Nicaea in 325 through five others to Nicaea II in 787. After that seventh council, the schism between Eastern and Western churches made fully ecumenical gatherings impossible, which has led the Eastern Orthodox churches to consider the age of the seven councils as closed, while the Roman Catholic church has continued to declare ecumenical councils in a series currently numbering twenty-one. The first four councils, reaching a climax at Chalcedon in 451, have long held a special doctrinal status for Western Christendom, partly because of the completeness of Christological doctrine that the Chalcedonian Definition is believed to have achieved. In the late sixth century, for example, Pope Gregory the Great (c. 540–604) claimed, at least rhetorically, that the sequence Nicaea-Constantinople-Ephesus-Chalcedon had a quasi-canonical status: "Just as the four books of the holy gospel, so also I confess to receive and venerate four councils."[11] The authority of the councils is surely closer to what the Thirty-Nine Articles of Religion claim than it is to what Gregory claims for them, but on any account, theology that

---

[10] Leo Donald Davis, *The First Seven Ecumenical Councils (325–787): Their History and Theology* (Collegeville, MN: Liturgical Press, 1983).

[11] Gregory the Great, Epistle 1, section 24.

knows how to honor its elders ought to make itself intimately familiar with the teachings of the ecumenical councils.

The ecumenical councils were convened to address numerous ecclesiastical issues, from the way bishops were appointed to the date of Easter.[12] But the leading issues were always doctrinal, as the provocation of various heresies forced the church to articulate its beliefs about God and Christ with increasing clarity and sharpness. Indeed, the quickest way to summarize the theological payoff of each of the first four councils is to enumerate the heresies anathematized at each of them: Arianism, Apollinarianism, Nestorianism, and Eutychianism. A slightly fuller account, still abstracting from the histories and protagonists, includes various elements.[13]

First Council: Nicaea I, in the year 325. As all the later councils are at pains to attest, the Council of Nicaea is the most important of the ecumenical councils. The heresy that provoked this epochal council was Arianism, the teaching that the preexistent Logos who took on flesh in the incarnation was not God, but a great and exalted creature. Since he was the Son of God, Arius argued, he must have come into existence from nonexistence, and prior to that he must not have existed. The Arian Christ is certainly a supernatural being, but just as certainly he is not actually divine. Arianism was rejected by the 318 bishops gathered at Nicaea under Emperor Constantine. Because Arius and his supporters were capable of making most scriptural language agree with their doctrine, the orthodox party pressed the extrabiblical term *homoousios* into service, meaning by it that the Son of God is of the same (*homo*) substance (*ousia*) as God the Father, or consubstantial with him. The goal of the Nicene theologians (including the rising generation that included the great Athanasius of Alexandria) was to assert the complete deity of

---

[12] Peter L'Huillier (*The Church of the Ancient Councils: The Disciplinary Work of the First Four Ecumenical Councils* [Crestwood, NY: St. Vladimir's Seminary Press, 1997]) examines the first four councils strictly from the point of view of their decisions about nondoctrinal matters related to polity and ecclesial oversight.

[13] For a fuller account, see Davis, *The First Seven*. For the official records of each council in a highly usable format, see *NL*. Popular summaries by Evangelical theologians include Peter Toon, *Yesterday, Today and Forever: Jesus Christ and the Holy Trinity in the Teaching of the Seven Ecumenical Councils* (Swedesboro, NJ: Preservation Press, 1996) and Gerald Bray, *Creeds, Councils and Christ* (Fean, Rossire, UK: 1984; repr. Christian Focus, 1997).

Jesus Christ in a clear and unequivocal way, which they did by placing this term into the creed that was produced at this council, calling Christ "the Son of God, begotten from the Father, only begotten, that is, from the substance of the Father, God from God, light from light, true God from true God, begotten not made, of one substance (*homoousios*) with the Father . . ." Lying behind this undertaking was a vision of what salvation entails: personal reconciliation with God and participation in God's own life. With that view of soteriology in place, the implicit soteriological axiom driving Nicaea and the entire conciliar theological tradition downstream from it is: *God alone can save.*[14]

Second Council: Constantinople I, in the year 381. The main thing the fathers of the first Council of Constantinople would want us to say about their work is that they reaffirmed the Council of Nicaea. Although the anti-Arian cause had prevailed decisively in the previous council, the middle decades of the fourth century saw the imperial church dominated by Arianism and various forms of semi-Arianism. By 381, however, the Nicene or Athanasian party had regained control; and this council, convened by Emperor Theodosius I, made its first order of business to reassert the creed from the Council of Nicaea. They revised it slightly by extending the article about the Holy Spirit and tightening up the terminology. The creed of 325 had included an anathema against all who teach that "the Son of God is of a different *hypostasis* or *ousia*" from the Father, obviously thinking of *hypostasis* and *ousia* as indicating the same reality. By 381, however, thinkers like the Cappadocian fathers had seen more clearly that a word like *hypostasis* should be reserved for referring to what there are three of in God. It is the faith of Nicaea as revised and extended in the creed of 381 that we commonly call today the Nicene Creed. Aside from this and the extended pneumatological article, along with an anathema against those "fighters against the Spirit," the Pneumatomachians, did Constantinople I teach anything new? It did take a stand against a new heresy, Apollinarianism, which was in some ways a kind of opposite error from Arianism. Apollinarius of Laodicea

---

[14] There is a small library of books about the Council of Nicaea. The best recent work is Lewis Ayres's *Nicaea and Its Legacy: An Approach to Fourth-Century Trinitarian Theology* (Oxford: Oxford University Press, 2006), and John Behr, *The Nicene Faith: Formation of Christian Theology* (Crestwood, NY: St. Vladimir's Seminary Press, 2004).

was a theologian who, beginning with the thought of the eternal Logos who is consubstantial with God the Father, described the incarnation as the Logos operating the physical body of Jesus. The human nature of Jesus Christ, on the Apollinarian account, was only a human body with no rational soul. Where you and I have rational souls, Jesus Christ had the eternal Logos. This "God in a bod" Christology has the obvious defect of recognizing the full deity of Christ at the expense of his full humanity. Apollinarianism was anathematized in the first canon of the council. Against Apollinarianism, the fathers of Constantinople had to confess the full humanity of Christ in a new, clear, and soteriologically relevant way. Behind the rejection of Apollinarianism was a vision of salvation represented by the soteriological axiom: "What is not assumed is not healed."[15] This axiom, articulated by Gregory of Nazianzus (who chaired part of the proceedings), presupposes that the Son of God saved humanity by "taking on" or "assuming" human nature into union with himself. Everything in human nature needs to be saved, so everything must be taken into union with Christ. In this light, if Christ had no human soul, the human soul is left unredeemed. It is worth noting the way Constantinople I argues for a scriptural teaching by using a new line of argument not directly advanced by the Bible itself.

Taken together, Nicaea I and Constantinople I establish, using new terms and new lines of argument, the full divinity and the full humanity of Christ. In both cases, the councils do this not as a speculative exercise, but under the guidance of soteriological axioms that trace the logic of redemption in Christ: *God alone can save us,* and *what is not assumed is not healed.* Already with the first two councils we have the full vertical reach of salvation, from God above all the way to humanity below. To say this much is already to say that Christ is of one essence with the Father by nature, and condescends to become of one essence with humanity by grace. He therefore, this one person, has both essences. Here in the fourth century, two-natures Christology has begun to emerge in the argument over salvation at these first two councils, though without the clarifying terminology that Chalcedon will bring. After Constantinople I, the ultimate terms of divinity and humanity

---

[15] Gregory of Nazianzus, "To Cledonius the Priest Against Apollinarius," in Edward R. Hardy, ed., *Christology of the Later Fathers*, LCC (Philadelphia: Westminster, 1954), 218.

were no longer in dispute. All subsequent parties would agree to them, and the question shifted to the way God and humanity in Christ, or, more formally, how the deity and humanity of Christ, are related.

Third Council: Ephesus, in the year 431. The heresy of Nestorianism provoked the third council, and Cyril of Alexandria (d. 444) was the key theologian at this council and the guiding spirit of the next two councils as well. There is a perennial question about whether Nestorius himself was a Nestorian. But for the sake of getting to the theological pay-off of the council, it is enough to describe Nestorianism as the type of Christological heresy that declares such a strict distinction between the divinity and humanity of Christ that it treats the two natures as separable. One of the many places this error becomes manifest is in the question of who Mary gave birth to. Nestorius had scruples about saying that Mary had carried and given birth to God (such that she could be called *Theotokos*, God-bearer), preferring instead a term he considered more precise and pious, *Christotokos*, Christ-bearer. Cyril discerned underneath this squeamishness a view of Christ which thought far too disjunctively about his human nature and his divine nature, as if they were two distinct persons within the one Christ. Nestorius had clear ideas about the difference between the human and the divine but seemed to be at a loss to account for how these two are unified in Christ. The one person who is Jesus Christ seems to be, for Nestorianism, the result of the incarnation or a way of talking about what these two vastly different entities, God the Son and the man Jesus, are doing together. Cyril's one central insight cut through this confusion: the eternal Logos, who existed before all ages and was consubstantial with the Father, is the active subject who takes on a perfect human nature. He, the hypostasis of the Logos, is the one who comes to be born of Mary and to die on the cross, and because he never ceases to be homoousios with the Father (he is God, having divine nature) or homoousios with his mother (he is human, having human nature), anything that can be said of one of his natures can be said about him, the Logos Jesus Christ. Behind this concern we may still see the Nicene soteriological axiom that *God alone can save us*, but it has taken on a more precise meaning with Cyril. For the sake of salvation, Cyril knew that the subject who undertakes all the acts of the incarnation must be the person of the Son.

Fourth Council: Chalcedon, in the year 451. Just as fourth-century Christology saw both an Arianism, which could not confess the deity of Christ, and an Apollinarianism, which could not confess his humanity, fifth-century Christology saw a swing from Nestorianism, which could not confess the hypostatic union of the two natures, and a Eutychianism, which could not confess their distinction. Eutychians (again treating the title as an ideal type of heresy)[16] certainly knew that divinity and humanity were not the same thing. But the miracle of the incarnation, and a virulent anti-Nestorian impulse, led them to view the result of the incarnation as the mixing of the two natures into the new nature of the incarnate Christ, a nature both divine and human. The Eutychians who were the subject of the fourth council's anathemas believed themselves to be loyal adherents of Cyril's theology, but they are best viewed as pushing the Cyrillian insight to a drastic extreme. Against this error, the fathers of Chalcedon anathematized "those who imagine a mixture or confusion of the two natures of Christ" and also "those who, first idly talk of the natures of the Lord as 'two before the union' and then conceive but one 'after the union.'" The mixing of the two natures imagined by Eutychianism does not produce a third substance equally identifiable as divine and human. Because divinity is infinitely larger than humanity, the result of the Eutychian mixing of natures is not an even compound but a mostly divine Christ. What soteriological motive lay behind Chalcedon's rejection of Eutychianism? This mixed-nature hypostasis after the incarnation, with an overpowering divinity more apparent than its submerged human nature, has some similarities to the Christ of Apollinarianism, at least insofar as an encounter with it is so directly an encounter with God that the

---

[16] It is clear enough that Eutyches himself was Eutychian, that is, that he viewed the divine and human natures as mingling and merging. But the description of this position that is built into Western histories of dogma is the term monophysitism, which is problematized by the ongoing existence of some ancient non-Chalcedonian churches today that are confessionally monophysite or miaphysite, yet do not commit the doctrinal errors described here. For the remarkable way the political, cultural, linguistic, and terminological situation has developed, see Dorothea Wendebourg, "Chalcedon in Ecumenical Discourse," *PE* 7 (1998): 307–32.

human element seems to undergo an eclipse. C. FitzSimons Allison has tried to capture this by calling Eutychianism the "religious withering of humanity."[17]

With Chalcedon, not only are the full scope of true divinity and true humanity in place, but also two opposite errors for how they can be related to each other in the hypostatic union are on the table. Through the first four councils, the fathers have faced all the hard questions and seen instances of most major mistakes that can be made. That hard-won clarity is part of what gives the Chalcedonian Definition its classic status as a balanced and far-sighted document. Consider the way the central section recapitulates more than a century of theological controversy and clarification:

> He was begotten before the ages from the Father as regards his divinity, and in the last days the same for us and for our salvation from Mary, the virgin God-bearer, as regards his humanity; one and the same Christ, Son, Lord, only-begotten, acknowledged in two natures which undergo no confusion, no change, no division, no separation; at no point was the difference between the natures taken away through the union, but rather the property of both natures is preserved and comes together into a single person and a single subsistent being . . .

Chalcedon does not solve every possible problem or offer extended metaphysical accounts of all its vocabulary. It does not even raise the host of psychological questions that fascinate us moderns. But it does accomplish a great deal. Perhaps the best metaphor for what Chalcedon accomplishes is that it provides definite boundaries on four sides (see figure 1.1, "Chacedonian Box"): on the top, it affirms Nicaea I (contra Arianism) by demanding that Christ is God, consubstantial with the Father. On the bottom, it affirms Constantinople I (contra Apollinarianism) by demanding that Christ is human, consubstantial with us. The soteriological axioms "God alone can save us" and "what is not assumed is not healed" mark out these boundaries. As for how

---

[17] C. FitzSimons Allison, *The Cruelty of Heresy: An Affirmation of Christian Orthodoxy* (New York: Morehouse, 1992), chap. 8.

Figure 1.1
"Chalcedonian Box"

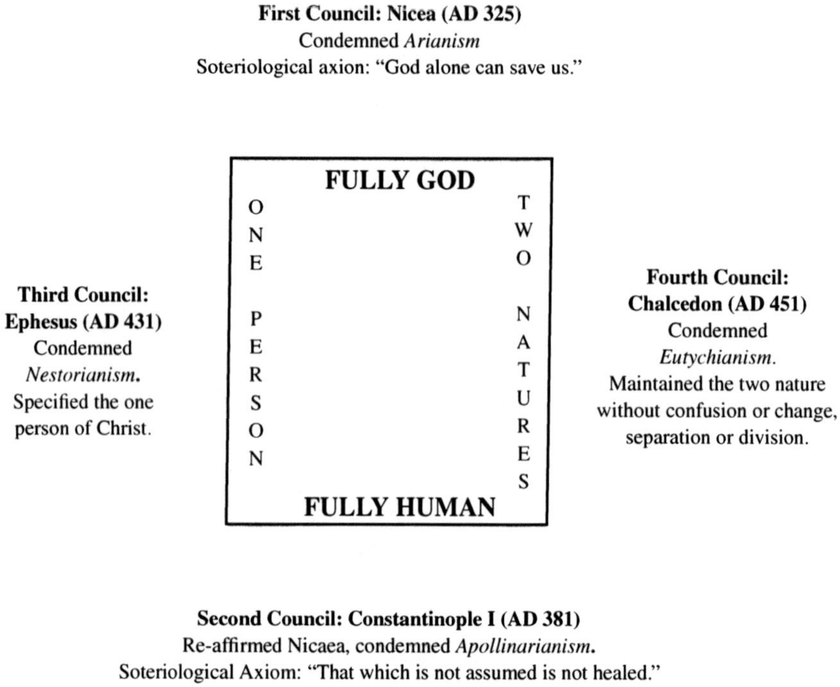

First Council: Nicea (AD 325)
Condemned *Arianism*
Soteriological axion: "God alone can save us."

Third Council: Ephesus (AD 431) Condemned *Nestorianism.* Specified the one person of Christ.

FULLY GOD

O N E P E R S O N

T W O N A T U R E S

FULLY HUMAN

Fourth Council: Chalcedon (AD 451) Condemned *Eutychianism.* Maintained the two nature without confusion or change, separation or division.

Second Council: Constantinople I (AD 381)
Re-affirmed Nicaea, condemned *Apollinarianism.*
Soteriological Axiom: "That which is not assumed is not healed."

the divine and human elements come together, Chalcedon marks out the right and the left with its four mighty negatives: no confusion and no change on the one hand (contra Eutychianism), but no division and no separation on the other (contra Nestorianism). In Christ, God and humanity neither merge nor diverge. In Christ, God and humanity are hypostatically united, and one of the Trinity dies our death on the cross, to rise again for us and our salvation. This is the way the Chalcedonian categories serve the gospel story. But one more thing is needed.

One Step Beyond Chalcedon: The Fifth Council

It is one thing to say that Chalcedon draws boundaries that mark the limits within which orthodox thinking on the incarnation can take place; but it is another thing to say that this is *all* Chalcedon does, emphasizing the negative, neutral, and empty character of the definition. The conventional wisdom of modern theology has usually treated Chalcedon in the latter way, as a self-canceling exercise in manipulating the conceptual categories of nature and person. It is fashionable among those who consider Chalcedon worth investigating (never mind those who do not) to think of the definition as having played itself out with its dialectical self-negations, so that now it serves as a venerable historical landmark and an invitation to do something new.

If the two natures (divine and human) and the four negatives (no confusion, no change, no division, no separation) mark the edges of the field, is there anything in the center, or is that the free zone for novelty and creativity in theological work today? I believe there is something already there at the center and that the Chalcedonian boundaries were established by the ecumenical councils in an awareness of what was at the center. When the bishops gathered at the councils, their tradition was to set up the book of the gospels in the seat of authority, and after Nicaea, the top item on the agenda of each subsequent council was to reaffirm the faith of Nicaea. At the center of the open space marked out by the boundaries of Chalcedon are two things: the apostolic narrative of the life, death, and resurrection of Jesus Christ; and the confession that this person in the gospel stories is an eternal person distinct from the Father, yet fully divine. What stands in the middle of the Chalcedonian categories is the biblical story of Jesus, interpreted in light of the Trinity. If we find the gospel and the Trinity stationed inside the Chalcedonian boundaries, what is it that we as theologians and Christians are supposed to do with them?

If Chalcedonian logic is correct, so far as it goes, then it requires us to take the next step. However, the "step beyond Chalcedon" that I am advocating is not the sheer backwards jump of a return to the

Bible—though that will be necessary and fruitful with the lessons learned from conciliar Christology. It is also not a sheer forward jump to new theological construction—though opportunities are likely there as well. Instead, the step beyond Chalcedon that I am advocating goes directly along the trajectory we have already been following and is nothing more than another step along the road of conciliar Christology, from the fourth council to the fifth. Furthermore, the step taken by the fifth council is itself not a new departure, and does not posit any new information beyond what is implicit in the Chalcedonian Definition. What Constantinople II (553) does is make explicit and thematic once again the trinitarian theology that has been the background of the four previous councils. It does this in three ways: (1) by bringing together Christological and trinitarian terminology, (2) by giving priority to the person in Christology, (3) and by telling the long story of salvation. We will return to these three ways of accomplishing the unification after a brief sketch of the council's work.

Trinitarian theology has been the background of the Christology of the ecumenical councils all along, and Christoph Schwöbel argues that this should have clued in theologians on the way Chalcedonian concepts were intended to work: "The fact that the clarification of trinitarian logic of the Christian understanding of God preceded the attempt at defining the boundaries of orthodox Christology should be seen as an important hint that elucidation of the doctrine of Christ necessarily presupposes the trinitarian understanding of God as its basis."[18] Consider the fact that the first thing the Nicene theologians had to do was make statements which straddle the line between Christology and the doctrine of the Trinity. To which category should we assign the confession, "Jesus is *homoousios* with the Father"? It is simultaneously Christology and trinitarianism, or better, it is Christology in trinitarian perspective. Brian Daley has issued a salutary warning that

> "Trinitarian theology" and "Christology" are modern
> terms, not ancient ones, and represent tracts in the theo-
> logical curriculum of the modern Western university rather

---

[18] Christoph Schwöbel, "Christology and Trinitarian Thought," in *Trinitarian Theology Today: Essays on Divine Being and Act*, ed. Christoph Schwöbel for the Research Institute in Systematic Theology, Kings College London (Edinburgh: T&T Clark, 1995), 121.

than categories of patristic discussion. Both of them are really about one thing: the distinctively Christian understanding of how God is related to the world and to history; how God can be both transcendent Mystery—ultimate, infinite, free of creaturely limitations, uncircumscribed by human thought—and also "Emmanuel," God-with-us, God personally encountered in Jesus, God speaking today in the scriptures and in the church.[19]

So the ecumenical councils were working both doctrines at once, for they were engaging the whole matrix of Christian thought at the level of the primal unities where the doctrines of God, Christ, and salvation are all mutually implicated.

Emperor Justinian convoked the fifth council, Constantinople II (553). Its main order of business was to reaffirm all that had been taught at previous councils, beginning with the teaching of Nicaea I and proceeding through Chalcedon. However, the participants at Constantinople II were especially concerned to reaffirm Chalcedon in a way that guarded it against misinterpretations. Because Chalcedon had clearly excluded radical Eutychianism and clearly distinguished between the divine and human natures, it had become possible for some thinkers to misinterpret the Chalcedonian Definition as teaching a form of Nestorian doctrine. For this reason, the heresy especially anathematized at Constantinople II is not a new one, but simply Nestorianism again, and the false teachers condemned were not church leaders actively propagating their doctrines at the time but writings from the past called the Three Chapters. The documents of the council report how the bishops in attendance listened to a reader rehearsing the teaching of Theodore of Mopsuestia:

> When all the blasphemies in his works were exposed, we were astonished at God's patience, that the tongue and mind which had formed such blasphemies were not straightaway burned up by divine fire. We would not even have allowed the official reader of these blasphemies to

---

[19] Brian E. Daley, "'One Thing and Another': The Persons in God and the Person of Christ in Patristic Theology," *PE* 15 (2006): 42.

continue, such was our fear of the anger of God at even a rehearsal of them (since each blasphemy was worse than the one before in the extent of its heresy and shook to their foundation the minds of their listeners), if it had not been the case that those who reveled in these blasphemies seemed to us to require the humiliation which their exposure would bring upon them. All of us, angered by the blasphemies against God, burst into attacks and anathemas against Theodore, during and after the reading, as if he had been living and present there.[20]

The blasphemies under consideration were similar to those of Nestorius, for by this time Theodore was recognized as the father of Nestorianism. Constantinople II published a series of anti-Nestorian anathemas in order to ensure that Nestorian ideas could find no shelter under the Chalcedonian Definition.

What positive soteriological insight was the motivating force at this council? The answer is simple: Cyril's insight, as stated at Ephesus (431), is that the active subject of the incarnation is the eternal Logos. If Chalcedon could be misinterpreted in a Nestorianizing direction, then Cyril's Christology would be marginalized, and much of the debate at this council was between a group of strict Cyrillians who emphasized the unity of the hypostasis of the hypostatic union and a group of dyophysites who emphasized the distinctness of the two natures in the union and worried about Cyril's influence. The day belonged, however, to the bishops who believed that Chalcedon and Cyril should go together, supporting each other and speaking with one voice. In the words of G. N. C. Frank, these bishops "argued for the inner cohesiveness of Cyril's thought and the Council's intention. These Cyrillian Chalcedonians represented the majority of bishops at Chalcedon . . . Finally in 553 at the Council of Constantinople [II], however, it was this Cyrillian Chalcedonianism which prevailed."[21]

---

[20] Tanner, "Constantinople II, 553," *NL,* 109. See also, Fairbairn's calmer presentation (pp. 93–94, below).

[21] G. L. C. Frank, "The Council of Constantinople II as a Model Reconciliation Council," *TS* 52 (1991): 644–45.

"Cyrillian Chalcedonianism" (or for that matter "Chalcedonian Cyrillism") is a mouthful, but it is what the fathers of Constantinople II meant when they confessed, "we accept the four holy synods, that is, of Nicaea, of Constantinople, the first of Ephesus, and of Chalcedon. Our teaching is and has been all that they have defined concerning the one faith."[22] In one sense, the accomplishment of the fifth council is purely conservative, gathering up the preceding tradition and declaring it to be one coherent teaching. But in another sense the fifth council represents progress beyond Chalcedon because it argues that the right way to interpret Chalcedon is in a broader Cyrillian context. That means that a strategic doctrinal emphasis on the distinction of the two natures of Christ must be situated within a primary commitment to the doctrine of the Trinity, and the resulting confession that the second hypostasis of the Trinity is the personal center of the hypostatic union. We said above that the positive theological achievement of the fifth council was to make explicit and thematic once again the trinitarian theology that has been the background of all orthodox Christology. We also mentioned three ways it did this: by bringing Christological and trinitarian terminology together, by giving priority to the person in Christology, and by telling the long story of salvation. These three moves flow naturally from each other.

Constantinople II issued fourteen anathemas that begin (rather oddly, until one sees the logic of the entire project) by reaffirming the doctrine of the Trinity. Nobody was denying the doctrine of the Trinity in the debates around the council, so the most likely reason for reaffirming it in the first anathema is simply to state up front the technical language. The fifth council brings together Christological and trinitarian uses of the word *person* in order to make clear that the person on the cross is the Son of God; the second person of the Trinity is the one person of the incarnation.[23] Everything hangs on the univocal use of *person* in the two contexts, as is appropriate for a theological project committed to Cyril's

---

[22] Tanner, "Constantinople II (553)" *NL*, 113.

[23] Brian E. Daley points out the connection between a strong statement of threeness in God and a strong statement of unity in Christ: "The more ancient authors emphasize the complex personal unity of Christ as the agent of salvation, the more they are forced to acknowledge the irreducible threeness of God, even to the point of having to conceive of Father, Son, and Holy Spirit as in some way ontologically ranked or subordinated, as sharing in the divine reality in differing degrees of fullness" ("One Thing and Another," 21).

insight into the identity of the incarnate one. Granting priority to the person of the incarnation forces the next move, which is to reintroduce the long story-arc of the incarnation, beginning in heaven and tracing the long descent from the Son's eternal begetting to his birth from the virgin Mary. This restoration of the trinitarian background of the long story-arc of descent and incarnation accounts for the pride of place given, in the second anathema, to the "two nativities" of the Word of God, "that which is before all ages from the Father, outside of time and without a body, and secondly that nativity of these latter days when the Word of God came down from the heavens and was made flesh."[24] Thus the clear categories of Chalcedon, with their tough logic articulating how the divine and human natures of Christ do and do not relate, are given life and sense by the doctrine of the Trinity, the priority of the person, and the long story of Christ's descent from heaven.

The powerful theology of the fifth ecumenical council has suffered from neglect, misunderstanding, and misrepresentation throughout the history of the church, but especially in Western theology during the modern period. When this theology has been taught at all, it has been taught poorly. But a retrieval of this council's theology is now underway, for a variety of reasons. In the above presentation, I emphasize the arguments made in the council itself, quoting its acts and anathemas. There is, however, a shorthand way of describing the heart of this council's theology; although couched in technical terms not used at the council itself, this description is worth introducing because it is the standard way of referring to fifth-council theology and because of its real explanatory value. I am referring to the anhypostatic/enhypostatic Christology. This terminology, derived from Leontius,[25] is not utterly opaque if one is

---

[24] Tanner, "Constantinople II (553)," in *NL*, 114.

[25] Or from another Leontius; the doctrine actually involves both Leontius of Byzantium and Leontius of Jerusalem, and there has been considerable argument in the past century over how the terminology is to be derived and applied. For an overview and reconstruction, see the excellent article by Dennis M. Ferrara, "'Hypostatized in the Logos': Leontius of Byzantium, Leontius of Jerusalem and the Unfinished Business of the Council of Chalcedon," *LS* 22 (1997): 311–27. The argument is extended in U. M. Lang, "Anhypostatos-Enhypostatos: Church Fathers, Protestant Orthodoxy, and Karl Barth," *JTS* 49 (1998): 630–57. Both Ferrara and Lang refute the overly scrupulous article by F. LeRon Shults, "A Dubious Christological Formula: From Leontius of Byzantium to Karl Barth," *TS* 57 (1996): 431–46, which has little merit in itself beyond casting "dubious" over the discussion, but which did provoke some very clear and helpful reconstructions. Whatever is historically demonstrable about the origin

already alert to the prevalence and importance of the word *hypostasis* in patristic Christology so far. If, as the theology of the fifth council argues, the eternal hypostasis of the Son takes to himself a perfect and complete human nature, what is the status of that human nature? Normally, any instantiation of human nature that we come into contact with is also a human person.

Is the human nature of Christ, therefore, also a human person? The Christology we are considering gives a twofold answer. On the one hand, the human nature of Jesus Christ is in fact a nature joined to a person, and therefore enhypostatic, or personalized. But the person who personalizes the human nature of Christ is not a created human person (like all the other persons personalizing the other human natures we encounter); rather it is the eternal second person of the Trinity. So the human nature of Christ is personal, but with a personhood from above. Considered in itself, on the other hand, and abstracted from its personalizing by the eternal person of the Son, the human nature of Jesus Christ is simply human nature, and is not personal. The human nature of Christ, therefore, is both anhypostatic (not personal in itself) and enhypostatic (personalized by union with the eternal person of the Son).

Modern theology has usually viewed this doctrine as a problem, and concluded that this is exactly the kind of unacceptable logical blunder one would expect to get into by taking Chalcedon seriously and trying to reconcile it with trinitarianism. In other words, the unacceptable conclusions of the fifth council (caricatured as "the impersonal humanity of Christ," or "Christ is a human being but not a human person," or "Christ is man but not *a* man") are taken as evidence that the Chalcedonian categories were always a bad fit for the Christian message. But medieval theology, from John of Damascus on, actually counted it as a strength and a confirmation of the fruitfulness of the Chalcedonian tradition. One obvious strength of the anhypostatic/ enhypostatic Christology is that it banishes forever the crypto-Nestorian tendency to find in the incarnation, alongside the second person of the

---

of the terminology, the doctrine and its key terms are present in John of Damascus' *De Fide Orthodoxa*, which is a solid beginning point for interaction with late patristic thought. See also Brian E. Daley, "A Richer Union: Leontius of Byzantium and the Relationship of Human and Divine in Christ," *SP* 24 (1991): 239–65.

Trinity undergoing human experiences, another person who is simply human. This shadowy figure lurks at the back of much modern Christology, a man descended from David and born to Mary—we could call him Adam Davidson Ben-Miriam—who somehow had to get out of the way when the eternal Son of God took over his personal existence. Having never existed, this character is stubbornly hard to eliminate from the conceptual fringes of any Christology that doesn't follow through Chalcedonian categories in light of the Trinity. Adam Davidson Ben-Miriam is the person Jesus would have grown up to be if he hadn't been the Son of God. Volumes of otherwise laudable historical Jesus research are dedicated to him. Yet no such person ever existed or ever could exist, for the human nature of Jesus Christ was nobody until the eternal Logos took it on as his own, personalizing (or em-personing or en-hypostatizing) it and making it a real man.

Jesus Christ is human, and Jesus Christ is a person. It is also true that Jesus Christ is a human person, but what the fifth council makes clear is that "a human person" cannot mean "his created human nature is personalized by a created human personhood." Instead, we can and must think in terms of the human nature of this divine person, the humanity of the hypostasis of the Son. After the powerful two-natures thinking honed at Chalcedon, it would be easy to imagine that the key to Christology is to double everything according to the logic of two perfect natures unconfused, unchanged, undivided, and unseparated. But at the center of the incarnation is the hypostasis of the hypostatic union, and no parallel thinking can apply to that hypostasis. The person involved in the incarnation is not derived by adding above and below, but comes down from above and takes to himself what is below. The parallelism appropriate to two-natures Christology only functions properly within a zone marked out by trinitarian thought. To say it in terms of the development of the last few councils: this one divine person (Ephesus 431) who is fully divine and fully human (Chalcedon 451) is the second person of the Trinity (Constantinople II 553). In one of the best recent defenses of this ancient doctrine, Dennis Ferrara summarizes the way the fifth council develops previous councils:

In simple terms: did Chalcedon pull back from and even "correct" the stark dogma of Ephesus or only specify it further so as to preclude the monophysite misunderstanding? More precisely: are we to read Ephesus' identification of Christ's divine person in the light of Chalcedonian diphysitism, or Chalcedonian diphysitism in the light of Ephesian identification of Christ's person? It was precisely this question that was decided in favor of Cyrillian orthodoxy by II Constantinople, a decision that would not have been possible without the theological breakthrough of Leontius of Jerusalem's doctrine of enhypostasis, which provided a theoretical basis for subordinating, without disavowing the advance made at Chalcedon, the duality of natures to the unity of person, and, most particularly, the humanity to the divine person.[26]

Ferrara goes on to specify that the doctrine of the anhypostatic/enhypostatic human nature of Christ enables us to affirm that Jesus Christ is a divine person and "that Christ's humanity has no independent, personal existence of its own; that, despite its consciousness and freedom, this human nature is not a personal 'who,' but exists precisely as the humanity of this divine subject. It is to acknowledge, accordingly, that Jesus Christ is not a human but a divine person, 'one of the Holy Trinity,' as II Constantinople says."[27] Finally, as a historical theologian he is concerned to underline the binding way in which "II Constantinople must be considered the Church's own authoritative interpretation of Chalcedon, one which compels us to read Chalcedonian diphysitism in light of Christ's primordial unity as divine subject. Accordingly attempts to use Chalcedonian diphysitism to justify a bipolar conception of Christ's person and identity, whether of a relational, process, or Spirit-Christology kind, are at best a relapse into pre-Ephesian confusion and at worst manifestly heterodox."[28]

If Ferrara is right about the fifth council being "the Church's own authoritative interpretation of Chalcedon," then anyone who gratefully

---

[26] Ferrara, "Hypostatized in the Logos," 324.

[27] Ibid., 325.

[28] Ibid.

receives theological guidance from the Chalcedonian Christology is obligated to engage also the anhypostatic/enhypostatic doctrine at least as a hypothesis worth conceptual testing. Of course, a later council one century removed from Chalcedon could be wrong about the intent of Chalcedon. But even if its historical claims are less solid than recent advocates have claimed, the theology of the fifth council generates a host of more or less detachable truth claims that are proving to be fruitful avenues of inquiry for contemporary projects in Christology.[29]

The anhypostatic/enhypostatic Christology has its own difficulties; it requires caution precisely because it makes such large claims across the whole range of central Christian doctrines and sets other concepts into motion whenever it is articulated. The fifth council has always been suspected of being a covert return to the Apollinarian error, because it seems that the human nature is missing something that it takes to be fully human: human personhood. H. R. Mackintosh called it "a finer species of Apollinarianism,"[30] but the fathers of the fifth council had already anticipated this charge in their fourteenth and final anathema, directed against anyone who "accuses holy Cyril of writing opinions like those of the heretical Apollinarius."[31] Anathematizing does not absolve Cyril of Apollinarianism, but the anathema at least shows that the fathers were alert to the charge and believed they did not fall prey to the error.

I believe this classic Christology is especially congenial to Evangelical theology and should become part of our basic conceptual equipment for thinking about Jesus Christ in trinitarian perspective. Most modern objections to it have come from theologians in the liberal tradition who have rejected it because of their strong historical-critical

[29] An impressive programmatic essay is Walter Kasper's "'One of the Trinity . . .': Re-establishing a Spiritual Christology in the Perspective of Trinitarian Theology," in *Theology and Church* (New York: Crossroad, 1989), 94–108. The most vigorous modern engagement with the anhypostatic/enhypostatic Christology is Karl Barth's incorporation of it into his lectures later published as the *Göttingen Dogmatics: Instruction in the Christian Religion* (Grand Rapids: Eerdmans, 1991); see the useful evaluation of Barth's discovery in Bruce McCormack, *Karl Barth's Critically Realistic Dialectical Theology: Its Genesis and Development 1909—1936* (Oxford: Oxford University Press, 1997).
[30] H. R. Mackintosh, *The Doctrine of the Person of Jesus Christ* (Edinburgh: T&T Clark, 1913), 218; cited in Ivor Davidson, "Theologizing the Human Jesus: An Ancient (and Modern) Approach to Christology Reassessed," *IJST* 3 (2001): 136.
[31] Tanner, "Chalcedon II (553)," 121.

agenda, an antimetaphysical outlook, or a program of demythologiza-
tion. Theologians who do not share these presuppositions would do well
to reinvestigate the doctrine.

In a recent attempt to rehabilitate and recommend the "somewhat
notorious" anhypostatic/enhypostatic Christology, Ivor Davidson reports
on the modern bias against it: "At first glance, such theology appears
anything but congenial to the affirmation of Jesus' humanity. Does it not
go out of its way to deny that Jesus is a human 'person,' and reduce his
humanity to the level of a 'nature' only—whatever that may mean post-
Darwin, Marx and Freud?" Here is an opportunity, it seems to me, for
theologians who have not given up on natures in general to get to work
and see if they can overcome the other objections. Any Christian thinker
who has somehow made it into the twenty-first century as an unrecon-
structed essentialist, or even as an unblushing substance dualist, will be
able to engage patristic thought on a shared metaphysical presupposition
inaccessible to much modern and postmodern theology.

Davidson continues: "A Christology which renders Jesus a union,
conjunction, synthesis (or whatever) of static 'natures' guaranteed more
or less constant stability by virtue of divine subjecthood surely trades . . .
on mythological descent-ascent motifs detached from the gritty realities
that are there in the gospels' own witness."[32] This, it seems to me, is the
place where Evangelicals and the fathers of the fifth council are able to
communicate directly with one another, because for the most part we
share an inability to be very embarrassed by the "mythological descent-
ascent motifs" that we use in confessing that one of the Trinity came
down from heaven and became human for us and for our salvation.[33] We
love to tell the story, our hymns attest in an irresistible rhyme, of how a
Savior came from glory. The long narrative-arc—from preexistence in
the Trinity, through the virgin birth, death, resurrection, and ascension—
is a scriptural motif that the fifth council's "Cyrillian Chalcedonianism"
makes possible.

---

[32] Davidson, "Theologizing the Human Jesus," 135–36.

[33] Davidson likely has Bultmann's arguments in mind, but recent rehabilitations of the
doctrinal impact of descent and ascent schemas include Douglas McCready, *He Came
Down from Heaven: The Preexistence of Christ and the Christian Faith* (Downers Grove,
IL: InterVarsity, 2005) and Douglas Farrow, *Ascension & Ecclesia: On the Significance of
the Doctrine of Ascension* (Grand Rapids: Eerdmans, 1999).

I have argued that Chalcedonian categories, the guidelines of classical orthodox Christology, are helpful and even necessary for giving a theological account of the gospel. In some ways, persuading contemporary Christians of that is not difficult, since some residual version of Chalcedonian two-natures Christology is always lurking just under the surface of Evangelical faith. I have also argued that Evangelicals should embrace the anhypostatic/enhypostatic Christology, even though the case is made more difficult because the conceptual framework of the fifth council is more demanding, and includes more elements which generate tension with the unreflective commitments held by most Christians. However, I believe that the Christological development of the fifth council, the anhypostatic/enhypostatic account of the perfect humanity assumed by the Son of God, has even deeper connections to the core commitments of Christian faith in the gospel. If the two-natures schema of Chalcedon risks being static, the fifth council throws it back into motion by affirming identity between the second person of the Trinity and the person who is the subject of the incarnation. If Chalcedon risks putting too much emphasis on the natures, the fifth council restores the Cyrillian focus on the person of Christ. If Chalcedon risks sounding like a description of component parts, the fifth council restores the plot line of the one who came from heaven above to take on human nature. It is a powerful, evangelical statement of the Christian claim "that our lord Jesus Christ, who was crucified in his human flesh, is truly God and the Lord of glory and one of the members of the holy Trinity."[34]

Jesus in Trinitarian Perspective: The Next Five Chapters

Each of the remaining chapters in this book approaches the task of doing Christology in a way that is informed by trinitarian thought and Chalcedonian categories. Each chapter can be read independently of the others, and each marshals its own evidence. A reader who is not persuaded to agree with one chapter will not necessarily have to reject the other chapters. In fact, there is considerable diversity of opinion among the authors, with a range of views represented on many of the details. Nevertheless, the

---

[34] Tanner, "Constantinople II (553)," *NL*, 118.

chapters have been carefully calibrated and arranged so that taken together they reinforce one another and develop a coherent line of argument regarding the person and work of the incarnate Son. Although each chapter is preceded by a summary (and a list of technical terms), it is worth noting here how the chapters work together in sequence.

J. Scott Horrell's chapter on "The Eternal Son of God in the Social Trinity" is the most directly trinitarian part of the book, focusing as it does not on the incarnation but on the eternal Trinity and the Son's place within it. Horrell's chapter leads the suite of three chapters on the person of Christ, and grounds the personhood of Christ in his eternal preexistence with the Father and the Holy Spirit. Horrell takes pains to articulate the particular position of the Son of God within the ordered fellowship of the immanent Trinity and is convinced that there is an ordered relationality and structure within that divine life that in no way jeopardizes the absolute ontological equality of the three persons. Although he speaks of the immanent Trinity, Horrell draws all of his evidence from the economic Trinity, a procedure he calls "heeding the metanarrative of social trinitarian revelation." His case for an eternally ordered set of relationships and roles (a *taxis*) among three centers of consciousness (a social Trinity) is stated very strongly and with extensive reference to alternative positions when appropriate. Readers may dissent from certain elements of Horrell's argument, yet retain the overall sense of just how secure the eternal personhood of the second hypostasis of the Trinity is, within the rich fellowship of Father, Son, and Spirit prior to the incarnation.

Donald Fairbairn's chapter, "The One Person Who Is Jesus Christ: The Patristic Perspective," is a bracingly direct engagement with patristic sources and current historiographical reconstructions of the Christology of the early church. Fairbairn is involved in a project of reclaiming Cyril of Alexandria as the key figure in the entire development of patristic Christology. Cyril's central insight is that the one person of Christ is the eternal person of God the Son, the second person of the Trinity. To make his case that Cyril is not only right, but was widely recognized to be right throughout the ancient church, Fairbairn dismantles some besetting stereotypes and clichés about the development of Christology, chiefly the notion that it is worthwhile to speak about an established

Antiochene school of Christology that included both orthodox and heretical thinkers. Nearly all the chapters in this book make some appeal to patristic sources, and one of the main contributions of Fairbairn's chapter is to provide historical rigor that grounds, supplements, and chastens the looser historical appeals of the other authors. However, Fairbairn is not a merely descriptive historian, and he makes a number of constructive doctrinal claims, including strong proposals for the way soteriology and Christology must interrelate, and the dictum that theology cannot treat a nature as if it were a person. Constructing Christology in trinitarian perspective is not an undertaking that just began in recent years, and Fairbairn helps recover the wisdom of the ancient Christian consensus on how it ought to be done.

Just as Fairbairn's contribution raises the historical standards of the volume, Garrett J. DeWeese's chapter, "One Person, Two Natures: Two Metaphysical Models of the Incarnation," raises the standards for philosophical clarity. DeWeese represents a version of contemporary analytic philosophy of religion that is attentive to revealed truth, submissive to doctrinal norms, respectful of tradition, yet impatient with ambiguity in theological language. Because he is concerned that Christian doctrine should defend itself against philosophical charges of incoherence, he points out some areas in which Christology should be articulated more carefully. He offers definitions of all the key terms of the Christological debate, such as *person*, *nature*, *mind*, and *will*, with special attention to ensuring that these terms are being used consistently, whether in Christology or trinitarianism. Not content merely to tidy up the terminology and describe various options, DeWeese advocates a model of the incarnation that seeks to do greater justice to the unity of the person of Christ than other currently available views stemming from certain medieval traditions. DeWeese's key move is to relocate some features of the incarnate life from the human nature of Christ to the divine person of Christ. This enables him to work toward a more unified description of the actions and experiences of the incarnate Christ, and away from an account too tied up in duality (two minds, two consciousnesses, two selves). DeWeese does his best to eliminate ambiguity without dispelling the mystery that necessarily adheres to the human experience of a divine person.

Bruce A. Ware's chapter, "Christ's Atonement: A Work of the Trinity," stands at the dividing line between the person of Christ and the work of Christ. Ware covers both in turn, arguing first that the doctrine of the Trinity is necessary for an adequate account of the identity of Jesus Christ the Savior, and second that it is also necessary if we are to understand the work the Savior accomplished. Ware's argument begins at the cross and poses trinitarian questions: How does the doctrine of the Trinity illuminate the way our salvation is accomplished in the life, death, and resurrection of this person? His argument proceeds by moving through the various trinitarian relationships (especially the Son to the Father and Spirit) and reexamining the biblical witness to see what explanatory light each passage throws on the person and work of Christ.

Klaus Issler's chapter, "Jesus' Example: Prototype of the Dependent, Spirit-Filled Life," is an essay in retrieving the notion of Jesus as our example and of discipleship as the imitation of Christ. Concerned that traditional Christological constructs can hinder this practical spirituality of imitation, Issler reexamines the biblical evidence and finds there a robust presentation of Jesus as a model for a true human experience of faith, dependence on God the Father, and personal interaction with the Holy Spirit. The trinitarian structure of Jesus' own incarnate life makes it possible for us to imitate Christ. On this basis and as the final plank in the cumulative argument of the book, Issler engages critics who consider the *imitatio Christi* motif to be a sub-Christian spirituality and answers their objections with a trinitarian account of the incarnation. Issler's reflection on Jesus as our example rounds out the book's treatment of the work of Christ by tracing the effects of Christ's work all the way down into the details of spiritual formation, based on the accomplished work of the incarnate Son.

We have taken care to make this book usable as an introduction to Christology by avoiding two extremes. On the one hand, we wanted to avoid rehashing standard views in a documentary fashion, whether as a four-views-of Christology resource or as a lowest-common-denominator resource. There is a place for these kinds of teaching, but we wanted an introduction to Christology that communicates more of the sense that this is an ongoing project. On the other hand, we did not want to stake out a new or experimental position, perhaps idiosyncratic or untested by critical feedback. There is place for that too in academic theology, but it is in professional journals rather than in introductory texts. To make *Jesus in Trinitarian Perspective* a text that we can use in introductory courses, we consistently wrote each chapter in a method-transparent way in order to model the work of theology for our readers. The decision to recruit an interdisciplinary team of scholars to ply their expertise in their own fields was part of the strategy for making the book maximally instructive as an introduction. Finally, we have identified in each chapter three axioms we consider normative for Christological work. In each case, we believe that even a reader who disagrees with some of the positions taken in a chapter will see the axioms as rules of thumb that should be followed, even if following them means reaching different material conclusions from the person who articulated them. Drawing out these axioms and identifying their binding claims on all Christology also helps each author distinguish what is axiomatic in their chapter from what is optional. Each of us have axes to grind and we disagree among ourselves; and some of our disagreements are about how important our disagreements are. Such is theology. Rather than retreat to purely descriptive work, however, we believe we have produced a text that not only is safe and trustworthy, but also exciting and filled with a sense of project.

For Further Reading

Davis, Leo Donald. *The First Seven Ecumenical Councils: Their History and Theology*. Collegeville, MN: Liturgical Press, 1983. If you are beginning to study the ecumenical councils, Davis provides a very readable overview that incorporates just the right mixture of history and doctrine. He has a slight tendency to exaggerate the importance of Rome.

Meyendorff, John. *Christ in Eastern Christian Thought*. New York: St. Vladimir's Seminary Press, 1987. Meyendorff's book begins with the fifth century, provides a very good Eastern perspective on the controversies around Chalcedon, and stretches to late Byzantium. Chapter 4, "God Suffered in the Flesh," is especially relevant.

Grillmeier, Aloys. *Christ in Christian Tradition*. Louisville: Westminster John Knox, 1975. This multivolume work is the best source for detailed investigations of each figure and movement involved. Grillmeier is unsurpassed on careful scholarship in the details, but he offers some large-scale generalizations about the history of Christology which are misleading.

Toon, Peter. *Yesterday, Today and Forever: Jesus Christ and the Holy Trinity in the Teaching of the Seven Ecumenical Councils.* Swedesboro, NJ: Preservation Press, 1996.

Bray, Gerald. *Creeds, Councils and Christ.* Fean, Rosshire, UK: Christian Focus, 1997. Originally published in 1984 by InterVarsity. These two short books provide popular-level summaries of the theological importance of the early councils, with less emphasis on history. Toon's book is a brief Christology, while Bray's is an introduction to the issues of authority involved in doing theology with the great tradition.

Study Questions

1. What guidelines does the author suggest for doing theology, and how do the various sub-disciplines of theology contribute? What is the role of the theological axioms offered in this book?

2. What is the biblical support for the councils of Nicaea (325) and Constantinople I (381)? For Ephesus (431) and Chalcedon (451)?

3. Why is the Chalcedonian Definition (451) such a fundamental theological statement for Christian orthodoxy still worth defending today?

4. How well does Chalcedon direct its readers to the most important things about Jesus Christ? Are there more important things which it omits or obscures?

5. What were the main Christological concepts introduced at fifth ecumenical council, Constantinople II (553), and what contribution do they make to understanding the Person of Jesus Christ?

6. What contribution can evangelical theologians make to the great tradition?

Part 1

THE PERSON OF CHRIST

2

THE ETERNAL SON OF GOD
IN THE SOCIAL TRINITY[1]

J. Scott Horrell

Chapter Summary

The purpose of the chapter is to contribute to how we think about God by tightening the relationship between the economic and immanent Trinity. My definition of *social model* of the Trinity is that the one divine Being eternally exists as three distinct centers of consciousness, wholly equal in nature, genuinely personal in relationships, and each mutually indwelling the other. I define *an eternally ordered social model* as the social model that, while insisting on equality of the divine nature, affirms "perpetual distinction of roles within the immanent Godhead." Broadly conceived within the metanarrative of biblical revelation, this entails something like the generous preeminence of the Father, the joyous collaboration of the Son, and the ever-serving activity of the Spirit.

Axioms for Christological Study

1. Speculations of trinitarian theology are not to supercede the metanarrative of divine revelation, particularly as revealed in Jesus Christ.
2. Ontological equality of the members of the Godhead and reciprocal indwelling of each in the other does not necessarily

---

[1] This chapter is a substantially revised version of "Toward a Social Model of the Trinity: Avoiding Equivocation of Nature and Order," *JETS* 47 (2004): 399–422. My thanks to Andreas Köstenberger and *JETS* for permission to revise it for this book.

preclude eternal relational order among the Father, Son, and Holy Spirit.

3. Biblical revelation points beyond mere economy to transcendent relationality, such that a univocal correspondence of the economic and immanent Trinity cannot be affirmed.

KEY TERMS

economic Trinity	immanent Trinity	person
nature	substance	social model
mutually indwelling	eternally ordered	social order
subordination	subordinationism	center of self-consciousness
ontological equality	eternal generation	eternal procession
roles	egalitarian	
Latin terms	*persona*	*substantia*
Greek terms	*hypostasis*	*ousia*
	monarchia	*perichoresis*
	taxis	

T he New Testament church was marvelously rich in trinitarian experience. As believers glorified the Father, they likewise exalted the incarnate Son, and this through the indwelling presence of the Holy Spirit. Reverence toward the Father, the Son, and the Spirit in the consciousness of the early church is reflected in over one hundred New Testament passages that speak of these three in what Christendom later would term "the Holy Trinity." But the *idea* of Trinity—that is, the conceptual language that helps us understand this biblical God—was so different from what had ever been thought before that it would take the concerted effort of the church through several centuries to frame the divine mystery. As we will see, that struggle to define God centered in the relationship of God the Son to God the Father. Yet even though the theological grammar was long in coming, it can never be said that the early church was not trinitarian. The threefold experience of the personal God is densely woven throughout the New Testament.

Today as well, every Christian experiences God as threefold. In prayer we address God as our Heavenly Father, the "High King of Heaven," with whom we are reconciled, adopted as children, and generously cared for. We pray in Jesus' name because through him we have access to God. Jesus is our brother who went before us, our supreme example, our high priest and mediator who intercedes for us to the Father. And all the while, the Holy Spirit within us motivates our prayer. The Counselor illumines, guides, and empowers what we say to God. He transcends our limitations. In a sense, then, like the early church we too experience the one God *above* us, *beside* us, and *in* us. Our Lord comes to us in different relations as three persons yet as the one and only God. "It is obvious but not trite to state," Miroslav Volf reminds us, "that the triune God stands at the beginning and at the end of the Christian pilgrimage and, therefore, at the center of Christian faith."[2]

Powerful as it may be, as the early church understood, experiencing God as tripersonal is not the same as *articulating* precisely what God has revealed of himself. Neither Jewish theology nor Greek philosophy provided the conceptual frameworks, much less the right words, needed to express what the church fathers were seeing in the Bible's witness of God as Father, Son, and Holy Spirit. All the early church agreed that God's ways are higher than our ways, and that the Infinite One stands beyond our reasoning capacities. Nevertheless, in a Greco-Roman world in which credible religion and philosophy required rational defense, and amidst the contentions by those on the edges of the church for suspect interpretations of the "Christian God," the church fathers were increasingly pressed to express and defend the very center of their belief—the doctrine of the triune God.

With time, Christian faith coalesced around the Nicene Creed as the definitive statement of the doctrine of the Holy Trinity. Although the Creeds never explicitly state the formula,[3] trinitarianism is often

---

[2] Miroslav Volf, "Being as God Is: Trinity and Generosity," in *God's Life in Trinity*, ed. Miroslav Volf and Michael Welker (Minneapolis: Fortress, 2006), 3.

[3] What we commonly call the Nicene Creed is the Niceno-Constantinopolitan Creed of 381. It is the received text from Chalcedon in 451, cited as the Creed "of the 318 fathers who met at Nicaea and that of the 150 who met at a later time." Differing somewhat from the creed actually written at Nicaea in 325, "the symbol of the Council of Constantinople" already appears in 374 in Epiphanius *Ancoratus* 120.

summarized with Tertullian's Latin description of *tres personae, una substantia*—"three persons, one substance"—or, in the evolving Greek terminology, three *hypostaseis* and one *ousia*. The Councils of Nicaea (AD 325) and Constantinople (AD 381) intended to define catholic belief about the nature of Christ and God while also protecting the mystery of God. In guarding divine mystery, the Niceno-Constantinopolitan Creed provides for a certain latitude regarding how the Godhead is to be understood. The councils provide the box, so to speak, outside of which there is no Christian orthodoxy and inside of which there is room for somewhat varied understandings (as this chapter explores). Down through Eastern and Western trinitarianism carefulness has marked most of these different views "within the box." Nevertheless, certain conceptions of how God is God in himself have been distant from Scripture. Too often speculative ideas of the Godhead have created a philosophic Trinity discussed among theologians but quite different from the one to which the average Christian relates.

Within the larger focus on Jesus in trinitarian perspective, the purpose of the present chapter is to contribute to how we think about God—and the place of the Son of God—by tightening the relationship between the economic and the immanent Trinity. That is, Scripture's record of God's revelation in human history ("the *economic* Trinity") should inform and control how we think about the eternal relations of the Godhead ("the *immanent* Trinity"). The structure of this chapter is as follows: An introductory section discussing two background issues lays a foundation for a threefold approach. Part 1 presents evidence for a social model of the Godhead, especially noting divine mutuality in Scripture. The Son, the Spirit, and the Father coexist in eternally self-giving relations. Part 2, after tracing current issues in social trinitarianism, investigates biblical data supporting eternal order in the Godhead. The roles of Father, Son, and Holy Spirit in revelation seem intentional rather than arbitrary; that is, God's self-disclosure in our finite universe is reflective of eternal divine relationships. Part 3 attempts a synthesis of the biblical evidences above, arguing for an "eternally ordered social model" of the Godhead. My definition of a *social model* of the Trinity is that *the one divine Being eternally exists as three distinct centers of consciousness, wholly equal in nature, genuinely personal in relationships, and each mutually indwelling the other.* I define an *eternally ordered social model* as the social model that, while insisting on equality of the divine nature, affirms "perpetual distinction of roles within the immanent Godhead." Within biblical revelation, this entails something like the generous preeminence of the Father, the joyous collaboration of the Son, and the ever-serving activity of the Spirit. I will argue that while hundreds of biblical texts affirm the *monarchia* of the Father, no texts sufficiently stand against it. Such a view corresponds in the deepest way with God's own self-disclosure as immanent Trinity, hence implying aspects of an eternal relationship of God the Son to God the Father.

Two Introductory Background Issues

Revelation and the Infinite

A key question in all discussion of divine ontology is whether biblical revelation can be taken as adequate to who and what God ultimately is.[4] While experiential and traditional arguments for the doctrine of the Trinity are helpful, neither can be ultimately decisive. Experiences may be variously interpreted. Christian traditions differ, and each tradition contributes a deeper metaphysical vocabulary forged within quite different cultural milieus. Most classical Christians will affirm that finally the Bible must ground and structure our understanding of God.[5] While there

---

[4] Nearly every recent theological discussion returns to Karl Rahner's assertion that the economic Trinity is the immanent Trinity, and the immanent Trinity is the economic Trinity, in *The Trinity*, trans. Joseph Donceel (new ed., New York: Crossroad, 1997), 80–120, esp. 99–103. See the helpful division of modern trinitarianism around Rahner's formula in Fred Sanders, *The Image of the Immanent Trinity: Rahner's Rule and the Theological Interpretation of Scripture* (New York: Peter Lang, 2004).

[5] If biblical revelation is primary, it is surprising that among the hundreds of works on the Trinity, until recently relatively few have been attentive to textual evidences for trinitarian doctrine. Works with substantial treatment of Scripture include George A. F. Knight, *A Biblical Approach to the Doctrine of the Trinity* (Edinburgh: Oliver & Boyd, 1953); Arthur W. Wainwright, *The Trinity in the New Testament* (London: SPCK, 1962); Royce Gordon Gruenler, *The Trinity in the Gospel of John: A Thematic Commentary on the Fourth Gospel* (Grand Rapids: Baker, 1986); Millard J. Erickson, *God in Three Persons: A Contemporary Interpretation of the Trinity* (Grand Rapids: Baker, 1995), 159–210; Peter Toon, *Our Triune God: A Biblical Portrayal of the Trinity* (Wheaton: Bridgepoint/ Victor, 1996); Gerald O'Collins, *The Tripersonal God: Understanding and Interpreting the Trinity* (Mahwah, NJ: Paulist Press, 2000), 11–82; John S. Feinberg, *No One Like Him: The Doctrine of God* (Wheaton: Crossway, 2001), 443–71; Ben Witherington III and Laura

may be hiddenness, incomprehensibility, and even *darkness* in God's self-revelation, there are no masks. The divine Being is not misleading the believer; there is no charade—as the incarnation and the cross powerfully testify. God is honest, true, and genuine in communicating himself. I presuppose that the economic Trinity as revealed in the Bible *accurately* represents to finite creation who and what God is but, at the same time, the economic Trinity is by no means *all* that is God. As classical theology confesses, language about God serves analogically but is inadequate for any exhaustive correspondence to the infinite. In the end, while many Christians emphasize the normative place of creeds and traditions, and others elevate the place of experience, an evangelical trinitarian will hold especially to the primacy of Scripture, with creeds and experience ranking secondarily. Our search necessarily requires intellectual humility before God's mystery which has, as Karl Rahner put it, a logic of its own.[6]

Nature and Person

Definitions of *nature* and *person* are enormously problematic, all the more as related to God. These philosophical terms attempt to describe what is revealed in Scripture and what believers have experienced in salvation history. For my purposes, the English words *nature* and *person* parallel the Greek terms *ousia* and *hypostasis* and the Latin *substantia* and *persona*—classical trinitarian grammar deemed equivalent for the East and West by Pope Damasus (366–84). The terms *nature* and *person* will be discussed from various Eastern and Western perspectives.

1. *Nature*. The *divine nature* may be defined as *the generic essence, universal property, or attributes of Godness manifest equally in the Father, Son, and Holy Spirit*. The term *homoousios* originally meant "of the same stuff," but it was adapted in most trinitarian usage to denote "of one substance." But what is "one substance"? The "nature" of the

---

M. Ice, *The Shadow of the Almighty: Father, Son and Spirit in Biblical Perspective* (Grand Rapids: Eerdmans, 2002); Brian Edgar, *The Message of the Trinity* (Downers Grove, IL: InterVarsity, 2004); Robert Letham, *The Holy Trinity: In Scripture, History, Theology, and Worship* (Phillipsburg, NJ: P&R, 2004), 15–85; Bruce A. Ware, *Father, Son, and Holy Spirit: Relationships, Roles, and Relevance* (Wheaton: Crossway, 2005); and John H. Fish III, ed., *Understanding the Trinity* (Dubuque, IA: ECS, 2006).

[6] See Rahner, *The Trinity*, 52–55.

divine nature, so to speak, was understood in two primary (albeit often exaggerated) senses.

The Eastern fathers placed the three *hypostaseis* as primary and the *ousia* in abstraction. Within this distinction, two subsets regarding the origin of *nature* are evident, even among the Cappadocians themselves. First, the Greek church both inherited and corrected aspects of second-century Logos Christology and Origen's doctrine of the eternal generation of the Son. Basil of Caesarea and Gregory of Nazianzus located the one divine nature, not in a unipersonal monad "in the manner of Aristotle,"[7] but in God the Father. As the unoriginated Origin and *fons totius divinitatis* ("source of the whole divinity"),[8] God the Father eternally begets the Son and gives eternal procession to the Holy Spirit.[9] Thus, in this first Eastern understanding of the divine nature, there are three *hypostaseis* that may each be called *God*; yet there is only one God, the Father, from whom the other *hypostaseis* forever derive their divine nature. The deity of the Son and the Spirit, eternal and full as it may be, is received from the Father. In this sense, God the Father has ontological priority but generously and eternally is the source of the fully equal deity of the Son and the Spirit.

The second Eastern conception of *nature* is defined by Gregory of Nyssa as a transcendent essence that itself unifies the Godhead. Rather than the Son and the Spirit's deity being derived from the Father, each member of the Godhead equally and eternally shares in this divine nature. Nevertheless, in *Not Three Gods*, Gregory argues that *no* term attempting to describe the divine nature signifies this nature in itself, as it remains utterly beyond human comprehension. We only know of the divine *ousia* by way of the divine operations through the three *hypostaseis* and their

---

[7] Gregory Nazianzen *Oration* 23.2.

[8] "He is, therefore, the source and origin of the whole divinity." From the Council of Toledo XI, AD 675. See *The Church Teaches: Documents of the Church in English Translation,* trans. John F. Clarkson, John H. Edwards, William J. Kelly, John J. Welch (St. Louis: B. Herder, 1955), 127.

[9] Gregory Nazianzen *Oration* 29.2 (On the Son): "a one eternally changes to a two and stops at three—meaning the Father, the Son, and the Holy Spirit. In a serene, non-temporal, incorporeal way, the Father is parent of the 'offspring' and originator of the 'emanation'— or whatever name one can apply when one has entirely extrapolated from things visible." See Thomas Hopko, "The Trinity in the Cappadocians," in *Christian Spirituality: Origins to the Twelfth Century,* ed. Bernard McGinn, John Meyendorff, and Jean Leclercq (New York: Crossroad, 1989), 263–70.

effects in finite creation. Nevertheless, Gregory of Nyssa insists, a real divine nature exists, albeit indescribable and unknowable. Similarly, Cyril of Alexandria and many subsequent Eastern trinitarians deny origination of the Son and the Spirit from the Father, even though the language of "beginning" (*arche*), "source" (*pege*), and "root" (*riza*) appears frequently. As refinement continued, the Greek church assumed the term *perichoresis*—the personal indwelling of each member of the Trinity in the other—as the primary sense of divine unity. Thus, in the East, either the divine *ousia* is directly derived from the Father, or it describes the sum of the attributes held in common by the Godhead (without necessarily denying a single substance). In both cases, the three persons are primary, each wholly manifesting the DNA of deity. They are three who are God yet one God. One or the other perspective of the divine nature is fundamental to a social theory of the Trinity.

In the Western church the typically Latin understanding of the divine nature begins with a single divine essence expressed in the subsistent relations of the Father, Son, and Holy Spirit. The divine essence, or single nature, has a reality concurrent with the three persons—this without admitting a quaternity. One might imagine two dimensions of a single divine reality, both the real substance of God and the real relations of Father, Son, and Holy Spirit. Such a perspective is reflected in nearly all Western theology from Augustine, and (especially) Aquinas to John Paul II and Benedict XVI.[10] As the recent *Compendium: Catechism of the Catholic Church* words it, "The three divine Persons are only one God because each of them equally possesses the fullness of the one and indivisible divine nature."[11] As a consequence, Western theology traditionally begins with a defense of the existence of God followed by long

---

[10] Pope John Paul II is said to have remained essentially Thomistic in his view of persons as relational subsistencies of the divine essence, in Antoine E. Nachef, *The Mystery of the Trinity in the Theological Thought of Pope John Paul II* (New York: Peter Lang, 1999), 171–98. However, both John Paul II and Benedict XVI have given significant attention to the three persons as in John Paul II's trilogy of volumes on the Father, Son, and Holy Spirit. Compared to his predecessor, Benedict XVI has written little on the Trinity, yet he was the editor of most of John Paul II's writings as well as the *Catechism of the Catholic Church* (1st ed., New York: Doubleday, 1995), which gives significant attention to the three persons of the Godhead.

[11] *Compendium: Catechism of the Catholic Church*, preface by Benedict XVI (Washington, DC: United States Conference of Catholic Bishops, 2006), part 1, q. 48.

discussions regarding the divine attributes before mention of the Holy Trinity. Colin Gunton has been especially acute in criticizing Augustine and Aquinas, with their stress on the divine nature, as having lost the personal three in the overwhelming one—or so philosophizing about the one God as to have lost true trinitarian faith and, consequently, setting the stage for European deism and atheism.[12] However perceived, the traditional Western view has been that the divine nature is not merely a unifying set of properties but something very close to an actual substance that is primary in uniting the three persons of the Godhead.

2. *Person.* If the term *nature* is difficult when we speak of God, the term *person* is all the more complex. Theologians such as Tertullian, the Cappadocians, Augustine, and Aquinas differ in their concepts of *person*,[13] even if modern and postmodern conceptions vary considerably more. Most Christians will agree that the architecture of human personality is grounded in the absolute personhood of the Father, Son, and Holy Spirit. But as the Trinity exists in partial hiddenness and mystery, so the *imago dei* entails aspects that are not reducible to mere rationality and volition, as some traditionalists would have it.

The Bible indicates a plurality of perspectives as to what constitutes a *person*, human or divine. In the divine and ideal sense, it seems best to define *person* as "a center of self-consciousness existing in relationship to others."[14] Trinitarian revelation suggests four specific aspects to help fill this out. Each divine *person* is constituted by (1) the essential nature of Deity ("the Word was God"), that is, the attributes (*ousia*) that distinguish God from creation; (2) full self-consciousness ("I Am"), the actual reality of self distinct from other persons, which in turn presupposes mental properties and internal relations; (3) unique relatedness ("the

---

[12] Colin E. Gunton, *The One, the Three and the Many: God, Creation and the Culture of Modernity* (Cambridge: Cambridge University Press, 1993); see also Jürgen Moltmann, *The Trinity and the Kingdom: The Doctrine of God*, trans. Margaret Kohl (San Francisco: Harper & Row, 1981), 129–222.

[13] See the remarkable historical survey of *person* in Stephen A. Hipp, *"Person" in Christian Tradition and in the Conception of Albert the Great: A Systematic Study of Its Concept and Illuminated by the Mysteries of the Trinity and the Incarnation* (Münster: Aschendorff, 2001).

[14] Chapters 3 and 4 by Donald Fairbairn and Garrett J. Deweese explore further the historical concepts of nature and person. Here I speak of "person" as manifest in the Godhead and only in a derived sense its ideal meaning for humanity.

Word was with God"), distinguishing each member of the Godhead from the others in I-thou relationships; and (4) *perichoresis* ("I am in the Father and the Father in me"), the mutual indwelling of each in the other without confusion of self-consciousness. Such a definition entails both ontological characteristics—i.e., those intrinsic to the divine nature and to individual self-consciousness—together with relationality and reciprocal real presence of each toward and in the other. Rather than the either/or of the West's Boethian individuality (*persona est naturae rationalis individua substantia*) or the postmodern perspective that *person* is a mere knot of relationships with no substance or nature in itself, it seems that both ontological and relational perspectives must be held together when we think of the tripersonal God. And I suspect, as well, these four categories parallel what is central to human personhood as intended by God.

With definitions of *nature* and *person* in place, situated with their historical variations, we proceed to a kind of dialectical discussion observing first the equality of trinitarian relations and then the differences. We conclude by drawing together these two biblical sets of evidence in order to correlate more adequately divine revelation in salvation history with what can be said of the eternal Godhead—thus the relationship of the eternal Son to the Father and the Holy Spirit.

Part 1: Toward a Biblical Social Trinitarianism

Clarification of the Son's role in relation to the Father and the Spirit is paramount in comprehending Jesus Christ's ministry and his death on the cross. A brief historical backdrop to a largely biblical study will help place our study in perspective.

Contemporary Divergence

With Eastern Orthodox influence growing in France in the 1930s through theologians such as Vladimir Lossky[15] together with the "social

---

[15] See Vladimir Lossky, *The Mystical Theology of the Eastern Church*, trans. Fellowship of St. Alban and St. Sergius (Fr. ed. 1944; Cambridge: James Clark, 1957; repr., Crestwood, NY: St. Vladimir's Seminary Press, 1976).

trinitarianism" of Oxford's Leonard Hodgson and others in the 1940s,[16] social models of the Christian Godhead have some precedence in twentieth-century Christendom. Far more dominant in the previous two centuries were either Schleiermacher's functional trinitarianism (merely describing Christian experience) or Karl Barth's conception of the Trinity as three "modes of being" with his characteristic resistance to the terminology of "three persons"—although Barth in various ways pointed the way toward social trinitarianism.[17] The past thirty years, however, have seen an extraordinary renewal of social trinitarian studies, notably through Jürgen Moltmann although the chorale has grown swiftly with many strong voices.[18] The choir around social model themes reached a first crescendo in the late 1980s and early 1990s. Moltmann, Leonardo Boff, John Zizioulas, Cornelius Plantinga Jr., Wolfhart Pannenberg, Catherine LaCugna, Colin Gunton, Ted Peters, Richard Swinburne, Millard Erickson, Robert Jenson, Miroslav Volf, and others wrote of God as three distinct persons, united as one through mutual indwelling.[19]

---

[16] Leonard Hodgson, *The Doctrine of the Trinity: Croall Lectures, 1942–1943* (New York: Scribner's, 1944).

[17] Gary W. Deddo, in *Karl Barth's Theology of Relations: Trinitarian, Christological and Human: Towards an Ethic of the Family* (New York: Peter Lang, 2001), 18–35, argues convincingly that although Barth resisted the terminology of "persons," he de facto treated the Father, Son, and Holy Spirit as "persons" in various forms of genuine relations.

[18] Overviews of modern trinitarianism include William J. La Due, *The Trinity Guide to the Trinity* (Harrisburg, PA: Trinity Press International, 2003); Stanley J. Grenz, *Rediscovering the Triune God: The Trinity in Contemporary Theology* (Minneapolis: Fortress, 2004); and Sanders, *The Image of the Immanent Trinity.*

[19] Although varying considerably, primary social trinitarian works include John Macmurray, *Persons in Relation* (New York: Harper & Row, 1961); Jürgen Moltmann, *The Trinity and the Kingdom*; Moltmann, *History and the Triune God: Contributions to Trinitarian Theology*, trans. John Bowden (New York: Crossroad, 1992); John D. Zizioulas, *Being as Communion: Studies in Personhood and the Church* (Crestwood, NY: St. Vladimir's Seminary Press, 1985); Leonardo Boff, *Trinity and Society*, trans. Paul Burns (Wellwood, Kent: Burns & Oates, 1988); Cornelius Plantinga Jr., "Social Trinity and Tritheism," in *Trinity, Incarnation and Atonement*, eds. Ronald J. Feenstra and Cornelius Plantinga Jr. (Notre Dame, IN: Notre Dame University Press, 1989); Wolfhart Pannenberg, *Systematic Theology*, vol. 1, trans. Geoffrey W. Bromiley (Grand Rapids: Eerdmans, 1991); Catherine Mowery LaCugna, *God for Us: The Trinity and Christian Life* (San Francisco: HarperCollins, 1991); Colin E. Gunton, *The One, the Three and the Many*; Gunton, *The Promise of Trinitarian Theology* (Edinburgh: T&T Clark, 1991); Gunton, *The Triune Creator: A Historical and Systematic Study* (Grand Rapids: Eerdmans, 1998); Ted Peters, *God—The World's Future: Systematic Theology for a New Era*, 2d ed. (Minneapolis: Fortress, 2000); Peters, *God as Trinity: Relationality and Temporality in Divine Life* (Louisville: Westminster John Knox, 1993); Richard Swinburne, *The Christian God* (Oxford: Clarendon, 1994); Millard Erickson, *God*

In the twenty-first century has come a second crescendo with a significant number of works espousing a largely social model of the Trinity by authors (many evangelical) Stanley Grenz, Stephen Seamands, Bruce Ware, LeRon Shults, Tom Smail, Marc Cardinal Ouellet, and again, Miroslav Volf.[20] With the popularity of the community model, however, various cautions have been raised concerning social trinitarianism in light of both patristic studies and philosophic concerns.[21]

Biblical Evidence

The New Testament explicitly includes the three divine persons together in at least 106 passages.[22] Scripture is in the language of finite humanity and, therefore, in one sense all biblical language is "economic," situated within culture and history. The Bible might be said to bring us revelation "from above" together with "from below"—albeit clarifying how far the language of Scripture can be projected to the eternal trinitarian relations is not easy. Nevertheless, I think we have to say that the terms used for the relationships between the members of the economic Godhead provide our most penetrating vista for understanding the immanent Trinity. I earlier defined the *social model* of the Trinity as the one

---

in Three Persons*; Robert W. Jenson, *Systematic Theology*, vol. 1, *The Triune God* (Oxford: Oxford University Press, 1997); and Miroslav Volf, *After Our Likeness: The Church as the Image of the Trinity* (Grand Rapids: Eerdmans, 1998).

[20] Stanley J. Grenz, *The Social God and the Relational Self: A Trinitarian Theology of the Imago Dei* (Louisville: Westminster John Knox, 2001); Grenz, *The Named God and the Question of Being: A Trinitarian Theo-Ontology* (Louisville: Westminster John Knox, 2005); Stephen Seamands, *Ministry in the Image of God: The Trinitarian Shape of Christian Service* (Downers Grove, IL: InterVarsity, 2005); F. LeRon Shults, *Reforming the Doctrine of God* (Grand Rapids: Eerdmans, 2005); Tom Smail, *Like Father, Like Son: The Trinity Imaged in Our Humanity* (Milton Keynes, Bucks, UK: Paternoster, 2005); Bruce A. Ware, *Father, Son, and Holy Spirit*; Marc Cardinal Ouellet, *Divine Likeness: Toward a Trinitarian Anthropology of the Family*, trans. Philip Milligan and Linda M. Cicone (Grand Rapids: Eerdmans, 2006); and contributions in Volf and Welker, eds., *God's Life in Trinity*.

[21] See T. W. Bartel, "Could There Be More Than One Lord?" *FP* 11 (1994): 357–78; Sarah Coakley, "'Persons' in the 'Social' Doctrine of the Trinity: A Critique of Current Analytic Discussion," in *The Trinity*, ed. Stephen T. Davis, Daniel Kendall, and Gerald O'Collins (Oxford: Oxford University Press, 1999), 123–44; Brian Leftow, "Anti-Social Trinitarianism," in *The Trinity*, 203–49; and Richard Cross, "Two Models of the Trinity?" *HeyJ* 43 (2002): 275–94.

[22] Fisher Humphreys, "The Revelation of the Trinity," *PRS* 33 (2006): 292, includes 120 New Testament trinitiarian passages, but not all directly mention all three persons. I count 106 passages (Humphrey's divides various texts); the listing will be available in my forthcoming book on the Holy Trinity.

divine Being eternally existing as three distinct centers of consciousness, wholly equal in nature, genuinely personal in relationships, and each mutually indwelling the other. Evidence for a distinctly tripersonal God is abundant, and for further discussion we need only a brief but important review as a foundation.

1. *Distinct centers of consciousness.* Hundreds of Old Testament passages record God speaking in the first person: "I am he. Before me no god was formed, nor will there be one after me. I, even I, am the LORD, and apart from me there is no savior" (Isa 43:10c–11). So it is revealing that the New Testament records the Father, the Son, and the Holy Spirit, each speaking as the divine "I."[23] How do Old and New Testament declarations of the "I" of God fit together? Each person of the Godhead is depicted as exercising intelligence (creating, instructing), volition (choosing, commanding), even emotion (joy, grief, anger). Yet these are not acting as one divine person in different manifestations, rather as three persons often in relation not only to finite created beings such as angels and humans but also in relation to one another. Certainly Jesus Christ acts in self-conscious awareness in the presence of God the Father, and this seems equally true of the Father in the presence of the Son. Of the trinitarian members, the least obviously personal is the Holy Spirit. Yet the "other Counselor" of John 14:16 *inhabits* (1 Cor 6:19), *comforts* (Acts 9:31), and *intercedes* for believers (Rom 8:14)—all profoundly personal acts. Equally telling is that, while blasphemy against the Father or the Son might be forgiven, blasphemy against the Holy Spirit (Matt 12:31) will not be forgiven. As Calvin observed, all the attributes of God are ascribed to the Holy Spirit as also to the Son.[24] As threefold distinct centers of self-consciousness, the Father, the Son, and the Holy Spirit appear as all that is God by nature yet also all that is personal, indeed tripersonal.

2. *Genuinely personal relationships.* Not only is the self-consciousness of each member of the Trinity discernable, but the divine persons also appear in unique relationship with one another. John's Gospel is particularly revealing.

---

[23] Among multiple texts, see (Father) 2 Pet 1:17; Rev 1:8; (Son) John 8:58; 10:30; 14:20; 17:4; Acts 9:5; Rev 1:17; 22:13,16; and (Spirit) Acts 10:20; 13:2.

[24] John Calvin, *Institutes of the Christian Religion* 1.13.14.

The Son and the Spirit were "with God." Jesus *sees* the Father (John 1:18; 3:11,32; 5:19,29,37; 6:46; 8:38), *hears* the Father (3:32,34; 5:30,37; 7:17; 12:49–50; 14:10), and *does* what the Father does (5:19–20; 6:38). The Spirit *speaks* what he hears, and *gives* what is the Son's (and the Father's) to the disciples (16:13–15; cf. 1 Cor 2:10–13). Whatever *seeing*, *hearing*, and *doing* imply regarding the immanent Trinity, the terms at least convey dynamic relationship each with one another.

They know and testify of each other. "The one who sent me is true, and you do not know him. I know him, because I am from him, and he sent me" (John 7:28–29; cf. 3:34; 8:55; 10:15; 17:25). Jesus knows the Father not because he is the Father, but rather because he enjoys deep affiliation with the Father. In a similar way, "the Spirit of God" *knows* the Father and is *known* by the Father (cf. 1 Cor 2:11–13; Eph 2:18), just as the same "Spirit of Christ" both knows the Son and is known by the Son (John 14:26; 15:26; Rom 8:9). Moreover, the Father *testifies* of the Son (John 5:36–37; 8:17), the Son of the Father (3:11,32; 17:6,26; 18:37), and the Spirit of the Son and the Father (15:26; 1 Cor 2:10–13; Gal 4:6). As the Spirit alights upon the Son to testify of him at his baptism (John 1:32–33) and will later be his witness (16:8–15), so the Son presents the Spirit (3:5–8), testifies of his coming (7:39; 14:16,26; 16:7–11,13), and sends the Spirit (15:26; 16:7; 20:22). Each desires to make the other known.

They exercise free personal choice. Intratrinitarian relationships appear neither obligatory nor mechanical but rather deliberate acts of volition on the part of each of the three persons. Jesus' prayers, for example, reflect distinctly I-Thou dialogue, together with free submission:[25] "Father, I thank you that you have heard me" (John 11:41); "Now my heart is troubled, and what shall I say? 'Father, save me from this hour'? No, it is for this very reason that I came to this hour. Father, glorify your name!" (12:27–28). Although the evidence is less obvious regarding the Holy Spirit and while complex trinitarian dynamics are in play, it seems that every member of the Godhead acts personally and freely (3:7–8; cf. 1 Cor 12:11).

They demonstrate self-rendering love. The Father *loves* the Son (John 3:35; 5:20; 15:9; 17:23–26), and the Son *loves* the Father (14:31).

---

[25] See also John 5:17,22,26; 8:26; 14:3.

Jesus declares, "I seek not to please myself but him who sent me" (5:30); "I always do what pleases him" (8:29); "The reason my Father loves me is that I lay down my life . . . I lay it down of my own accord" (10:17–18). Likewise, the Father *glorifies* the Son (8:50,54; 13:32; 17:1,5,22,24), the Son *glorifies* the Father (13:31–32; 14:12; 17:1,4), and the Spirit *glorifies* the Son (16:14) and thereby the Father. Far from the selfish role some-times mistakenly projected onto the Father, the Father *honors* the Son (5:23; 12:26) and the Son *honors* the Father (5:23; 8:49), such that their honor and glory are inextricably bound with one another and overflow to all who believe (12:26; 13:31–32; 17:1,22,24). As Moltmann convinc-ingly argues in *The Crucified God*, it is Jesus' suffering and death on the cross that split open the very idea of the Hebrew God and now makes untenable a unipersonal God, especially one who is impassible in the sense of many classical interpretations.[26] The relationship of Jesus Christ with the Father and the Spirit rolls back the roof of our human existence for us to peer into the self-giving love between the Father, the Son, and the Spirit. That there is nevertheless order within the reciprocity of the Trinity's self-giving love will be argued below in part 2.

3. *Each mutually indwells the other.* On occasion in John's Gospel, Jesus declares, "the Father is in me and I in the Father" (John 10:38; cf. 14:20; 17:11,21–23). A striking passage is John 14:8–12; when Philip asks to see the Father, Jesus responds, "Don't you know me, Philip, even after I have been among you such a long time? Anyone who has seen me has seen the Father . . . Don't you believe that I am in the Father, and that the Father is in me?" So present is the Father in Jesus that, without con-fusing the persons, Jesus can declare that to see him is to see the Father. Likewise, the Spirit is in Jesus and will later be described as the Spirit of the Son, the Spirit of Christ. Yet the Son is distinct from the Spirit (4:10–14; 7:37–39; 14:16; 20:22), as the Spirit is from the Father (1 Cor 2:10–13).

Although the idea appears in Gregory of Nazianzus and is devel-oped in Maximus the Confessor, it is John of Damascus who popu-larizes the term *perichoresis* to describe the coinherence or mutual

---

[26] Jürgen Moltmann, *The Crucified God: The Cross of Christ as the Foundation and Criticism of Christian Theology*, trans. R. A. Wilson and John Bowden (London: SCM Press, 1974), 200–90.

indwelling of the members of the Trinity.[27] To presuppose on rational grounds, as some do today,[28] that one person cannot inhabit another seems to fall short of the biblical portrayal not only of the Godhead but also of the indwelling of a human being by either the Holy Spirit or, for that matter, a demonic spirit. It is *perichoresis*, the personal interpenetration of each member of the Godhead in the other—each inviting and indwelling—that best explains how three self-conscious persons can also be one in consciousness, thought, will, and action. So intrinsic is this perichoretic unity that God acts as the one and the three. While each person ever possesses distinct mental properties and unique relation to the others, the entire Holy Trinity coexists in communitarian and complete harmony. Although not resolving the mystery, the doctrine of *perichoresis* helps explain the unity of the divine mind and will without slipping into either modalism or tritheism into which other solutions tend to fall.

In summary, as grounded in the New Testament, a *social model* of the Trinity is that in which the one divine Being eternally exists as three distinct centers of consciousness, wholly equal in nature, genuinely personal in relationships, and each mutually indwelling the other. Today most theologians have abandoned phrases such as Barth's three divine "modes of being" or Rahner's "manners of subsistence," because they prove inadequate to describe the complex, vivid relationships between the Father, Son, and Holy Spirit of a nuanced social model.

If a social theory of the Holy Trinity fits the biblical pattern, as argued above, how are we best to understand the apparently ordered personal relations within the Trinity? Frequently, a social model is presumed to include a democratic or egalitarian conception of the immanent Trinity.

---

[27] John of Damascus *De Fide Orthodoxa* 1.8; Verna Harrison, "Perichoresis in the Greek Fathers," *St. Vladimir's Theological Quarterly* 35 (1991): 53–65; and Michael O'Carroll, *Trinitas: A Theological Encyclopedia of the Holy Trinity* (Wilmington, DE: Michael Glazier, 1987), 68–69. In the West the Latin term *circuminsession* (from *insedere*) emphasizes abiding reality, rest, of each member of the Godhead in the other; the similar *circumincession* (from *incedere*) captures the dynamic circulation of trinitarian life from each person to the other.

[28] E.g., William Lane Craig, in J. P. Moreland and William Lane Craig, *Philosophical Foundations for a Christian Worldview* (Downers Grove, IL: InterVarsity, 2003), 587.

Indeed, such an assumption is almost endemic in many circles. But does such a theory find sufficient mooring in the Bible itself?

Part 2: Biblical Evidences for Eternal Order in the Godhead

In Scripture, neither the ontological equality of the members of the Godhead nor the reciprocal indwelling of each in the other necessarily precludes an eternal relational order among the Father, the Son, and the Holy Spirit. Social trinitarians who largely concur with the relational model (Part One) divide around several issues that are helpful to review prior to evaluating biblical evidences for an eternal relational order in the triune God.

Contemporary Divergence among Social Trinitarians

Social models of the Godhead can be variously categorized. Almost all concur that divine unity should be understood in terms of *perichoresis*, a fairly uncontested historical consensus in the East as well as in the West (although understood somewhat differently in each). Contemporary social models of the Godhead divide, admittedly not always neatly, around three major issues.

1. *The Father as origin*. Does the very deity of the Son and the Spirit derive from the Father? That is, does the Father have ontological priority in the Godhead so that he eternally gives equal deity to the Son and the Spirit? Such a position is implied in the Nicene Creed's description of the Son as "of the substance of the Father, God from God, Light from Light, true God from true God . . ." Yet though this view is well-attested among Eastern Orthodox theologians (Basil of Caesarea, Gregory of Nazianzus, John Zizioulas) and a few like Richard Swinburne in the West, the majority of Western trinitarians insist that the answer must be no. If the Son's or the Spirit's divinity is ontologically derived from another, then it cannot be equal to the deity of the unoriginated Originator, the Father.[29]

---

[29] Gregory of Nazianzus struggled with the implications of his own position, particularly before the Arianism he was fighting: "I should like to call the Father the greater, because from Him flow both the equality and the being of the equals . . . but I am afraid to use the word Origin, lest I should make Him the Origin of inferiors, and thus insult Him by precedencies of honour. For the lowering of those who are from Him is no glory to the Source." *Oration 40* (On Holy Baptism), 43.

2. *Ontological equality and social order.* The second issue is related to the first and is the most significant in terms of both the history of trinitarianism and the present discussion. Even if the Son and the Spirit are not *essentially* derived from the Father, is there a sense in which the persons in the immanent Trinity have an eternal social order (Gk. *taxis*)? Or put another way, is there a characteristic way in which each member of the Godhead experiences *koinonia*? Is the Father somehow ever the "head," the designer from whom all else flows? Is the Holy Spirit always glorifying the other in his activity (even as he is Lord)? Is the Son forever colaborer alongside the Father (even as coregent)? That virtually all Christianity from at least the fifth century has confessed the *eternal generation* of the Son and the *eternal procession* of the Spirit indicates (but does not oblige) an order in the immanent Godhead. From the Cappadocians to the Puritan John Owen, from Karl Barth to Avery Cardinal Dulles, some form of eternal divine *taxis* is frequently defended and arguably is the dominant perspective of how the Godhead, the immanent Godhead, has been understood in Christian history—certainly in popular theology.[30]

Augustine seems to hold the converse position, at least according to Peter Lombard's quotation of him in the *Sentences*: "As the Son was made man, so the Father or the Holy Spirit could have been and could be now."[31] There is such equality in the Trinity that, in another universe, the divine order could be switched or terms such as Father, Son, and Holy Spirit altogether changed for other analogies. The reasoning is, as Millard Erickson words it, that while there may be "metaphysical identity" between revelation on earth and what God is in heaven, there is not necessarily "epistemological identity."[32] According to this argument, we cannot project roles assumed in God's economic revelation to knowledge of eternal roles in the immanent Trinity. Indeed, to ascribe to the Trinity eternal roles—for example, "subordination" of the Son to the Father—is

---

[30] Kevin Giles, although Western in his approach and adamant against any suggestion of eternally ordered relations in the Godhead, gives a substantial listing of Protestant and Evangelical scholars over the centuries and today who affirm eternal order. *Jesus and the Father: Modern Evangelicals Reinvent the Doctrine of the Trinity* (Downers Grove, IL: InterVarsity, 2006), 18–39.

[31] *Sentences* 3.1.3, cited in Jenson, *Systematic Theology*, 1:112.

[32] Erickson, *God in Three Persons*, 309.

akin, as Giles deems it, to ancient Arianism and hence in some sense heretical. In fact, to ascribe *any* eternal order to the Godhead would necessarily make one divine person superior, consequently another inferior. Thus a logical leap is justified that opens a discrepancy between, on the one hand, the biblical history that suggests strong order among the Father, Son, and Spirit, to the immanent Godhead on the other hand which cannot admit any eternal order if there is to be true equality.

We might call this particular social model of the Trinity "egalitarian trinitarianism," and it includes two subgroups: those who accept the creedal and traditional language of *begetting* and *procession*—therefore some form of eternal distinction between the members of the Trinity—and noncreedalists who reject such terms and, therefore, have few criteria at all for distinguishing among the members of the Godhead in their eternal relations.[33] But whether the specific terms of *begottenness* and *procession* are themselves exegetically applicable (although all classical Christianity has assumed them), is, I think, somewhat beside the point. The greater issue is whether the revelation of the economic Trinity, historically perceived as hierarchical, in fact reflects ultimate *ordered* (taxiological) relationship in the immanent Trinity. As those above, many have reviewed the biblical and historical evidence and concluded that it does not.

3. *Trinity becoming in time.* A final issue in our overview of social models of the Godhead is whether one can properly even speak of an immanent Trinity. Is God truly three persons in eternal relationship? Or is God triune only in relation to creation? Is the concept of God as Trinity inextricably bound up in cosmic or human history and, therefore, not intrinsic to God himself? Or does the divine Being only come to self-fulfillment as Trinity in time—for example, in the eschaton or "Omega Point"? Or, again, as various modern theologians contend, can one simultaneously affirm a truly *immanent* Trinity and yet also interpret God as *becoming* Trinity through salvation history? Assuming a paradigm shift in God's relation to time, not a few theologians today conceive of

---

[33] J. Oliver Buswell, *A Systematic Theology of the Christian Religion* (Grand Rapids: Zondervan, 1972), 107–10; Wolfhart Pannenberg, *Systematic Theology*, trans. Geoffrey W. Bromiley (Grand Rapids: Eerdmans, 1991–1997), 1:305–7; John Feinberg, *No One Like Him*, 488–92; Erickson, *God in Three Persons*, 309–10; Craig and Moreland, *Philosophical Foundations*, 594.

God's own self-identity as defining itself in history[34]—indeed, remarkably, in the human history of this tiny planet.

Our specific concern is with the second question: Can the persons of the immanent Trinity possess complete ontological equality yet also eternal social order? Is there any eternally distinguishable relationship of God the Son within the Holy Trinity? What might biblical testimony indicate?

Biblical Evidence for Eternal Order in the Godhead

The Bible presents the Father, Son, and Holy Spirit with different primary activities in relation to the world, for example, in creation, salvation, and sanctification. My efforts are directed to New Testament teachings that seem to be windows opening beyond the economy of the incarnation. In no sense is my treatment full-orbed, rather it is admittedly selective within the perichoretic social model of part 1.

1. *Divine giving.* A helpful vision of intratrinitarian relationships is seen in the Greek verbs translated "give" (*didomi* and *paradidomi*). These occur 378 times in the Greek Testament, about thirty times pertinent to trinitarian relations. The pattern of the New Testament is expressed in James 1:17, "Every generous act of giving, with every perfect gift, is from above, coming down from the Father of Lights." If the Father is the Giver, what does he give? In brief, God the Father gives the Son his name (John 17:11–12; Phil 2:9–11), his words and works (John 5:36; 12:49), authority (Matt 9:6; 28:18; John 17:2), "life in himself" (John 5:26), judgment (5:22,27), his rule and kingdom (Luke 1:31–33; Acts 13:34), "all things" (Matt 11:27; Luke 10:22; John 3:35; 13:3), suffering (Matt 26:39–40;

---

[34] The following works affirm some form of an immanent Godhead but tie it to God's "becoming" through activity as the economic Trinity; divine fulfillment (or self-actualization) comes ultimately in the eschaton. Eberhard Jüngel, *The Doctrine of the Trinity: God's Being Is in Becoming*, trans. Horton Harris (Edinburgh: Scottish Academic Press, 1976); Jüngel, *God as the Mystery of the World: On the Foundation of the Theology of the Crucified One in the Dispute between Theism and Atheism*, trans. Darrell L. Gruder (Grand Rapids: Eerdmans, 1983); Jürgen Moltmann, *The Trinity and the Kingdom*; Moltmann, *The Coming of God: Christian Eschatology*, trans. Margaret Kohl (Minneapolis: Fortress, 1996), 257–339; Wolfhart Pannenberg, *Systematic Theology*, 1:309–19; Robert W. Jenson, *The Triune Identity: God According to the Gospel* (Philadelphia: Fortress, 1982); Jenson, *Systematic Theology*, 1:217–23; Bruno Forte, *The Trinity as History: Saga of the Christian God*, trans. Raul Rotondi (New York: Alba House, 1989); Ted Peters, *God as Trinity*; Peters, *God—The World's Future*, 107–14, 129–46, 318–21. See discussion in Sanders, *The Image of the Immanent Trinity*, 83–112.

John 18:11), glory (John 17:22), the disciples (10:29; 17:6–12; 18:9), all believers (6:37–39; 10:27–30; 17:24), and the Revelation (Rev 1:1). What does the Son *give* to the Father? Jesus gives the Father thanks (Luke 10:21; Matt 26:27–28; 1 Cor 11:23–24); his own spirit/life (Luke 23:46); and the eschatological kingdom over which he will reign (1 Cor 15:24). As for the Holy Spirit, nowhere do the verbs above refer to the Father or the Son *giving* to the Spirit. Nevertheless Jesus says of the Spirit, "He will glorify me, because he will take what is mine and declare it to you" (John 16:14). We see, too, that both the Son and the Spirit themselves are *given* by the Father to the world and/or believers (Luke 11:13; John 3:16; Rom 8:11,14–17). While other words might also be studied, *didomi* and *paradidomi* exemplify typical New Testament language of intratrinitarian activity, language evidenced not only of the incarnate Christ of the Gospels but of the resurrected and glorified Son as well. One concludes that the economic relationships between the Father, the Son, and the Spirit are as patently unlike (or nonegalitarian) as they are personal.

2. *Johannine language.* The brevity of this chapter does not allow extended commentary on the traditional language of begetting and procession. Whereas the primary meaning of the related passages likely concerns the economic Trinity,[35] the church fathers were attempting to describe with biblical language the greater movement in the eternal God that they were seeing in Scripture. Two of the most repeated phrases in John's Gospel are that the Son *comes/came from* (22 times) the Father and, again, is *sent by/from* (44 times) the Father (or "above," "heaven").[36] Not only does the Son *come* from the Father. The Spirit of truth also *comes* from the Father (15:26; 6:7–8,13), described as one who "goes forth" or "proceeds" (*ekporeuetai*) from the Father (15:26). While *ekporeuetai* seems most properly to indicate the sending forth of the Spirit to

---

[35] Various times the Bible records the Father's voice "You are my son" and often adds the phrase "today I have begotten you," found in the present tense; see Ps 2:7 in Matt 3:17; 17:5; Mark 1:11; Luke 3:22; 9:35; Acts 13:33; Heb 1:5; 5:5; 2 Pet 1:17,18. In John's Gospel, God is designated the Father (121 times) and Jesus the Son. One thinks of a Father *generating* or *begetting* a Son. Thus, it might be natural that *monogenes* ("one of a kind") was confused by the church fathers with *monogennetos* (from *gennao*, "beget, bear").

[36] See key texts for *sent*: John 5:23–24,37–38; 6:38–39; 7:28–33; 8:16–18; 12:44–45,49; 14:14,16; 16:5,7; 17:21–25; 20:21; *comes/came*: 5:31; 6:38–42,50–51; 8:39,42; 15:27–30; 18:38. Added to this are the 12 times when the same idea is implicit as Jesus enters "into the world."

believers by the Father,[37] it was extrapolated as scriptural language to fit a larger pattern of Spirit-Father-Son relatedness. The Spirit is always going forth from the Father, as well as being promised, sent, or breathed out by the Son (15:26; 16:7; cf. 14:26). Very well, some may argue, but all this evidence merely speaks of the economic Godhead. My point is that no texts indicate any other trinitarian order, for example, the Father being sent by the Son. God the Father repeatedly is presented as the *fons divinitatis*, the divine source from which all else flows in the history of the world and, evidently, within the trinitarian activities as a whole.

3. *The Apocalypse.* The movement of the book of Revelation slowly unfolds the restored glory of the Son (cf. John 17:5). Nevertheless, in stark contrast to the trinitarian language of John's Gospel (1:1–3), the Apocalypse begins with peculiar language: "The revelation of Jesus Christ, which *God* gave him to show his servants . . ." More striking still is the language of Revelation 1:5b–6: "To him [Jesus Christ] who loves us and freed us from our sins by his blood, and made us to be a kingdom, priests serving *his God* and Father . . ." (italics added). In the Apocalypse, the testimony to Christ's absolute deity is ambiguous at first and crescendos at the end (22:13). The central place of "the Lord God the Almighty" (4:8) is retained throughout as "the one who is seated on the throne." The study of *thronos* in the book is instructive. The term appears as the reigning place of the Father (distinctly) about thirty-five times. Yet as overcomer, Jesus Christ speaks of "my throne" (3:21a) and, again, as having "sat down with my Father on his throne" (3:21b). Twice he is seen "at" or "in the center" of the divine throne (5:6; 7:17), and the divine presence on the new earth is described as "the throne of God and of the Lamb" (22:1,3). What might this indicate? In that titles of the Father are ascribed to Jesus (22:13) together with his reign with God, the deduction of the church fathers seems justified: Jesus is "very God from very God." At the same time, while "God and the Lamb" share glory, power and authority, the role of the Father continues as "the Lord God the Almighty" (21:22). Behind the Son sits the Father who cedes highest honor to his Son—innately worthy, now fully glorified in and by all creation. While surely the Apocalypse continues the economic revelation

---

[37] See D. A. Carson, *The Gospel According to John* (Leicester: InterVarsity, 1991), 529.

of God in "heaven" and on earth, one must ask to what extent is it licit to shift away from the implications of such language regarding the Son in relation to the Father when conceptualizing the immanent Trinity. Surely some discontinuity between an economic and an eternal subordination of the Son is necessary. But the absolute discontinuity of egalitarian trinitarian theology seems not to be justified.

4. *The ends of all creation.* Insofar as I can see, the final window within cosmic history as to what might be glimpsed of the immanent Godhead is found in 1 Corinthians 15:24–28 NIV:

> Then the end will come, when he [the Son] hands over the kingdom to God the Father after he has destroyed all dominion, authority and power. For he must reign until he has put all his enemies under his feet. The last enemy to be destroyed is death. For he 'has put everything under his feet.' Now when it says that 'everything' has been put under him, it is clear that this does not include God himself, who put everything under Christ. When he has done this, then the Son himself will be made subject to him who put everything under him, so that God may be all in all.

Although some have interpreted the "God" of the phrase "that God may be all in all" as trinitarian, it is well known that *theos* in Paul almost always designates the Father, and there is little exegetical evidence to suggest otherwise in this passage. As implied in previous texts on divine mutuality, there is a sense of both/and rather than either/or in the Son's relationship to the Father: in the community of the Godhead, the Son is both equal to yet submissive to the Father. Pannenberg comments, "The lordship of the Son is simply to proclaim the lordship of the Father, to glorify him, to subject all things to him. Hence the kingdom of the Son does not end (Luke 1:33) when he hands back lordship to the Father. His own lordship is consummated when he subjects all things to the lordship of the Father and all creation honors the Father as the one God."[38] In my

---

[38] Pannenberg, *Systematic Theology*, 1:313. Yet having affirmed the eternal "begottenness" of Son by the Father, Pannenberg without biblical warrant then presses divine mutuality too far: "By handing over lordship to the Son the Father makes his kingship dependent on whether the Son glorifies him and fulfils his lordship by fulfilling his mission. The self-distinction of the Father from the Son is not just that he begets the Son but that he hands

judgment, the reign of the Son under the monarchy of the Father visible in 1 Corinthians 15 reflects in some sense the immanent trinitarian relations. The bookends of the entire created order are constituted on one end by the command of the Father for creation itself through the Son and the Spirit (John 1:3; Col 1:16; Heb 1:3; Ps 33:6; etc.) and, on the other end, by the consummation of the created order through the Son and the Spirit (Rev 22:17) and its return to God the Father.

In summary, social models of the immanent Trinity vary substantially, the greatest historical tension existing around whether there is an eternal monarchy in relation to God the Father or whether the trinitarian persons in eternity exercise wholly equal roles. Whether the Niceno-Constantinopolitan Creed's language of eternal origin-generation-procession, Augustine's social analogy of lover-beloved-love itself (or for that matter all of his psychological models), or Karl Barth's revealer-revealed-revealedness, Christian history has repeatedly formed analogies of trinitarian relations with immanent implications. The biblical evidence repeatedly moves us this way by affirming divine *taxis* through which the Godhead has made itself known. In other words, nearly everything confirms trinitarian order and nothing appreciably suggests otherwise.

Part 3: An Eternally Ordered Social Trinitarianism

I have defined an eternally ordered social model of the Trinity as affirming both equality of the divine nature and also "personal distinction of roles within the immanent Godhead." Such a position protects the mutual koinonia of equally divine members of the eternal Trinity, while also reflecting the plurality of dispositions of Father, Son, and Holy Spirit testified in virtually all Scripture. In fact, all traditions embrace as normative the trinitarian language of origin, generation, and procession—although the terms themselves only hint of something beyond our grasp (as well they might, God being God). This correspondence between economic revelation and the immanent Godhead suggests the generous preeminence of the Father, the joyous collaboration of the Son, and the ever-serving

---

over all things to him, so that his kingdom and his own deity are now dependent upon the Son. The rule of the kingdom of the Father is not so external to his deity that he might be God without his kingdom" (313).

activity of the Spirit—again, all within the self-givingness of the divine fellowship. Such a proposal attempts to respect the complexity of God's own self-description in Scripture, even though it is most difficult for us philosophically to hold full equality of nature together with eternal differences in communal order. But all speculation of what God is like in transcendent otherness is perilous and, therefore, must be based soundly upon the only sure foundation of the Bible. Gender polemic, political correctness, and rhetoric around progressive versus traditional perspectives can distract from the greater question of God's very being.[39]

Parts 1 and 2 have established both the loving relationality of the social Trinity as well as the hierarchical order of the Godhead that characterizes the economic Trinity in all relations to creation. Several concluding observations are in order.

Heeding the Metanarrative of Social Trinitarian Revelation

Of the multiple texts that mention the Father, Son, and Holy Spirit in various combinations, not many appear intentionally arranged as a theology proper (e.g., Matt 28:19; 1 Cor 8:4–7; Eph 1:3–14). Most of the passages seem casually expressive of the bountiful threefold experience

---

[39] Implications of trinitarianism for conjugal, familial, ecclesial, and societal order are frequent themes across a wide gamut of theologies, from Hans Urs von Balthasar, *Theo-Drama: A Theological Dramatic Theory*, vol. 3, *Dramatis Personae: Persons in Christ*, trans. Graham Harrison (San Francisco: Ignatius, 1992), 283–360; Marc Cardinal Ouellet, *Divine Likeness*; Bruce A. Ware, *Father, Son, and Holy Spirit*; and Wayne Grudem, *Evangelical Feminism and Biblical Truth* (Sisters, OR: Multnomah, 2004), 405–43; to Kevin Giles, *The Trinity and Subordinationism: The Doctrine of God and the Contemporary Gender Debate* (Downers Grove, IL: InterVarsity, 2002); Giles, *Jesus and the Father*; Giles, "The Subordination of Christ and the Subordination of Women," in *Discovering Biblical Equality: Complementarity without Hierarchy*, ed. Ronald W. Pierce and Rebecca M. Groothius (Downers Grove, IL: InterVarsity, 2004), 334–52; Ray S. Anderson, *The Shape of Practical Theology: Empowering Ministry with Theological Praxis* (Downers Grove, IL: InterVarsity, 2001), 35–131; Gavin D'Costa, *Sexing the Trinity: Gender, Culture and the Divine* (London: SCM Press, 2000); and many feminists, including Elizabeth A. Johnson, *SHE WHO IS: The Mystery of God in Feminist Theological Discourse* (New York: Crossroad, 1992). Interestingly, some like William Lane Craig deny eternal submission of the Son but affirm marital complementarianism. Conversely, others affirm the eternal subordination of the Son yet deny its relatedness to gender order in family and church— Craig S. Keener, "Is Subordination Within the Trinity Really Heresy? A Study of John 5:18 in Context" *TJ* 20 (1999), 39–51. Although I think gender issues appear related (1 Cor 11:3), this study has the single intent of understanding the triune God (and the theologies attempting to do so) grounded especially in Scripture, the only sure word we have.

with God in the early church. That is, there is no particular literary order in which the members of the Godhead are mentioned in the Scriptures. Yet it might be said that, although all three persons may in some sense be present in every divine act, the Bible never admits an inversion of the roles of the Godhead. Certainly, enough is said in Scripture to affirm the equal deity of the Son and the Spirit with the Father. But the order of the economic Godhead appears largely inviolable in the flow of the Bible itself. God the Father reflects generous preeminence. The Father loves the Son and gives everything to him, yet the Father is not left empty or without lordship for having given all things out of infinite fullness. Behind the *monarchia* of Jesus Christ the King of kings looms the *monarchia* of God the Father Almighty. While coregent, the Son is collaborator, taking up what is given from the Father, and rejoicing in the communion of the Father. The Son, too, is fully God and exercises that deity, but there are no hints of the Father's retirement.

"The fellowship of the Holy Spirit" appears more complicated when turned Godward. Augustine's designation of the Spirit as gift and love in the Godhead seems appropriate if taken as actively personal, yet this Spirit is also holy and ever desirous of glorifying the Son and the Father. While the Holy Spirit may be "the Spirit of YHWH," "the other *parakletos*," and the revealer of the deep truths of God, there is no evidence anywhere, to my knowledge, that the Spirit would ever exercise authority over the Father.

The flow seems steadily from the Father through the Son and in the Spirit, then back toward the Father through the Son and in the Spirit. Surely if personal order is ultimately contingent or external to God's very being then Scripture would provide at least some evidence, but this is elusive. Before the abundant metanarrative of all divine revelation, the burden of proof rests with those who contend something other than an eternal social order in the Godhead.

The Epistemological Problem

Although many historic Christians might appeal to tradition and experience as theological sources for knowledge that God is constituted as Trinity, the confession of Evangelicals is that the only infallible source of knowledge is Scripture. If all infallible knowledge of God comes from Scripture, and if Scripture never contradicts the pattern we have seen of Trinitarian order, then how else does one know the nature of the immanent Trinity?[40] On what basis does one affirm a transcendent Godhead of a different relational order or no order at all? What would be the criteria for its verification apart from the structure of revelation? Reason and language are, of course, essential to understanding. We always interpret the text within our human settings, always bound by limitations. But the warning here is that we recognize our finitude when forming a speculative trinitarianism disjunctive with the data of the text. Philosophic arguments that a true equality of nature necessitates ultimate equality of social order are neither rationally required nor harmonious with God's self-revelation. Conversely, to insist on equality of eternal roles and order in spite of biblical evidence is methodologically parallel to that of heterodox theologians who reduce God to their own mental paradigms. When philosophic reasoning divorces a theology of the immanent Trinity from the revelation of the economic Trinity, it may have journeyed to where we dare not go.

Dangers of an Egalitarian Godhead: Collapse of Personal Distinctions

The argument in parts 1 and 2 has clarified the biblical testimony regarding both equality of nature with real distinction of roles. These two poles stand in tension and serve as a helpful dialectic that leads to a reasoned biblical synthesis. The two poles also remind us of exaggerations in historic and contemporary trinitarianism—eternal egalitarianism and eternal subordinationism.

1. *History's road toward an egalitarian Trinity.* Reflecting the Apostles' Creed, the Niceno-Constantinopolitan Creed appears to set forth a trinitarian hierarchy. Yet as theology continued to evolve, concepts of the immanent and the economic Trinity became increasingly difficult

---

[40] The repeated weakness of egalitarian trinitarians—among whom I counted myself for various years—is finding any modicum of biblical evidence for affirming an eternal divine democracy. Dozens of textual arguments to the contrary are simply dismissed as necessarily economic in nature. Thus philosophic arguments or appeals to historic and contemporary theologians override biblical testimony. One of the few efforts at a biblical defense for an egalitarian Godhead is Giles, *Jesus and the Father*, 93–128; less directly, Gruenler, *The Trinity in the Gospel of John.*

to hold together. We have seen that Gregory of Nyssa rejected Basil's and Gregory of Nazianzus' locating the divine *ousia* in the Father, yet the younger Cappadocian did not escape his own continuous language of "origin," "begottenness," and "procession." Likewise, Augustine was observed as sometimes stating that nothing tangibly distinguished the three subsistences of the Godhead (each identically possessing the single *ousia*), yet he, too, would return repeatedly to the language of origin. As especially the Western church increasingly focused on the priority of the divine essence over the three subsistent relations, the diversity of roles in the Godhead was minimized.

    2. *Godhead without internal distinctions.* Robert Jenson writes, "The Augustinian supposition that there is no necessary connection between what differentiates the triune identities in God and the structure of God's work in time bankrupts the doctrine of the Trinity cognitively, for it detaches language about the triune identity from the only thing that made such language meaningful in the first place: the biblical narrative."[41] Scripture gives no indication that behind the economic hierarchy, there is arbitrary choice of trinitarian roles (although God is surely as free as he is intentional). There is no hint that the three, to put it brashly, "flip a coin" to see who will do what, although each is completely God. There is never indication that in some future eon or in some deep blue past, the Son plays the role of the Father or the Holy Spirit plays the role of the Son, even though we say that each indwells the other. The creedal terminology of *origin*, *begetting*, and *proceeding* is admittedly not satisfying, but to strip it away for a kind of democratic triumvirate leaves no distinguishing relations between the divine persons. If each member is foremost in everything, then real differentiation is gone. Gerald O'Collins comments: "The relational quality of personhood in God entails acknowledging that the three persons are persons in different ways. Because of the intradivine order of origin (in that the Son and the Holy Spirit are not the origin of the Father), there is an asymmetry between them. They are ordered to one another in an asymmetrical way. The self-

---

[41] Jenson, *Systematic Theology*, 1:112. Certain passages of Augustine lean against Jenson's accusation, which may better be aimed at Aquinas.

giving of the Father, which is the condition of the self-giving of the Son, for example, happens in a way that cannot be reversed."[42]

A social model of the Godhead that does not recognize eternal differentiation of the Father, Son, and Holy Spirit based firmly in divine revelation loses all significant distinction. Indeed, an egalitarian model entirely collapses the meaning of the divine names that distinguishes one divine person from the other. Conversely, an eternally ordered social model of the Trinity argues that the activities and roles of each member visible throughout divine revelation are analogously correspondent with the immanent triune relationships. This would mean, for example, that the Son's role in salvation history is reflective of his eternal relationship with the Father and the Spirit.

Dangers of Subordinationism: The Loss of Intratrinitarian Koinonia

1. *Subordinationism as heresy and nonheresy.* Classical subordinationism is Arianism and designates the essential inequality of nature between the three persons. Christian faith precludes this by defining the *divine nature* as the generic essence, universal property, or attributes of Godness manifest equally in the Father, Son, and Holy Spirit. Subordinationism of essence constitutes a historical heresy outside of our discussion. However, the term *subordination* has also been employed to denote a role of eternal obedience of God the Son to God the Father. Typically such a view affirms that the roles of the Son and the Spirit are wholly volitional. In spite of sometimes sharp accusations against this view,[43] the position that one member of the Godhead eternally and freely defers to another can hardly be construed as a historical heresy! Nor does unbound submission of equally divine persons necessarily denote inferiority (any more than it denotes superiority). Nevertheless, in a fallen

---

[42] O'Collins, *The Tripersonal God*, 179; see Rahner, *The Trinity*, 23.

[43] Giles, *The Trinity and Subordinationism*, 21–31; and *Jesus and the Father*, 32. In response, Letham, in *The Holy Trinity*, 489–96, says, "In the end, Giles's argument collapses. It is self-defeating. He has to point to the submission that he calls (rightly) on us all to display. So he says repeatedly that 'voluntary subordination is godlike' ([*The Trinity and Subordination,*] 18, 21, 116, 117). . . . Giles misses the point that if the Son submits to the Father in eternity, his submission could hardly have been imposed on him, for he is coequal with the Father, of the identical being. He submits willingly. . . . If he did so in the Incarnation without jeopardy to his deity, why is this not so in eternity?" (495).

world, the term *subordination* immediately implies hierarchy, top-down authority, power over another, subjugation, repression, and inequality. With Robert Letham, I think it is a term better abandoned when speaking of the divine immanent relations, particularly if understood as excluding the mutual volition of the Son and the Spirit in any activity of the Godhead.[44] But not to be abandoned is the trinitarian pattern.

2. *Perils of functional subordinationism.* An exaggerated or ill-defined subordinationism of divine roles can violate, it seems to me, not the *homoousios* of God, but the generous character of God seen in the many New Testament passages affirming the Godhead's self-giving and reciprocity (part 1). First, therefore, a functional subordinationism may overstate hierarchy and minimize divine mutuality, including the deep goodness of the Father in relation to the Son and the Spirit.

Second, certain traditional models of a hierarchical Godhead surely minimize differences between the economic and the immanent Trinity. To insist upon univocal correspondence of the economic to the immanent Trinity misses the path, because Scripture itself (although economic in nature) opens up beyond creation history. Revelation points beyond mere economy to transcendent relationality. Hans Urs von Balthasar observes that it is ultimately the immanent Trinity that grounds and supports the economic: "Otherwise the immanent, eternal Trinity would threaten to dissolve into the economic; in other words, God would be swallowed up in the world process."[45] Too narrow a correspondence between the economic and immanent Godhead can distort a sufficient vision of the triune God—whether by evolutionary trinitarians who immerse divine self-fulfillment in salvation history, or by traditionalists who too tightly interpret trinitarian hierarchy while disregarding biblical evidence for divine mutuality. Therefore, trinitarian theology must secure together what is implied regarding the immanent Godhead while also being faithful to the general pattern of God's revelation in time and space.

In the end, theories about the immanent Trinity serve as nets by which we seek to better understand the grace and justice of the triune God in human history. As majestic and engaging as some theories may be, they must continually be subject to and purified by the biblical witness.

---

[44] Letham, *The Holy Trinity*, 480–82, 492–3.

[45] Von Balthasar, *Theo-Drama*, 3:508.

So while theories of the immanent Trinity will not simply duplicate the economic Trinity, they will reflect the economic Trinity in an embracive macrostructure that is faithful to God's Word.

Toward a Deeper Sense of Trinitarian Fullness

1. *Nature and person.* Our linguistic distinctions between nature and person sometimes appear artificial before the infinite triune God. In one sense, God is perfect in very nature, and perfect nature cannot become better nor will it become worse. Yet not only are the persons of the Godhead constituted themselves by nature but also in reciprocal relationship with the other: the Father is the Father in relation to the Son, and the Son to the Father. In yet another sense, the Father, Son, and Holy Spirit forever choose to be themselves in relation to the others—this according to each person's innate dispositions as well as the unifying nature of the Godhead. We might conclude, then, that God exists as Trinity by *nature*, by *relationship*, and by *choice*.

2. *Ordered collaboration.* In the midst of the social-model euphoria over the last three decades that often emphasized totally synonymous divine relations, certain theologians continued to ask this question: in what sense does the coming of the Son and the Spirit disclose eternal relations in the immanent Trinity?[46] The fact that one of the Trinity became incarnate and as God-man obeyed, suffered, and died suggests something beyond mere economy of salvation. Indeed, the incarnation, the cross, and the resurrection shape the Holy Trinity's most remarkable self-disclosure. Of course, in the Son we are shown the love of God the Father (John 3:16). Equally precisely, however, the *kenosis* is the Son's revelation of himself. His willing subjection to the Father in human history must surely reflect some sense of eternal disposition. Similarly, if the activity of the Spirit reveals the character of the Spirit, then what the Godhead has disclosed in revelation history aligns with the intrinsic inclinations of the three persons as immanent Trinity. To say otherwise would deny that God's revelation is ultimately true to God's own reality.

---

[46] Rahner, *The Trinity*, 21–30, 34–38; Pannenberg, *Systematic Theology* 1:308–27; Grenz, *Theology for the Community of God*, 86–88; Jenson, *Systematic Theology*, 1:108–14; Peters, *God—The World's Future*, 110–14; while answers may vary, each sees eternal distinctions in the Godhead.

The Bible not only reveals the innate disposition of each member of the Godhead, on every side it also manifests an order of divine relationship. We have seen in part 1 divine mutuality: not only does the Father request of the Son but the Son requests of the Father; the Son obeys the Spirit as the Spirit obeys the Son. However, as we saw in part 2, the structure of divine relations seems undeniably ordered. Every Pauline letter in the New Testament, for example, salutes the readers with blessings from "God our Father" and the "Lord Jesus Christ"; and the same epistles affirm economic hierarchy in the Godhead with phrases such as "the head of Christ is God" (1 Cor 11:3). Therefore, in detecting the central trinitarian design of Scripture, the mutuality and equality of the Godhead must be held in tension with trinitarian social order. God is love, and each person of the Godhead is mutually self-giving toward the other. Yet these shared personal relations do not exclude what appears to be an ultimately collaborative pattern—indeed, a joyful, deliberate pattern.

3. *Trinitarian life.* Could the Holy Trinity eternally experience within its own inner life both the call-to-do and the doing-response—the giving with the receiving—all in ordered unity and profoundly mutual trust? Both initiation and response appear together in the Godhead with each person freely exercising their innate inclinations and desires. Each loves, each is self-rendering, each serves, but within a harmonious order reflective of the dispositions of the Father, the Son, and the Holy Spirit. Thus, decree and reply—loving ordination and engaging response—might be thought of as both at once in God, as a free and cherished ordination and submission, an activity hardly conceivable in a fallen world but profoundly beautiful in the triune confidence. I submit, then, that the economic Trinity, the Trinity of biblical revelation, points toward an extraordinary abundance in the eternal *koinonia* where the divine persons are completely themselves in perichoretic harmony. Rather than an imposed order, this is an authentic, generous order. And this order of heaven is reflected in God's revelation on earth. To the contrary, by insisting on eternal egalitarian roles that stand in contrast to the divine economy in the Bible, we may, rather than honor the Son and the Spirit, in fact displease them.

Conclusion

The present proposal, not at all strange to most Christian history, is an attempt to better conjoin our idea of God outside creation with the revelation of God inside creation. Jesus Christ is "the reflection of God's glory and the exact imprint of God's very being" (Heb 1:3). The incarnation of the Son of God is the most extraordinary act of divine transparency in human history. Through Jesus we move toward understanding the profound triune reality of the infinite, personal God.

I have defined an *eternally ordered social model* of the Trinity as the social model that, while insisting on equality of the divine nature (part 1), affirms "distinction of roles within the immanent Godhead" (part 2). Such a perspective in simple terms suggests (part 3) the generous preeminence of the Father, the joyous collaboration of the Son, and the ever-glorifying activity of the Spirit.[47] Such a definition, it was insisted (again part 1), must stand together with the infinitely rich self-givingness and reciprocity of the Godhead. The *social model* of the Trinity designates that the one divine Being eternally exists as three distinct centers of consciousness, wholly equal in nature, genuinely personal in relationships, and each mutually indwelling the other. The two definitions are not contradictory but attempt to better frame the mystery of the trinitarian relations.

My primary assertion is that the speculations of trinitarian theology are not to supercede revelation. Rather, the divine mystery must be framed within decidedly biblical truth. On the one hand, egalitarian Trinitarians rightly emphasize the self-giving, perichoretic relations of the Godhead but wrongly minimize the biblical pattern of internal distinctions among the persons, with its implications regarding the immanent Trinity. On the other hand, subordinationist trinitarians correctly perceive that the economic relations of the Father, Son, and Holy Spirit carry implications for the eternal Godhead but often err in presuming univocal correspondence with the immanent Trinity or in neglecting biblical witness regarding the generous mutuality of the trinitarian persons. If the Bible affirms and is not contradictory to an eternally ordered social trinitarianism, then

---

[47] The author recognizes that he has not explicitly defended these divine roles but only the structure in which greater refinement can be made. Nor, given divine reciprocity, does he wish to imply that each member of the Godhead *exclusively* assumes these roles.

efforts to present either an egalitarian Godhead or an overly subordinationist Trinity are misguided. Surely radiant truths can be discerned from social models of the Trinity for our understanding of self and interpersonal relationships. However, philosophic arguments that true equality of nature necessitates equality of order are an equivocation of the two. To those who would furthermore project Western assumptions regarding equality and freedom to remodel God in democratic ideals, we must insist that God's Word judges culture and not vice versa. Conversely, those who on the basis of a hierarchical model of the Trinity justify political oppression or autonomous masculine rulership in familial and ecclesial settings do not grasp the self-sacrificing nature of the Father as well as of the Son and the Spirit.

The two pictures of the Christian Godhead, the economic and the immanent, often leave believers confused. In Western Renaissance paintings such as Masaccio's *The Holy Trinity* (1425), God the Father is often depicted holding his dying Son from behind the cross with the Spirit coming forth from his mouth as a dove. In the Eastern church, Rublev's renowned *Old Testament Trinity* (c. 1415) portrays three nearly equal figures, each with head deferred slightly to the next around the sacred chalice in the center.[48] Are the divine persons distinguishable or virtually identical? Even when we repeat the declaration of the Council of Florence (1438–1445) that "no one of them either precedes the others in eternity, or exceeds them in greatness, or supervenes in power,"[49] we still likely pray to the Father, through the Son, in the Holy Spirit. The immanent Trinity of speculative theology can seem quite distant from the economic Trinity of the Bible and Christian practice. This chapter

---

[48] See Jürgen Moltmann, *Experiences in Theology: Ways and Forms of Christian Theology*, trans. Margaret Kohl (Minneapolis: Fortress, 2000), 305–6. Contra Moltmann's interpretation of the three as indistinguishable, at close inspection, in Rublev's icon each member of the Godhead is quite distinguishable by chronology, colors, and posture, with priority of the Father on the left, the Son above the cup, and the Holy Spirit.

[49] *Concilium Florentinum: Documenta et Scriptores* (Rome: Pontifical Oriental Institute, 1940–1971), quoted in O'Carroll, *Trinitas*, 112–13. Balancing the oft-quoted Florentine credo above, the papal bull *Laetentur coeli*, July 6, 1439, declares: ". . . all likewise profess that the Holy Spirit is eternally from the Father and the Son, and has his essence and his subsistent being both from the Father and the Son, and proceeds from both eternally as from one principle and one spiration."

has attempted to tighten our appreciation for a social model of the Trinity together with the biblical pattern of ordered divine relationships.

In the end, the implications of confessing that one of the Trinity died on the cross are breathtaking. Jesus Christ is the Rosetta Stone that translates in many respects all of reality, but especially and most amazingly, the reality of God's very existence as Holy Trinity.

For Further Reading

Davis, Stephen, Daniel Kendall, and Gerald O'Collins. *The Trinity*. Oxford: Oxford University Press, 1999. Advanced. From an interdisciplinary symposium on the Trinity in 1996, this is a remarkable collection of articles by a broad spectrum of scholars. Gerald O'Collins's opening chapter, "Holy Trinity: The State of the Questions," tightly packages twelve primary issues today.

Grenz, Stanley J. *Rediscovering the Triune God: The Trinity in Contemporary Theology*. Minneapolis: Augsburg, Fortress, 2004. Intermediate. An informed generous reading of modern Trinitarians from Schleiermacher to the present, preface to Grenz's larger recent volumes on the implications of Trinitarian theology for humanity today.

Letham, Robert. *The Holy Trinity: In Scripture, History, Theology, and Worship*. Phillipsburg, NJ: P&R, 2004. Intermediate. From a Reformed perspective, this substantive work is the best holistic exposition of the doctrine of the Trinity today, demonstrating significant scholarship not only in biblical and historical theology but also in current theology and trinitarian praxis.

O'Carroll, Michael. *Trinitas: A Theological Encyclopedia of the Holy Trinity*. Wilmington, DE: Michael Glazier, 1987. An exceptional reference work to the terminology, issues, and significant theologians engaged in the development of trinitarian dogma. From a historical Roman Catholic perspective, it lacks references to recent trinitarian development.

Volf, Miroslav, and Michael Welker, eds. *God's Life in Trinity*. Minneapolis: Fortress, 2006. Intermediate. Eighteen scholars from diverse perspectives interact with Jürgen Moltmann, helpfully exploring current issues in trinitarian theology.

Study Questions

1. Explain what is meant by "economic" and "immanent" Trinity.
2. How does the author define a social model of the Trinity?
3. What is the biblical evidence for a social model of the Trinity?
4. What is the biblical evidence for eternal order in the Godhead?
5. How does the author define an eternally ordered social model of the Trinity?
6. In contrast to the author's eternally ordered social trinitiarianism, explain egalitarian and subordinationist trinitarianism, benefits of each view, and how each view addresses potential problems.

3

THE ONE PERSON WHO IS JESUS CHRIST
The Patristic Perspective

Donald Fairbairn

Chapter Summary

We can no longer legitimately view the Christological controversy as a clash between two equally represented "schools,"
leading to a compromise at Chalcedon that settled the matter
in a largely negative way. Rather, the Christological controversy was an expression of the outrage that most of the church
felt toward the unacceptable Christology of a tiny minority of
people, one of whom (Nestorius, the catalyst for the controversy) happened to be in a very influential position as bishop
of Constantinople. That outrage expressed itself negatively in
Nestorius's condemnation at the Council of Ephesus in 431
and led positively to the consistent doctrinal formulations at
Chalcedon in 451, Constantinople II in 553, and Constantinople
III in 680–81.

This chapter presents Cyril of Alexandria (ca. 375–444), the
key figure in the entire controversy, as the Christian church's
most significant Christological teacher. Furthermore, it will be
argued that the progression of the controversy after Cyril's time
was a development of his own thought, not a departure from it
or a correction of it. Stated simply, Cyril's fundamental insight
into Christology was that the one person of Christ is in fact God
the Logos, the second person of the Trinity. Furthermore, Cyril

specifically and consistently elaborated the implications of this truth for the way we understand the suffering of Christ: it was truly God the Son who died for us on the cross.

Axioms for Christological Study

1. All doctrine should be intimately and clearly connected to soteriology.
2. Any Christology that purports to be biblical and consistent with the early church must assert that the one person in Christ is God the Logos.
3. One must not treat a nature as if it were a person. Rather than stating that the human nature of Christ died on the cross, one must assert that God the Son died on the cross through the human nature he had assumed into his own person.

KEY TERMS

the Logos	person	nature
schools of Antioch and Alexandria	impassible	

Latin terms	*persona*

Greek terms	*prosopon*

I n this chapter, I hope to help illuminate the question of how Jesus should be understood in trinitarian perspective by focusing on the heart of the early church's discussions about Christ, discussions which came in the fifth century. My thesis is that the fifth-century Christological controversy was not a conflict about whether Christ was one person or whether he had two natures, divine and human, since everyone at the time recognized both the unity and duality of Christ (although most of them did not use the words *person* and *nature* to describe these). Nor was it a clash between two equally represented "schools" (Antioch and

Alexandria) that ultimately compromised with each other in agreeing to the Chalcedonian Definition in AD 451. Instead, the controversy was fundamentally about *who* the one person of Christ was. The church as a whole was united in affirming that the one person of Christ was in fact God the Logos, the second person of the Trinity, and those who opposed this consensus comprised only a small minority of Christendom.

In the process of making my case, I will argue that the key figure in the entire Christological controversy, and indeed the Christian church's most significant Christological teacher, was Cyril of Alexandria (ca. 375–444);[1] and that the progression of the controversy after Cyril's time was a development of his own thought, not a departure from it or a correction of it. Furthermore, Cyril specifically and consistently elaborated the implications of this truth for the way we understand the suffering of Christ: it was truly God the Son, one of the persons of the Trinity, who died for us on the cross. When one recognizes that the fundamental issue of the controversy was *who* the one person of Christ was, and when one accepts the centrality of Cyril's place in the controversy, then it becomes clear that the Council of Chalcedon in 451 and the Second Council of Constantinople in 553 were consistent with each other and were Cyrillian in substance, even though they did not use Cyril's terminology.[2]

In order to achieve this purpose, I will need to do several things. First, I will discuss why contemporary theologians and theological students should care about the patristic Christological controversy. Given that we affirm *sola scriptura*, why does it matter whether we understand Chalcedon correctly, as long as we understand the biblical teaching on Christ correctly? Second, I will explain and critique the common view that the Christological controversy was a clash between two equally represented schools, leading to a compromise at Chalcedon. Third, I will address the soteriological concerns that lay at the heart of the contro-

---

[1] Lionel Wickham asserts: "The patristic understanding of the Incarnation owes more to Cyril of Alexandria than to any other individual theologian. The classic picture of Christ the God-man, as it is delineated in the formulae of the Church from the Council of Chalcedon onwards, and as it has been presented to the heart in liturgies and hymns, is the picture Cyril persuaded Christians was the true, the credible, Christ." Lionel R. Wickham, Introduction to *Cyril of Alexandria: Select Letters*, trans. Lionel R. Wickham, OECT (Oxford: Clarendon, 1983), xi.

[2] Throughout this chapter, I will often refer to the ecumenical councils simply by their place names; e.g., "Ephesus," "Chalcedon," and "Constantinople II."

versy. Fourth, I will examine Cyril's Christology itself and demonstrate its fundamental consistency at the level of ideas, in spite of admitted problems with his terminology. Fifth, I will examine the Chalcedonian Definition in light of the soteriological and Christological ideas I have discussed. And finally, I will address the need for consistency between the way we describe the incarnation and the way we describe the atonement. By doing these things, I hope to show how fruitful it can be for Christian theologians today to attend to the early church's (and particularly Cyril's) picture of our Savior.

Before I begin the body of this chapter, there is one further introductory matter I must address, namely, the question of what we mean by the word *person*. Dr. DeWeese's chapter of this book will address this question from a more philosophical perspective, and I do not intend to invade the territory he will explore. Instead, I would like simply to point out that in the patristic period, the word *person* could be understood in two very distinct ways. First, a *person* could be understood merely as a united personal appearance. Two of the Greek and Latin words for person (*prosopon* and *persona*, respectively) both meant "mask" and referred to the mask that an actor wore in order to assume a given character, a given appearance.[3] In this understanding, one could say that Christ was a single person, but this would mean little more than the obvious fact that the Jesus whom people could see, hear, and touch appeared as one man. In actuality, this understanding asserts, he was really two different subjects, the Logos and the man Jesus, appearing together as one *prosopon*. But a second, and very different, patristic way of understanding the idea of person was to see a person as an active subject who *does things* and *to whom things happen*. This is the idea of person that dominated the fifth-century discussions of Christ. It was obvious that he *appeared* as a single character, but at heart, who was the active subject who did things and to whom things happened? To ask the question differently, who was born, the Logos or the man Jesus? Who died, the Logos or the man Jesus? This deeper sense of the word *person* is what I will discuss in this chapter, and as a result, I will use the word *person* and the explanatory phrases "active subject" and "personal subject" interchangeably. With

---

[3] In ancient drama, the same actors played many different parts in the same play, and they distinguished their various roles by wearing different masks.

this understanding of *person* in mind, I will now turn to the tasks I have set for myself in this chapter.

Why Should Contemporary Theologians Care about the Patristic Controversies?

I am often asked why present-day Christians, or even contemporary theologians, should care about the church fathers. My standard answer is that what we think the Bible says is influenced by what we think the church has said the Bible says. (You may want to read that sentence again, slowly.) More specifically, what we today consider important to say about Christ is strongly influenced by what we believe the early church thought important to say. Almost no contemporary Christians ever say that the Council of Chalcedon was wrong about the incarnation. Instead, most orthodox theologians exhibit great respect for the Chalcedonian Definition and regard it as one of the definitive statements of the biblical teaching about Christ. As a result, if we today have misunderstood what the patristic controversies actually dealt with and have thus misunderstood where the significance of the Chalcedonian Definition actually lies, then our very respect for the early church could lead us to problems in our own Christology. To state it differently, if we believe that Chalcedon was biblical, and if we believe that Chalcedon said "x" and only "x," then we are strongly predisposed to say that the Bible teaches "x" and only "x" about Christ. We might then find "x" in Scripture, even if "x" is not *all* that the Bible says about Christ, or even if "x" is not an *accurate* statement of what the Bible says.

Furthermore, even Christians who have never heard of Chalcedon are still influenced by what the current scholarly world thinks Chalcedon meant to affirm. For example, many Christians think that the main thing we need to affirm about Christ is that he is both God and man, that he is one person who has two natures. Where does this conviction come from? It comes, whether we realize it or not, from contemporary theologians' assumption that the major product of patristic Christological controversy was the Chalcedonian Definition's statement that, in Christ, the two natures are united without confusion, without change, without division, without separation. And where does

84

this assumption come from? It comes from contemporary theologians' belief that the Christological controversy dealt primarily with the questions of whether Christ was a single person and whether he possessed complete and distinct divine and human natures.

Notice carefully what is happening here. Recent scholars have made an assumption about what the primary issue in the Christological controversy actually was, an assumption that may or may not be correct. That assumption has led them to look for a particular statement in the Chalcedonian Definition. This in turn has led them to declare what that definition's major point was, and that declaration has then led all of us to make assumptions about what Scripture primarily teaches us about Christ. We read the New Testament looking simply for assurances that Christ is God and man at the same time; and we do this because we have absorbed the idea, propagated by contemporary scholars and reflected in virtually all church history and historical theology books, that this is the main thing the Christological controversy was about.

However, as I have already claimed, and as I hope to show in this chapter, a union of two natures in one person is not the only thing, or even the primary thing, the Chalcedonian Definition and the early church were asserting about Christ. I believe that Chalcedon said much more than this, and if I am correct, then the better we understand the fullness of what Chalcedon and the early church were actually saying, the more likely we will be to look for the fullness of what the Bible itself says about Christ. The controversies of the patristic period in general, and the Christological controversy in particular, matter to us because our understanding of them influences our understanding of Scripture. Whether we like it or not, whether we admit it or not, we are prone to find in Scripture what we *think* the early church believed Scripture to be saying about Christ. But if what we think they saw in Scripture is not what they actually saw in Scripture, then we could find ourselves reading the Bible looking for something that the early church did not find there, something that may or may not be there. We could potentially misunderstand the biblical teaching because we have unwittingly misunderstood the patristic church's understanding of that biblical teaching. This, in a nutshell, is why theologians and theological students today should care about patristic debates such as the Christological controversy.

The Two-Schools Approach to the Christological Controversy

Before I can probe more deeply into what I (and others) believe was actually happening in the Christological controversy, I need to address the view of that controversy that has led us to see Chalcedon in the way I described above. For much of the twentieth century, the commonly accepted approach to the Christological controversy saw it as a clash between two competing schools of thought—the school of Antioch, which emphasized the full humanity of Christ, and the school of Alexandria, which focused on the deity of Christ and had problems seeing him as fully human.

Good Guys vs. Bad Guys

In this understanding, the Antiochenes usually come off looking like the good guys: it is asserted that the reason they recognized the full humanity of Christ was that they took Scripture literally and acknowledged the importance of history. In contrast, the Alexandrians often come off looking like the bad guys, since we are told they cared little for history, allegorized the Bible, and allowed their philosophical interests to dominate their thought. When Christians today see these assertions (especially that the Antiochenes took Scripture literally), we are naturally prone to favor Antioch over Alexandria. This way of describing the controversy suggests that the clash between these two schools led to a back-and-forth struggle and that the key event, the writing of the Chalcedonian Definition, was a compromise between the two schools. This idea in turn leads theologians to look at the Chalcedonian Definition primarily in negative terms. It was not an attempt to say who Christ is, as much as it was an attempt to say how one may *not* speak of him, to rule out obviously unacceptable Christologies.

One could open virtually any twentieth-century work on church history or historical theology and find this view presented, and a noteworthy example is Roger Olson's *The Story of Christian Theology*. In the section of that work dealing with the Christological controversy, two of

Olson's chapter titles are "The Schools of Antioch & Alexandria Clash over Christ" and "Chalcedon Protects the Mystery."[4] Notice how different is the impression these titles generate than if the chapters were entitled "The Church Reacts to Nestorius" and "Chalcedon Proclaims Who Christ Is." We fail to see the fullness of what Chalcedon is saying because we are conditioned to regard it as mainly a negative document produced as a compromise between competing schools. Furthermore, seeing the Antiochenes as the good guys inclines one to see Cyril of Alexandria as the ultimate bad guy, the man who squashed the valid insights of the Antiochene school for the sake of political ambition. As a result, Cyril's theology is rarely even read by Western theologians,[5] even though he is arguably the greatest theologian in the history of the Eastern church and is today enjoying a significant surge in attention from patristics scholars.

It would be almost impossible to overstate the widespread influence of this two-schools approach, but patristics scholarship over the last generation has demonstrated convincingly how inaccurate the approach is. In fact, patristics scholars now recognize that the entire notion of a uniform and well-represented Antiochene school is problematic. The major figures thought to have belonged to this school are Eustathius of Antioch, Diodore of Tarsus, and John Chrysostom in the fourth century, and Theodore of Mopsuestia, Nestorius, John of Antioch, and Theodoret of Cyrus in the fifth century. Of these, the ones whose thought sparked the Christological controversy were Theodore and especially Nestorius. Early in the twentieth century, scholars usually regarded these thinkers as very similar to one another in possessing a recognized, uniform exegetical method that led them to see Christ in a uniform way.[6] But careful study of these writers' exegesis over the past half century has shown that the differences among the Antiochenes were greater than the differences

---

[4] Roger E. Olson, *The Story of Christian Theology: Twenty Centuries of Tradition & Reform* (Downers Grove, IL: InterVarsity, 1999). See especially 233–35 for Olson's view of Chalcedon as a compromise.

[5] Notice the fact that there is no volume on Cyril of Alexandria in the *NPNF²*, far and away the most readily available collection of patristic writings in English.

[6] One of the best examples of this earlier way of viewing the "schools" of Antioch and Alexandria comes in Richard V. Sellers, *Two Ancient Christologies: A Study in the Christological Thought of the Schools of Antioch and Alexandria in the Early History of Christian Doctrine* (London: Society for Promoting Christian Knowledge, 1940).

between them and the Alexandrians. For example, Theodoret of Cyrus was much more likely to find Christ prefigured in a given Old Testament passage than was Theodore of Mopsuestia, thus making Theodoret less "literal" than Theodore in the minds of contemporary scholars, but making Theodoret more *Christian* in the mind of the early church.[7] Another poignant example is that Eustathius (one of the early so-called Antiochenes) gives Origen (the examplar of the Alexandrian allegorizers) a thorough tongue lashing on the grounds that Origen interprets the account of Saul and the witch of Endor (1 Sam 28) too literally.[8] If one moves beyond the stereotype of calling the Antiochenes literal and historical and branding the Alexandrians as allegorizers, then one finds that the so-called Antiochenes are no more likely to take Scripture literally than are the Alexandrians. Patristics scholarship today is calling into question the very idea that there was a uniform Antiochene school of literal, historical exegesis.[9] As a result, that scholarship is undermining the idea that the Antiochenes were the good guys who came to their conclusions simply by reading the Bible well.

The So-Called Antiochenes: Not a Well-Represented School

Once the notion that the Antiochenes were necessarily the good guys has been taken off the table, and thus the incentive to see them as being well represented in the early church has been removed, then it quickly becomes apparent that the controversy was not primarily about taking the Bible literally vs. allegorizing Scripture, or about whether Christ is a single person with two natures. Rather, the controversy was fundamentally about whether God the Logos was personally involved in human experience. This concern implies the question of who the personal subject of Christ was: was Christ God the Son, who was also somehow human, or was he the man Jesus, who was also somehow divine?[10] If one

---

[7] See Frances M. Young, *From Nicaea to Chalcedon: A Guide to the Literature and Its Background* (Philadelphia: Fortress, 1983), 285–86.

[8] See Frances M. Young, "The Rhetorical Schools and Their Influence on Patristic Exegesis," in *The Making of Orthodoxy: Essays in Honour of Henry Chadwick*, ed. Rowan Williams (Cambridge: Cambridge University Press, 1989), 194–95. Young is citing Eustathius's work *On the Witch of Endor and Against Origen* (PG 18:613–73).

[9] I summarize much of this recent patristics scholarship in my forthcoming article "Patristic Exegesis and Theology: The Cart and the Horse" in *WJT* 69:1 (Spring 2007): 1–19.

[10] For a summary of scholarly opinions on what the central issue of the controversy

regards this as the fundamental question, then it is clear that there were few people who actually deserved to be called "Antiochene." Instead, most of the so-called Antiochenes agreed fully that the Logos is the personal subject of Christ, and this places them very much at odds with Theodore and Nestorius. Much of my own recent work has sought to demonstrate this, and I would like to illustrate this point here by briefly examining one crucial passage each from John Chrysostom, John of Antioch, and Theodoret of Cyrus, all alleged to be members of the "Antiochene School."

In Chrysostom's homily (probably preached in 399) on the crucial Christological passage Philippians 2:5–11, he clearly distinguishes actions that are befitting for humanity from those that are befitting for deity, but he ascribes all of these actions to the person of the Logos. He declares: "Speaking here of his divinity, Paul no longer says, 'he became,' 'he took,' but he says, 'he emptied himself, taking the form of a servant, being made in the likeness of men.' Speaking here of his humanity he says, 'he took,' 'he became.' He became the latter [i.e. human], he took the latter; he was the former [i.e. God]. Let us not then confuse or divide. There is one God, there is one Christ, the Son of God. When I say 'one,' I mean a union, not a confusion; the one nature did not degenerate into the other, but was united with it."[11]

Several things are noteworthy here. First, Chrysostom equates God, Christ, and the Son of God ("there is one God, there is one Christ, the Son of God") in a way that makes clear that he sees the Logos as the subject of Christ's person. Second, he applies both being and becoming/taking to the person of the Logos. Third, he distinguishes being (who the Logos is in his deity) from becoming (what the Logos does in his humanity). The statements "he became" and "he took" do not apply to Christ's deity: Christ did not become God or take deity upon himself, since he always was God. Rather, the Son of God became man and took the form of a

---

was, see my book *Grace and Christology in the Early Church*, OECS (Oxford: Oxford University Press, 2003), 6–11.

[11] Chrysostom, *Homilies on the Epistle to the Philippians* 7.3. The Greek text may be found in *PG* 62:177–298. An English translation may be found in *NPNF¹*, 13:184–398. This passage is in *PG*, 62:232; *NPNF¹*, 13:214–15. This translation and all other translations of patristic writings in this chapter are ones for which I bear final responsibility, although I have consulted published translations when they were available.

servant upon himself. Chrysostom insists that the one born of Mary was in fact God the Son, the second person of the Trinity.[12]

In November of the year 430, prior to the Council of Ephesus, John of Antioch wrote a letter to his friend Nestorius, in which he sought to convince him to accept the title *Theotokos* for Mary. In the most crucial passage of that important letter, John writes: "If one suppresses this title or what it signifies, then it necessarily follows that neither is God the one who has taken on himself the unsearchable economy for our sake, nor is God the Logos the one who manifested such a great love for us in emptying himself and taking the form of a servant. But these are things which the divine Scriptures affirm in connection with God's love for us, when they declare that the pre-existent, eternal, and only-begotten Son of God descended in an impassible manner to be born from the virgin."[13]

Here John makes it absolutely clear that he believes Scripture teaches that the Logos himself was the one born of Mary, and the reason this is so crucial is that only then can God be the one who has accomplished our salvation, the one who has emptied himself and become incarnate on our behalf. John of Antioch (like Chrysostom) sees salvation as an act of God's condescension, and so he (again, like Chrysostom but not like Theodore and Nestorius) views Christ's personal subject as that of the Logos himself.

Theodoret of Cyrus's Christology has puzzled theologians both in his own time and more recently, and there has long been disagreement about whether his view of Christ was acceptable. But to summarize and simplify a very complicated discussion, I believe that Theodoret's normal pattern was to see the Logos as the one person in Christ. Only in some of his most polemical writings against Cyril does he slide away from this view.[14] A good example of his normal way of viewing Christ

---

[12] See my fuller discussion of Chrysostom's Christology in *Grace and Christology in the Early Church*, 204–11. See also the assessment of Camillus Hay, "Antiochene Exegesis and Christology," *ABR* 12 (1964): 16–17. Hay argues that although Theodore and Chrysostom were fellow students and friends, their Christologies were dramatically different.

[13] John of Antioch, *Epistle to Nestorius*. The Greek text may be found in *ACO*, tom. 1, vol. 1, pars 1, pp. 92–96. There is no English translation of the entire letter, but I translate the significant portions of it and offer an explanation of its theological significance in my article "Allies or Merely Friends? John of Antioch, and Nestorius in the Christological Controversy," *JEH* 58:3 (July 2007).

[14] For the details of this debate and my own attempt to resolve it, see my article, "The Puzzle of Theodoret's Christology: A Modest Suggestion," *JTS* 58:1 (April 2007).

comes in a letter written in the winter of 431–32, shortly after the Council of Ephesus. Theodoret claims: "Therefore, we say that our Lord Jesus Christ is the only-begotten Son of God and firstborn. On one hand he is only-begotten, both before being made man and after being made man; but on the other hand, he is firstborn after his birth from the virgin . . . The divine Scriptures state that God the Logos alone was begotten from the Father; but the Only-Begotten also becomes first-born, by taking our nature from the virgin and deigning to call 'brothers' those who have trusted in him. In this way the same one is only-begotten in that he is God, but firstborn in that he is man."[15] This passage makes clear that Theodoret sees the events of the incarnation and life of Christ as happening to one personal subject, the Logos. This Logos who was eternally begotten of the Father has now been born of Mary. The one who had no brothers because he was God's *only* Son now counts us as his adopted brothers.

It is quite significant that Chrysostom and John of Antioch see the person of Christ as being the Logos and that Theodoret normally does so, since as I have mentioned, all three of them have generally been considered major representatives of the Antiochene School. If these three men are not really Antiochenes, then who *does* belong to this "school"? We are left with Diodore, Theodore of Mopsuestia, and Nestorius as the only real "Antiochenes," and these three men were all condemned by the church for heretical Christology. One cannot legitimately argue that the "Antiochenes" were a bona fide school or that Antiochene Christology was well represented in the fifth century and accepted by the church. When one acknowledges that the central issue in the debate was that of who the person of Christ was, and when one defines Antiochene Christology as that which sees the man Jesus as the personal subject of Christ, then one recognizes that the Antiochenes constituted only a tiny minority of the church, a minority which the rest of the church deemed to be heretical. Therefore, it is not legitimate to see the Chalcedonian Definition as a compromise document mediating between two schools; it was part of a consistent line of doctrinal development that began with

---

[15] Theodoret of Cyrus, "Epistle C4." The critical text, with French translation, may be found in Theodoret of Cyprus, *Correspondance*, ed. Yvan Azéma, SC 429 (Paris, Editions du Cerf, 1998), 122. An English translation is in *NPNF²*, 3:329.

Nestorius's condemnation at the Council of Ephesus in 431 and continued after Chalcedon with the formulations of Constantinople II in 553
and Constantinople III in 680–81.

Therefore, if the two-schools approach is unacceptable and if the controversy really was not fundamentally about whether Christ was fully human
as well as fully divine, then what is a better way to view the Christological
controversy? I have argued that the fundamental question was whether the
one person of Christ is God the Son. In order for us to grasp the full significance of this question, we need to examine it in more detail, paying close
attention to the soteriological concerns that lie behind it.

Fifth-Century Soteriology: The Handmaiden to Christology

I believe one of the most fundamental theological axioms is that *all
doctrine should be intimately and clearly connected to soteriology*. It is
a great mistake to isolate various Christian doctrines one from another,
and this mistake is particularly dangerous when one is dealing with the
trinitarian and Christological controversies. Too often these patristic debates are presented as if they were primarily attempts to arrive at the
best philosophical vocabulary for speaking of God and Christ. But fundamentally, these debates were not about philosophy; they were about
salvation. I contend that at the deepest level, the church's thought process
in the fourth and fifth centuries was an attempt to answer the question,
"What does God have to be like in order to give us the kind of salvation
that we Christians know (from Scripture and the Holy Spirit's witness)
we have?" To state this another way, the church was not simply asking
what language the Bible will or will not allow us to use when we speak
of God or Christ, although that was part of the question. The church was
also asking what the Bible says about our salvation, and thus what it
must say or imply about the One who grants us that salvation. Differing
perceptions of what salvation actually is and how it is accomplished are
closely related to different perceptions of who can accomplish that salvation. At the level of what the church *said* about Christ, the issue was
Christological. But at the level of *why* the church said what it said about
Christ, the underlying issue was soteriological. In this way, one may call
patristic soteriology the handmaiden to patristic Christology, and I be-

lieve it is very important for us to grasp the soteriology that lay behind the church's Christology in order to understand that Christology itself.

When the fifth-century church rejected Nestorianism, it was condemning a particular way of understanding what salvation is and how it is achieved, and the church (including some so-called Antiochenes such as Chrysostom and John of Antioch) was asserting a different soteriology. The soteriology behind Nestorianism finds its best and clearest expression not in Nestorius himself, but in his teacher Theodore of Mopsuestia, who died in 428 just as the Christological controversy was about to break loose. The soteriology that the church affirmed finds its clearest expression in Cyril of Alexandria, although Cyril's view was not just his own, but was the consensus of the whole church at the time. As a result, in this section, I would like to summarize Theodore's soteriological concerns briefly and then examine Cyril's soteriology in a bit more detail.

Theodore of Mopsuestia and the Human Ascent to the Second Age

At the heart of Theodore's thought lies his concept of the "two ages," two radically different states of humanity.[16] The first age is one of mutability, corruption, and sin; the second age is one of immutability, incorruption, and perfection. Theodore argues that the first age is the one in which God has created us, and thus it is a good age; but the second age is the one to which we aspire, and it will be a vastly superior age. This concept of the two ages implies that for Theodore, the fall was not an actual event in which humanity abandoned an earlier perfect condition. Rather, the fall is a reflection of humanity's state from the beginning. Thus, in Theodore's thought, salvation is not a restoration of fallen humanity to a previous condition, but rather the elevation of humanity to an entirely new condition. In keeping with these ideas, Theodore places almost no emphasis on salvation as a believer's present possession, but instead sees salvation almost entirely as a future condition, a possession that will be ours only in a future world, but toward which the believer must strive in this world.

Another important idea in Theodore's thought is his belief that God does not actually give us the blessings of the second age, nor does he give

---

[16] For a discussion of Theodore's soteriology and an examination of the most important texts from his writings demonstrating his thought, see Fairbairn, *Grace and Christology in the Early Church*, 29–40.

the Holy Spirit himself to believers. Instead, God gives us what we need in order to attain to that age ourselves. As a result, one can see that in Theodore's soteriology, human effort plays a very significant role. God did not simply give humanity fellowship with himself at creation; he set before humanity the task of aspiring to a higher age. Similarly, God does not simply restore humanity to fellowship with himself at the beginning of salvation; he gives us what we need to seek the second age ourselves. One can say that for Theodore, God plays an assistive, auxiliary role in salvation, and the primary role belongs to humanity: we ascend from the first age to the second age with God's help.

Cyril of Alexandria and the Gift of Divine Communion

In sharp contrast to Theodore's concept of the two ages, Cyril (as well as most of the church) understands human history as a drama of creation, fall, and restoration. He emphasizes very strongly that God created humanity in mature fellowship with himself, that we lost this blessing through the sin of our first parents (an *actual* fall, rather than merely a metaphorical one as in Theodore), and that God himself came into our world through the incarnation in order to restore us to the condition he had given us initially. In this way, Cyril sets himself up to place much more emphasis on God's action in accomplishing our salvation than on our own action: God *gave* us the initial beatitude; we lost it, and he *gives it to us anew* in salvation. Furthermore, Cyril's understanding of what salvation actually entails is quite different from Theodore's. Theodore focuses on our ascent to a perfect *human* age, but he has virtually no concept of human participation in divine life or even of human fellowship with God. In his mind, what we achieve in the second age is a state of human perfection and immortality. In contrast, Cyril sees salvation primarily as our sharing fellowship with God.

A few passages from Cyril's *Commentary on John*, probably written in the mid-420s,[17] will serve to illustrate these points. As Cyril comments on John 17:18–19, he explains Jesus' prayer by asserting, "From the Father

---

[17] The Greek critical text of this work may be found in *Sancti patris nostri Cyrilli archiepiscopi Alexandrini, in d. Joannis evangelium: Accedunt fragmenta varia necnon tractatus ad Tibersium diaconoum duo*, ed. P. E. Pusey (Oxford: Clarendon, 1872). An English translation may be found in LoF, vols. 43, 48.

he sought for us that holiness which is in and through the Spirit, and he desires what was in us by the gift of God at the first age of the world and the beginning of creation to be rekindled to life in us again." Cyril explains that at creation, God gave life to Adam by breathing his Spirit into him, and he continues: "He desires, therefore, the nature of man to be renewed and re-formed, as it were, into its original likeness, by communion with the Spirit, in order that, by putting on that original grace and being re-shaped into conformity with him, we may be found able to prevail over the sin that reigns in this world."[18] Here, it is clear that God gave himself to us at creation through his Spirit, thus fashioning our initial image after his own image. Furthermore, Cyril uses the word *again* and four verbs beginning with the prefix "re-" in order to show that salvation is a return to the participation in the Holy Spirit which he gave humanity initially.

The passage above shows not only that salvation is a restoration to the condition God originally gave humanity, but also that this condition involves participation in God. Earlier in this commentary, Cyril has made clear what he means by this participation. Commenting on John 1:13, Cyril explains the difference between the way the Son is begotten of God and the way Christians are. He writes: "When he had said that authority was given to them from him who is by nature Son to become sons of God, and had hereby first introduced that which is of adoption and grace, he can afterwards add without danger [of misunderstanding] that they were begotten of God, in order that he might show the greatness of the grace that was conferred on them, gathering as it were into natural communion those who were alien from God the Father, and raising up the slaves to the nobility of their Lord, on account of his warm love toward them."[19]

In this passage, two things are noteworthy. First, Cyril sharply distinguishes the true Son, the Logos, from Christians who are adopted sons and daughters of God. We are not begotten of God in the same way that the Logos is. He is the unique Son of God, but we are children of God by adoption and grace. The second noteworthy thing is that even though we are "merely" adopted, God grants us to share in the natural commu-

---

[18] *Commentary on John* 11.10 (Pusey, *Sancti patris nostri Cyrilli*, 2:719–20; LoF, 48:535–36).

[19] *Commentary on John* 1.9 (Pusey, *Sancti patris nostri Cyrilli*, 1:135; LoF, 43:106).

nion that has existed from eternity between the Father and the Son. To state this differently, God does not simply grant us *a* relationship with himself, or *some kind* of fellowship with himself. Instead, he grants us to share by grace in *the very same* fellowship that the persons of the Trinity share by nature. To be saved, to participate in God, is to share this very communion. In Cyril's mind, this is what God has given humanity at creation, and what he gives us anew in salvation.[20]

Even from this very brief survey, it should be clear how startlingly different Theodore's and Cyril's soteriologies are. For Theodore, and for his student Nestorius, salvation is largely the human task, with God's assisting grace, of ascending from an imperfect human age to a perfect human age. In this understanding, there is no particular need for God to enter human life personally in order to save humanity. We need a human example and trailblazer, not a divine Savior. As a result, Theodore and Nestorius write of Christ as the man who has received aid and cooperation from the Logos, so that he can himself ascend to the second age and blaze the trail that we will follow in ascending to that age ourselves. In marked contrast, Cyril (as well as the church as a whole) sees salvation as God's action to give humanity participation in the very communion that the persons of the Trinity share. In order to do this, God the Son himself must personally step into human history. Thus, it is clear that the soteriologies behind Theodorean/Nestorian and Cyrillian Christologies profoundly influence the respective understandings of who the personal subject of Christ is: Theodorean Christology sees that person as the man Jesus, who is indwelt by God the Son in order to receive the aid he needs to blaze the trail we follow, but Cyrillian Christology sees the personal subject as God the Logos himself, who has assumed humanity into his own person in order to grant human beings the fellowship he shares with the Father and the Spirit. With these soteriologies in mind, I now turn to Cyril's Christology itself.

Cyril of Alexandria's Christology

I have already claimed above that Cyril asserts the one person of Christ to be God the Logos, and I insist that this is a fundamental axiom

---

[20] I give a much more extensive discussion of this idea in chapter three of *Grace and Christology in the Early Church.*

for any Christology that purports to be biblical and consistent with the early church. It is now time to elaborate on that claim by examining Cyril's Christology in some detail. In this section, I would like to look at three major ways in which Cyril indicates that the personal subject of Christ is the Logos.

Two Infamous, but Misunderstood, Assertions

Cyril is probably most infamous as the champion of two great slogans, the title *Theotokos* ("bearer of God") for Mary and the phrase "one incarnate nature of God the Logos." These two slogans have given Cyril quite a bad reputation among many recent theologians, since they seem to imply that he foreshadowed the excessive attention to Mary characteristic of medieval Christianity, and that he was the father of what we refer to as the "Monophysite heresy." However, I suggest that we have quite badly misunderstood what Cyril meant by these slogans. When one understands them properly, it becomes clear that Cyril uses both of them to affirm that the Logos is the personal subject of Christ.

The question of whether one may call Mary *Theotokos* was actually sparked the Christological controversy initially. In Cyril's first letter at the outbreak of the controversy (written early in 429),[21] he asks poignantly: "If our Lord Jesus Christ is God, how is the virgin who gave birth to him not the bearer of God?"[22] He goes on to argue that since anyone who has received the grace of the Holy Spirit can be called "Christ" (i.e., "anointed one"), the mother of any Christian could be called *Christotokos*, but only Mary can be called *Theotokos*.[23] From these passages it is clear that Cyril's point is to proclaim the uniqueness of the Son whom Mary bore: He is God the Logos himself in human form. In this way, Cyril safeguards the distinction between the way we become sons of God and the way Christ is Son of God.

---

[21] Cyril's letters may be found in *PG* 77:9–390, and critical texts of some of them may be found in various places. Most useful for general purposes is Wickham, *Cyril of Alexandria: Select Letters*, which includes both critical texts and English translations of the most important theological letters. English translations of all the letters may be found in FaCh, vols. 76, 77. Subsequent citations from the letters will reference the best text available and the most convenient English translation.

[22] *Epistle* 1 (*ACO* tom. 1, vol. 1, pars 1, p. 11; FaCh, 76:15).

[23] *Epistle* 1 (*ACO* tom. 1, vol. 1, pars 1, p. 14; FaCh, 76:20).

In the autumn of 430, Cyril issued twelve anathemas, the first of which condemned anyone who refused to call Mary *Theotokos*. The next year, just before the Council of Ephesus began, he explained this anathema by writing: "Certain people have denied his birth according to the flesh, that birth which took place from the holy virgin for the salvation of all. It was not a birth that called God into a beginning of existence but one intended to deliver us from death and corruption when he became like us. This is why our first anathema cries out against their evil faith and then confesses what is the right faith, saying that Emmanuel is truly God, and for this reason the holy virgin is the bearer of God."[24]

Here we see that to Cyril, a denial of the title *Theotokos* constitutes a denial of the saving economy. The Logos did not receive the beginning of his divine existence from Mary, since he was eternally begotten from the Father, but he was born a second time "for the salvation of all," in order to free us from death and corruption.[25] For Cyril, as for most of the fifth-century church, the title *Theotokos* was not so much a statement about Mary as it was a way of demonstrating the true deity of Christ. The truth behind the title *Theotokos*—that the one born of Mary was the same person who had been eternally begotten from the Father—is crucial precisely because only this Son can share with us the communion he has with the Father. According to Cyril, this truth, this concept of salvation, will be in jeopardy if one denies Mary the title.

In his controversial writings, Cyril uses the infamous slogan "one incarnate nature of God the Logos" at least nine times, and I will look briefly at one of these passages. After the split produced by the Council of Ephesus, Cyril, John of Antioch, and others worked diligently to come to terms and bring about a reunion of the separated parties. The result of those efforts was the Reunion Formula, a statement that spoke of a union of two natures in Christ. Cyril signed the statement in 433, a fact that infuriated some of his supporters who regarded his slogan "one incarnate nature" as a test of orthodoxy. Cyril's response to one such supporter, Acacius of Melitene, is very revealing. Cyril asserts: "When we have the

---

[24] *Explanation of the Twelve Chapters* 6 (*ACO* tom. 1, vol. 1, pars 5, p. 17). There is an English translation in John A. McGuckin, *St. Cyril of Alexandria: The Christological Controversy*, SVC 23 (Leiden: E. J. Brill, 1994), 282–93.

[25] In Greek, as in many languages, there is a single word for the two English words *born* and *begotten*.

idea of the realities from which is the one and unique Son and Lord Jesus Christ, we speak of two natures being united; but after the union, the duality has been abolished and we believe the Son's nature to be one, since the Son is one, yet become man and incarnate. Though we affirm that the Logos is God on becoming incarnate and made man, any suspicion of change is to be repudiated entirely because he remained what he was, and we are to acknowledge the union as totally free from merger."[26]

One should notice that Cyril refers to both "two natures" and "one nature" in Christ, and this fact should immediately lead us to recognize that there is more than one way to use the word *nature* (*physis* in Greek). When Cyril speaks of two natures, he is referring to deity and humanity, and he repudiates any thought that these have changed or become confused through the incarnation. But when he speaks of one nature after the union, he is referring to a single sonship; and he makes this connection between Christ's single nature and his single sonship explicit by writing, "we believe the Son's nature to be one, since the Son is one." The Son is one as a person, the second person of the Trinity. In this way, the Son's *physis* is one.

This suggests that the "one nature" formula functions as a means of pointing to the fact that when considered in personal terms, Christ is a single entity, the Father's natural Son. Thus, Cyril's use of the "one nature" slogan does not constitute a rejection of Christ's true humanity or a belief that the humanity has been absorbed into his deity and lost. Rather, he uses the word *physis* in the sense that Chalcedon would later give to *hypostasis*: Christ as a single personal subject, the Logos-made-man. Although Cyril himself uses *physis* in this way, he is not opposed to using the word to refer to the divine and human realities in Christ. He can comfortably speak of one nature and two natures in the same paragraph, because he is able to clarify the different senses of the word.

Christ Is the Natural Son of God

In addition to the expressions I considered in the previous section, another common way that Cyril shows that the Logos is the person of Christ is by insisting repeatedly that Christ *is* the natural Son of God. He is not just Son by virtue of having a divine nature (after all, no one

---

[26] *Epistle* 40 (*ACO* tom. 1, vol. 1, pars 4, p. 26; FaCh 76:160–61).

speaks of a nature as being a son or daughter; only a person can be a son or daughter), nor did he receive deity, sonship, or grace from the outside. Furthermore, Cyril contrasts Christ's natural sonship with believers' sonship by grace, and he argues that if Christ were not Son by nature, he would not have been able to make us sons and daughters or to give us grace. Of the many passages in which Cyril emphasizes these truths, two are especially noteworthy. In Cyril's paschal letter for the year 436,[27] he discusses Jesus' trial, at which the crowd tells Pilate that Jesus has made Himself out to be God's Son (John 19:7). Cyril argues: "He did not make himself out to be God's Son, but he truly was so. For he possessed the quality of sonship not from the outside, nor as something added, but as being the Son by nature, for this is what we must believe. For we are sons of God by adoption as we are conformed to the Son who has been begotten [of the Father] by nature. For if there were no true Son, who would remain to whom we could be conformed by adoption? Whose representation would we bear? Where indeed would the resemblance be, if we were to say that the original did not exist?"[28]

Here it is clear that adoption is not a matter of divine fiat; it is a conformity that God gives us to the true Son. If there were no true Son, then there would be no one to whom we could become conformed, and therefore we could not become adopted sons and daughters. And since Cyril insists overwhelmingly that the only true, natural Son of God is the Logos, it is clear that Christ is that very Logos.

The second passage comes in *Epistle* 55, written around the year 438. Cyril alludes to Philippians 2:6–8 and argues that those who postulate two sons distort the meaning of the mystery: "He is not someone who after being empty attained fullness; instead he humbled himself from his divine heights and unspeakable glory. He is not a humble man who was exalted in glory, but rather he was free and took the form of a slave. He is not a slave who made a leap up to the glory of freedom; he who was in the Father's form, in equality with him, has been made in the likeness of men. He is not a man who has come to share the riches of God's like-

---

[27] Each year it was customary for the bishop of Alexandria to write a paschal letter to inform the churches when Lent would begin and when Easter would be celebrated that year. Cyril's paschal letters are preserved in *PG* 77:401–981.

[28] *Paschal Letter* 24:3 (*PG* 77:896b). There is no English translation of this letter.

ness."[29] One should notice that only if there is a genuine Son who has moved from his own wealth to our poverty can we become sons of God. Personal downward movement of the Logos is the only thing that can enable us to receive God himself and become his children. No elevation of a man to divine status would accomplish anything for us, but such an elevation of the man Jesus to divine status is precisely what Theodore and Nestorius teach. In their soteriology, that is all we need, and we can follow in the footsteps of that man so as to reach the second age. But if one sees salvation as God's action to give us his own natural fellowship, then God himself must come down to us through the incarnation. Therefore, Christ must be, and is, the natural Son of God, the second person of the Trinity.

The Logos Personally Experienced Human Life

One of Cyril's most common ways of referring to the incarnation is to speak of the Logos as uniting flesh (that is, humanity) to his own person, so that the humanity of Christ is the Logos's own flesh. The word "own" (*idios* in Greek) then becomes Cyril's keyword for stressing that the Logos himself is personally present on earth with us through the humanity that he has made his own. His humanity is not a distinct person, but instead a set of properties that the Logos possesses after the incarnation, so that the Logos himself can personally live as a man. Thus one can say unequivocally that God the Logos was born, the Logos suffered, the Logos died on the cross and was raised (all of which statements Theodore and Nestorius refuse to make). I will give three examples of this pattern.

In his second letter to Nestorius, written early in 430, Cyril denies that a man was born and then the Logos descended onto him, and he argues instead that the Logos "was united with flesh in her [Mary's] womb and so is said to have undergone birth according to the flesh, so as to appropriate the birth of his own flesh."[30] Here Cyril makes clear that it is the Logos himself who undergoes birth from Mary, although this birth obviously did not constitute the origin of his divine substance. Instead, the birth (or more properly, the conception) constituted the origin of his

---

[29] Wickham, *Cyril of Alexandria,* 112–13.
[30] *Epistle* 4 (Wickham, *Cyril of Alexandria,* 6–7).

flesh, his humanity, but the person who underwent this human birth was God the Son.

Even more dramatically, in another writing from 429, Cyril comments on Acts 20:28: "Do you hear the way the apostle clearly proclaims the deity of the crucified one? For he says that we are to be shepherds of the church of God, which he purchased through his own blood. Not that he suffered in the nature of his deity, but that the sufferings of his flesh are ascribed to him because the flesh is not that of some other man, but is the Logos's own. Therefore, since the blood is said to be God's blood, then clearly he was God, clothed with flesh."[31]

The biblical phrase translated "his own blood" is somewhat ambiguous; it could mean either "the blood of his own [Messiah]" or "God's own blood." Cyril interprets the phrase (correctly, in my opinion) as referring to God's own blood which the incarnate Logos shed on our behalf on the cross. Similarly, in a writing from just before the Council of Ephesus in 431, Cyril insists: "Even though the Logos of God the Father is so [i.e., impassible] essentially, he made his own the flesh that is capable of death, so that by means of what is accustomed to suffer he could assume sufferings for us and on our account, and thus liberate us all from death and corruption."[32]

These passages are striking, because Cyril attributes not merely human birth, but even human suffering to the divine person, the Logos. Because the flesh/humanity was the Logos's own, the suffering was the Logos's personal suffering which he underwent through that humanity. Clearly, Cyril sees the Logos as the personal subject of Christ.

These bold assertions do not mean that Cyril has abandoned his belief in the Logos's impassibility; he insists that the Logos suffers in his flesh, not in his own nature. But his understanding of salvation as God's giving us himself demands that he affirm the Logos's personal presence in the lowest depths of human experience. Indeed, it is precisely in the depths that we need God's presence, and if God were not to meet us there, we would have no hope of grace, adoption, or salvation, as Cyril under-

---

[31] *Against Those Who Do Not Give Mary the Title "Theotokos"* 22. The Greek text of this work may be found in *ACO* tom. 1, vol. 7, pars 19–32. There is no English translation. This passage is in *ACO* tom. 1, vol. 1 pt. 7, pars 29.

[32] *Explanation of the Twelve Chapters* 31 (*ACO* tom. 1, vol. 1, pars 5,25).

stands these. Only if God the Logos himself has personally descended to the lowest point of human experience can God meet us where we are, in order to fill us with his presence, with his grace, with himself.[33]

In these three ways, Cyril presses home his fundamental insight, the truth that considered as a person, Christ is God the Son. The humanity created and united to the Logos in Mary's womb subsists in the *hypostasis* of the Logos, so that one may truly say God the Son was born, suffered, died, and was raised. As we have seen, Cyril's understanding of Scripture and his concept of salvation lead him to say this. Only if the person who meets us in our lowly human condition is truly God's unique Son, the Logos, can we receive from him the communion he has with the Father. As Cyril sees it, the Theodorean/Nestorian Christ can do no more than point the way to God; he cannot bring God to humanity, since he is not God himself but merely a graced man. Cyril's understanding of salvation (as well as that of the church as a whole) demands that God's presence in our world be personal and direct, which in turn requires that God himself, the Logos, be the one personal subject in Christ.

Cyril and Chalcedon

When one understands the difference between Theodore's and Cyril's soteriologies, and when one grasps Cyril's insistence that the Logos is the one person of Christ, then one is able to look at the Chalcedonian Definition in a significantly new way. One is now able to see that it was not merely a compromise document mediating between two schools that were at loggerheads with each other, and thus one is no longer forced to view it simply as a negative statement designed to do nothing more than exclude "extremes" like Nestorianism and Eutychianism. Rather, one may now see the Definition as a positive statement of the Church's consensus faith, a faith that had been expressed well by Cyril and others of his time.

---

[33] For an assessment of Cyril's Christology and soteriology very similar to mine, see Thomas F. Torrance, *Theology in Reconciliation: Essays Towards Evangelical and Catholic Unity in East and West* (London: Geoffrey Chapman, 1975), 161.

With this in mind, let us now look directly at the Chalcedonian Definition.[34] The text, as I translate it and highlight key recurring phrases, reads as follows:

> Therefore, following the holy fathers, we all unite in teaching
>> that we should confess **one and the same** Son, our Lord Jesus Christ.
>
> **This same one** is perfect in deity, and **the same one** is perfect in humanity;
>> **the same one** is true God and true man, comprising a rational soul and a body.
>
> He is of the same substance as the Father according to his deity,
>> and **the same one** is of the same substance with us according to his humanity,
>> like us in all things except sin.
>
> He was begotten before the ages from the Father according to his deity,
>> but in the last days for us and our salvation,
>> **the same one** was born of the virgin Mary, the bearer of God, according to his humanity.
>
> He is **one and the same** Christ, Son, Lord, and only-begotten,
>> who is made known in two natures unconfusedly, unchangeably, indivisibly, inseparably.
>
> The distinction between the natures is not at all destroyed because of the union,
>> but rather the property of each nature is preserved
>> and concurs together in one *prosopon* and *hypostasis*.
>
> He is not separated or divided into two *prosopa*,
>> but is **one and the same** Son, the only-begotten, God the Logos, the Lord Jesus Christ.
>
> This is the way the prophets spoke of him from the beginning,
>> and Jesus Christ himself instructed us,
>> and the council of the fathers has handed [the faith] down to us.

---

[34] The Greek text of the Chalcedonian Definition may be found in many places. Perhaps the most accessible is Philip Schaff, ed., *CC*, 2:62–63. Schaff also includes an English translation.

From the portions printed in boldface type, one can see that the phrases "the same one" and "one and the same" occur a combined eight times. Clearly the dominant statement of the definition is that Christ is one and the same. The one who is consubstantial with the Father is the same one who is consubstantial with us. But to whom, to what personal subject, do these statements refer? Many interpreters have argued that Chalcedon does not address the question of who the personal subject of Christ is. But notice that the definition is structured around three parallel framing statements, each of which begins with the affirmation "one and the same." Notice also that these statements become more explicit as the definition goes along. The first reads "one and the same Son, our Lord Jesus Christ," the second "one and the same Christ, Son, Lord, and only-begotten," and the third "one and the same Son, the only-begotten, God the Logos, the Lord Jesus Christ." The increasing specificity of the statements makes clear that the person who is one and the same is the Logos, the only-begotten himself.

In light of this, all of the "same one" statements must be read as referring to the Logos himself. Who is perfect in deity? The Logos. Who is perfect in humanity? The Logos after the incarnation. Who is of the same substance with both the Father and us human beings? The Logos. Who was begotten twice, once from the Father before the ages, and once in time from the virgin Mary for our salvation? The Logos. Who is revealed to us in two unconfused, unchanged, undivided, unseparated natures? The Logos. All of these statements refer to the person of the Logos, God the Son.

Furthermore, one should notice that the three framing statements effectively divide the definition into two parts. The first part establishes the personal identity of the Savior: he is the one who was eternally begotten of the Father, who has also become fully human in order to accomplish our salvation. The second part introduces new terminology for describing the deity and humanity of Christ by assigning the word *physeis* ("natures") to his two elements (deity and humanity) and the words *prosopon* and *hypostasis* to his single person. This latter part of the definition is its new contribution to Christology. Taking its cue from the way Pope Leo the Great and the Western church have written about

Christ in Latin, Chalcedon implicitly draws a line between *physis* and *hypostasis* in Greek, insisting that *ousia* and *physis* will subsequently be used of Christ's "twoness," and *hypostasis* and *prosopon* of his oneness. (Prior to this time, Cyril, Nestorius, and most other theologians had used *physis* and *hypostasis* as synonyms.) This is a major terminological improvement over Cyril, and it is a significant contribution on the part of the Chalcedonian fathers, but this is emphatically not the main thing the definition is asserting. The framing statements, the eightfold repetition of the phrases "the same one" and "one and the same," and the assertions in the first half of the definition all show that its major thrust is to proclaim that the one who was born for our salvation is the same one who had been eternally begotten from the Father.

As a result, it should be clear that when scholars claim that the union of two natures without confusion, change, division, or separation is the primary assertion of the Chalcedonian definition, these scholars are confusing its new contribution with its primary emphasis. Of course, what is new deserves our attention, but in this case, focusing so much on what is new has led us to miss what is most emphasized. Accordingly, we have claimed incorrectly that the Chalcedonian Definition does not identify who the one person of Christ is. I believe it does make that identification, though not as explicitly as will be the case later at Constantinople II. And if I am correct about this, then the consensus reflected in Chalcedon is more specific than we normally realize, and in fact, that consensus is Cyrillian. Cyril, Chalcedon, and the vast majority of the fifth-century fathers were united in seeing the Logos as the one person of Christ.

Christology and Atonement: The Need for Consistency

We have seen that one major reason Cyril insists that the Logos is the personal subject of Christ is that in his mind, if the one who suffered and died on the cross were not the second person of the Trinity, then Christ's death would have had no power to accomplish our salvation. It had to be God's own blood that was shed on the cross for us to be redeemed. Of course, Cyril is well aware that suffering is unbefitting for God, that God is impassible. Nevertheless, his reading of Scripture and his concept of salvation demand that he say the one who suffered on the cross was indeed God the Son, even if he cannot explain how the impassible God could suffer. Indeed, he does not try to explain this. Instead, Cyril speaks of "impassible suffering" and frequently affirms, "Let the mystery be adored in silence."

On this point, Cyril has repeatedly been criticized and even ridiculed. About the year 447, Theodoret smirked, "Who in his right mind would ever put up with such ridiculous riddles? No one has ever heard of an impassible passion, or of an immortal mortality."[35] Theodoret's argument is that impassible suffering is a contradiction in terms, and so if one is to be consistent, then one must interpret the death of Christ in such a way as to avoid any notion that an impassible God has suffered. And many contemporary Christians would agree. In fact, I do not think it is an exaggeration to say that in the West today, *most* theologians do one of two things. Many affirm God's impassibility and either say simply that "Christ suffered" or assert that it was not the divine nature that suffered; it was the human nature that died on the cross. Others reject altogether the idea that God is impassible and argue for a passible God who is capable of suffering in his own nature, such that it truly was God who suffered on the cross.[36] Behind both of these more recent views lies the conviction (shared by Theodoret in the fifth-century) that Cyril is being flatly inconsistent when he speaks of "impassible suffering."

But *is* Cyril being inconsistent here? Or is it perhaps Theodoret and his recent heirs who are the inconsistent ones? From Cyril's point of view, "impassible suffering" is not so much an inconsistency in itself (as Theodoret and others claim), as it is an appeal to paradox in order to affirm a greater consistency—that the same person was born and suffered, even if we cannot imagine how God could suffer. To state this a

---

[35] Theodoret of Cyrus, *Eranistes* 3. The Greek text of this work may be found in Theodoret of Cyrus. *Eranistes: Critical Text and Prolegomena*, ed. Gerard H. Ettlinger (Oxford: Clarendon, 1975). There are English translations in *NPNF²* 3:160–249 and FaCh 106. This passage is found in Ettlinger, ed., *Eranistes*, 218; *NPNF²* 3:229.

[36] Alister McGrath gives a typical discussion of this issue, attributing an inflexible belief in God's impassibility to the patristic and medieval church and an insistence on God's passibility to Luther and much of the contemporary theological world. See Alister E. McGrath, *Christian Theology: An Introduction*, 3rd ed. (Oxford: Blackwell, 2001), 273–78, 364–66. For a more detailed and nuanced discussion, see Paul Gavrilyuk, *The Suffering of the Impassible God: The Dialectics of Patristic Thought*, OECS (Oxford: Oxford University Press, 2004). Virtually the entire book deals with the issue of how one may and may not say that God suffers.

different way, Theodoret and many contemporary theologians complain that one is being inconsistent if one speaks of an impassible person (the Logos) suffering. But Cyril's response to this criticism is that it would be a much greater inconsistency to say that the person who was born (the Logos) was not the person who suffered on the cross. If it was God the Son who was born, then it must have somehow been God the Son who died as well. From Cyril's point of view, Theodoret is falling into a huge inconsistency by trying to avoid a smaller inconsistency (or better, by trying to avoid a paradox). He is swallowing a camel even as he strains out a gnat. To bring this idea closer to home, I should point out that many contemporary theologians are guilty of this same inconsistency. When one affirms that God the Son was truly born of Mary, virtually no conservative theologian objects. But when one affirms that God the Son died on the cross, most conservative theologians balk.[37] Why? I think there are two major reasons for this.

The first reason, I believe, is that we have subconsciously confused that which pertains to a nature and that which pertains to a person. It is perfectly true that suffering is not fitting for the divine nature. But it is not correct for us to move from that statement to the assertion that therefore only the human nature died on the cross. Why not? Because suffering and death are not things that happen to a *nature*; they are things that happen to a *person*. One of Cyril's greatest insights (even though he did not express it with the terminology I am using here), an insight that I believe is another fundamental axiom of Christology, is *that one must not treat a nature as if it were a person*. A person, or what patristics scholars call a personal subject, is the entity who can be born, live, die, and be raised. A nature is not such an entity. Instead, a nature is a set of characteristics appropriate to either deity or humanity. God the Logos possessed such a set of divine characteristics prior to the incarnation, and thus we say that he possessed the divine nature. At the moment of the incarnation, that same God the Logos took into his own divine person a complete set of human characteristics and components—including everything that pertains to humanity—so that from then on he is said to possess a human nature as well. That human nature, that set of human

---

[37] See McGrath's discussion referenced in the previous note, especially 364–65.

characteristics, is what enables the divine person, the Logos, to suffer and die on the cross.

Cyril and the fifth-century church insist that it would be contradictory to say that God the Son suffered *as God*, in his divine nature. But God the Son could and did suffer in his human nature, *as man*. Indeed, the primary reason he took that human nature upon himself was precisely so that he, the second person of the Trinity, could suffer in our place. Impassible suffering is thus a paradox, not a contradiction. But to say that the Son was born of Mary, and then to say that merely the human nature suffered, would be a contradiction. In spite of his lack of terminological precision, Cyril had his finger on this truth and expressed it more clearly than virtually anyone else in the fifth century. In his view, if God did not himself accomplish our salvation, then we could not be saved. And in order for God to accomplish our salvation, he had to come down personally to live, die, and be raised as a man on our behalf.

A second closely related reason why most contemporary scholars refuse to say God the Son suffered on the cross is that they balk at Cyril's idea that the humanity of Christ is not a person per se, but rather a set of characteristics enabling the Logos to live as a man. (This idea is often expressed by the phrases "anhypostatic humanity" and "enhypostatic humanity," as described in the first chapter of this book.) Many contemporary scholars assert, and many contemporary Christians often seem to agree, that a human nature subsisting in the person of the Logos is not a real humanity; that Christ could not really be human unless he were a man independent of the Logos. This objection flows from an understanding of what it means to be human that is virtually universal, but from a Christian point of view, disastrous. Contemporary thinkers mistakenly think that one is truly human only if one is independent of God, and tragically many Christians today unconsciously accept this recent concept of what it means to be human without realizing how thoroughly un-Christian it is. From a biblical point of view, none of us were meant to be independent of God. True humanity, humanity as God meant it to be, involves life in dependence on God. Therefore, a person whose humanity actually subsists in the person of the Logos and who lives a life of utter dependence on the Trinity is not a less-than-human person, as much recent scholarship asserts. Such a person is the most fully human person there is.

Cyril and the fifth-century church recognized this. They saw, as we all too often fail to see, that salvation is something utterly beyond our fallen human capacity to achieve. We do not need help to save ourselves. We need someone else to come down to do that for us. The person who did that, the only person who *could do* that, was God the Son. He accomplished our salvation by assuming humanity into his own person, so that he—the second person of the Trinity—could live a human life and accomplish for us what we could not do ourselves. In doing this, he was the most fully human person in history, and he accomplished the salvation of the human race.

To affirm, therefore, that it was really God the Son who died on the cross is to be consistent—consistent with the early church's concept of what salvation was, consistent with what the early church said about the incarnation, consistent with what we need in order to be saved. Admittedly, the church's major consensual document about Christology, the Chalcedonian Definition, does not say directly that it was God the Son who died on the cross. But I have argued that Chalcedon does clearly state that it was God the Son who was born for our salvation. If one is to be consistent, if one is to state clearly what Chalcedon implies but leaves unstated, then one must go on to say that it was God the Son who died. This is what Cyril, the primary human mind behind the Christology of Chalcedon, did say explicitly. This is what Constantinople II, proclaiming itself to be nothing but an interpreter of Chalcedon, did say explicitly. This is the faith of the patristic church.

Conclusion

Of course, we do not believe that something is true just because Cyril, Chalcedon, or Constantinople II said it. We must, and we will, always evaluate patristic Christology in light of Scripture. But we must understand before we can evaluate. I hope this chapter has helped the reader to understand more clearly what the early church was actually saying about Christ. In the process, I hope the reader has begun to recognize that there could be problems with what *we* normally say about Christ.

Have we let a contemporary definition of what it means to be human skew our understanding of the Bible's claim that Christ is man? Have we unwittingly treated Christ's human nature as if it were a person in and of itself, and have we thus misread Scripture's treatment of Christ's death? Have we let a mistaken notion of what the patristic church actually meant blind us to what both the patristic church and the Bible really say about Christ?

At heart, what we are asking is the question of who cried out in despair, "My God, my God, why have you forsaken me?" Much contemporary theology says, or at least implies, that it was the man Jesus who said these words because the Logos had abandoned him. But I am convinced that the patristic church claimed, and was correct to claim, that it was God the Son incarnate who cried these words. The one hanging on the cross was God the Son, forsaken by God the Father. It was God the Son, bearing in his own person the weight of his rejection by his own Father, a rejection that we deserved to bear eternally. If this is correct, then that moment was the most awful, stunning, terrible, and yet amazing moment in history. And if this is right, then in order for the gospel to shine most clearly and powerfully in our proclamation and our theology, we need to say directly and unambiguously that the one who died on the cross in our place was indeed one of the persons of the Trinity.

For Further Reading

Fairbairn, Donald. *Grace and Christology in the Early Church*. OECS. Oxford: Oxford University Press, 2003. In this book, I explain in much more detail many of the ideas that I have summarized in this chapter. In particular, the book extensively addresses the connection between soteriology and Christology by considering the concept of grace in Cyril's thought and that of John Cassian.

Gavrilyuk, Paul L. *The Suffering of the Impassible God: The Dialectics of Patristic Thought*. OECS. Oxford: Oxford University Press, 2004. This book explores the patristic understanding of divine impassibility in order to explain the paradox of God's "impassible suffering" on the cross. The book does not deal with enough evidence to be entirely convincing to patristics scholars, but its lack of evidential depth actually makes it more accessible to the nonspecialist than are most books in its class, and I believe its conclusions are exactly right.

Meyendorff, John. *Christ in Eastern Christian Thought*. Rev. ed. Crestwood, N.Y.: St. Vladimir's Seminary Press, 1975. (French 1st edition, 1969.) This book primarily deals with the period after the fifth century, but it makes an outstanding case for seeing Chalcedon and Constantinople II as consistent with each other. Meyendorff distinguishes more sharply than I do between the way the Eastern and Western churches of the sixth century understood Chalcedon. The way he argues the Eastern church understood Chalcedon is the way I believe the whole Church understood it.

O'Keefe, John J. "Impassible Suffering? Divine Passion and Fifth-Century Christology." *TS* 58 (1997): 38–60. This article adeptly summarizes and criticizes the typical "two-schools" approach to the Christological controversy, and it highlights the centrality of the question, Did God actually suffer on the cross? O'Keefe's understanding of the Christological controversy is very similar to mine.

Torrance, Thomas F. *Theology in Reconciliation: Essays Towards Evangelical and Catholic Unity in East and West*. London: Geoffrey Chapman, 1975. This book deals extensively with both Cyril and his fourth-century predecessor Athanasius. Torrance sees Athanasius and Cyril as providing a central axis from which both East and West subsequently departed (the East by paying too much attention to the Cappadocians, and the West by following Augustine too exclusively). If Torrance is right, and I think he is, then the entire church today would do well to listen more carefully to the voices of Athanasius and Cyril.

Wickham, Lionel R., ed. and trans. *Cyril of Alexandria: Select Letters*. OECT. Oxford: Clarendon, 1983. This book contains outstanding English translations of Cyril's most important theological letters. The notes and the introduction help the nonspecialist to navigate the history of the Christological controversy and thus to place Cyril's letters in their proper context.

Study Questions

1. Why is it problematic to posit a "clashing two-schools approach" to understanding Chalcedon?
2. Explain Cyril of Alexandria's main affirmations about salvation and about Jesus' identity.
3. What difficulty has there been in making the claim that God the Son died on the cross? How can you defend this claim?
4. What role can patristic thought have in contemporary Christological study?

4

ONE PERSON, TWO NATURES
Two Metaphysical Models of the Incarnation

Garrett J. DeWeese

Chapter Summary

The second person of the Trinity, the divine Logos, is eternally a person with a divine nature. Indeed, given that the divine nature includes aseity, the union of the person of the Logos and the divine nature is an essential union, while the union of the Logos and human nature is contingent—that is, the Logos would still be the second person of the Trinity apart from the incarnation. The set of properties that define human nature are exemplified by the divine person, and so in a very unambiguous sense, Jesus is *fully* (but not *merely*) human. I will discuss two metaphysical models of the incarnation—one historical, one contemporary— which I believe do give content to the two-nature formula.

On the standard model, not only does Christ's human will threaten to disappear, but Christ's entire human mind as well. The unintended result of this line of thinking is that Christ's human will/mind/consciousness becomes little more than a theoretical entity with no observable consequences in the life of Christ. Christ's exemplary role as a perfect man simply evaporates. On the contemporary model, a person has a mind and a will, and a nature does not. Thus, Christ had one mind and one will, which belong to his divine person.

Axioms for Christological Study

1. Christ is one person with two natures; therefore, whatever goes with natures, Christ has two of, and whatever goes with persons, he has one of.

2. Attempts to explicate the Chalcedonian Definition do so from the standpoint of a particular metaphysics; the differences between medieval and contemporary metaphysics will result in different models of the incarnation.

3. Models of the incarnation are conceptual structures that aim at being faithful to biblical and orthodox theological claims and at rebutting of charges of incoherence or implausibility directed at the doctrine of the hypostatic union.

KEY TERMS

person	nature	universals
substance	properties	relations
identity	center of consciousness	Nestorianism
Apollinarianism	will	mind
dyothelite	monothelite	
Latin terms	*prosopon*	*persona*
Greek terms	*hypostasis*	*ousia*

T he Christian doctrine of the incarnation claims that the eternal Son of God, the second person of the Trinity, became fully a man, Jesus of Nazareth; that in doing so he did not for a moment cease to be fully God; and that he did this "for us and for our salvation."

These are astonishing claims, and challenging ones, claims that force Christians to think hard about how they can be true. The creeds of the church, both ancient and modern, require Christians to believe the doctrine of the incarnation—that is, to accept as factually true the proposition that Jesus Christ was simultaneously God and man. At least since the Council of Chalcedon in 451, this has been understood to mean that both divine and human natures were united in one person.

115

On its face this proposition seems incoherent. John Hick objects:

> Orthodoxy insisted upon the two natures, human and divine, coinhering in the one historical Jesus Christ. But orthodoxy has never been able to give this idea any content. It remains a form of words without an assignable meaning. For to say, without explanation, that the historical Jesus of Nazareth was also God is as devoid of meaning as to say that this circle drawn on paper is also a square. Such a locution has to be given semantic content: and in the case of the language of incarnation every content thus far suggested has had to be repudiated. The Chalcedonian formula, in which the attempt rested, merely reiterated that Jesus was both God and man, but made no attempt to interpret the formula. It therefore seems reasonable to conclude that the real point and value of the incarnational doctrine is not indicative but expressive, not to assert a metaphysical fact but to express a valuation and evoke an attitude.[1]

But Hick's "reasonable conclusion" cannot be shared by orthodox Christians for the very reason that led the early church to assert the two-nature claim in the first place, namely, that our salvation depends in a very profound way on Jesus' being both fully man and fully God. This is the theological axiom that links soteriology and Christology; it is not merely a metaphor intended to evoke an attitude. Both Fred Sanders and Donald Fairbairn, in their respective chapters, have demonstrated—conclusively, I believe—that the axiom has been so intended and so understood throughout church history.

How then should a Christian respond to Hick's objection that the Chalcedonian formula is meaningless? Hick's challenge is a philosophical one, specifically, that the two-nature claim has no metaphysical meaning; worse, that it is as blatantly self-contradictory as the claim that "this circle is a square." My aim in this chapter is to respond as a philosopher to this philosophical challenge. I will discuss two metaphysical

---

[1] John Hick, "Jesus and World Religions," in John Hick, ed., *The Myth of God Incarnate* (Philadelphia: Westminster/John Knox Press, 1977), 178.

models[2] of the incarnation—one historical, one contemporary—which I believe can give content to the two-nature formula, and thus show that the formula is not incoherent after all. And while my preference for the contemporary model will be apparent, I will not claim that the other is so wrong-headed as to be irrational or unorthodox. The difference between the two lies in differing background metaphysical commitments.

Doing this will take us on a quick historical scurry through certain ecumenical councils (for a more leisurely tour, see the chapters in this book by Sanders and Fairbairn) and selected medieval theologians, and then into contemporary analytical philosophical theology. Any one of these issues can be—indeed, has been—developed in itself as a full-length book, so my discussion will necessarily be summary.

First, though, and subject to further amplification below, I need to define roughly certain terms which figure prominently in the discussion.

- A *person* is an individual with suitably complex mental capacities. Sometimes the biblical word *soul* is used as synonymous with person.

- A *nature* is a set of characteristics which belong to an individual and determine just what kind of individual it is. For the purposes of this paper, *nature* and *essence* may be taken as synonyms. The term *nature* is a philosophical one and has no clear biblical parallel, although it may be argued that the entire worldview of Scripture presupposes the existence of natures.

- A *mind* is the immaterial part of a person, consisting of at least the capacities of consciousness, thought, belief, desire, emotion

---

[2] By *model* I mean a theoretical construct which is recognized to be analogical, which is used to aid understanding of data or experience, and which contributes to the extension of understanding of a theory. Ian Barbour defends the use of the term *model* in both science and religion: "Models and theories are imaginative human constructs. Models, on this reading, are to be taken seriously but not literally; they are neither literal pictures nor useful fictions but limited and inadequate ways of imagining what is not observable. They make tentative ontological claims that there are entities in the world something like those postulated in the models." Ian G. Barbour, *Religion and Science: Historical and Contemporary Issues* (San Francisco: HarperCollins, 1997), 115–24. John Frame discusses and demonstrates the use of models as well as analogies in his work in theology proper, even saying in connection with a discussion of models of the Trinity, "I think that godly speculation can have an edifying function." John M. Frame, *The Doctrine of God* (Phillipsburg, NJ: P&R, 2002), 725.

and volition. Sometimes the biblical word *soul* is used for all or part of a person's mind.

- A *will* is a capacity of the mind by which the person acts to cause something to come about. Often the will causes a bodily action, but sometimes the will causes certain mental states or processes, as when we "will" ourselves to think about something.

The Ecumenical Councils: Formulation

Terminological Considerations

One might hope that any Christological confusion could be cleared up if we simply got clear on the technical vocabulary of the church councils. But as anyone who has plunged into the issue knows, that hope is futile. There are, I suggest, a number of reasons for this.

First, *usage*, and consequently common (lexical) meaning, changes through time, and it is unwarranted to assume that the language of Nicaea (325) or Chalcedon (451) fixed the meaning of even technical terms such that they are univocal with the language of Constantinople III (681), for example. Richard Swinburne notes the problem with respect to *psyche*: "When 'thinking soteriologically,' [the Fathers] wished to affirm that Christ had a human way of thinking and acting. When thinking of 'the unity of Christ's person,' they wished to affirm that there was only one individual. But the Fathers were insufficiently sensitive to the different possible understandings of ψυχή [*psyche*] (soul) arising from the Greek philosophical systems which they used. For Plato, as for me, the soul is an entity separate from the body. For Aristotle it is a way of thinking and acting."[3] The problem of slippery meaning is exacerbated by the difficulties inherent in translation from Greek to Latin and back. The familiar shifting senses of *prosopon*, *persona*, and *hypostasis* illustrate this difficulty.

Second, as the *theological context* changed, the connotations of terms changed as well. As the debate between Arians and Nicenes like Athanasius was settled, new disputes were engendered with the rise of Apollinarians, Nestorians, Eutychians, monothelites, and the like. No one desired to be heretical, so new terms were introduced that putatively

---

[3] Richard Swinburne, *The Christian God* (Oxford: Oxford University Press, 1994), 252.

retained the orthodox understanding but shaded the meaning slightly in one direction or another, and subsequent polemical rejoinders added terms to shade meanings back in the original direction. So for example, the *ousia* of Nicaea was seen to be inadequate in Christological formulations, and was supplemented by *physis* at Chalcedon.

Third, similarly, the *changing philosophical context* altered the meaning of terms. The attempts to understand what, precisely, the God-man Jesus was necessarily involved the use of philosophical terms and concepts. But as the background metaphysical systems changed, so did the meanings of those terms. As John Marenbon notes, "For Aristotle, *hupostasis* means a substance, in the sense of a thing (for example, a particular man or tree) which acts as a substrate for accidents (literally the word means 'something which stands under'). But this Aristotelian meaning was stretched and altered by Plotinus and his [Neoplatonic] followers."[4] Neoplatonism countenanced uninstantiated universals; Aristotelianism admitted only immanent universals, and the nominalism of, say, William of Ockham or the Lutheran scholastics, rejected universals altogether. Once certain terms were baptized by the councils into the status of orthodoxy, the different schools continued to use the terms, but with different metaphysical connotations.

The best illustration of the alterations wrought on a theological term by changes in philosophical contexts is the key term *nature*: the early Platonic understanding of a *nature* as an abstract thing had been replaced by the fifth century with a reified conception of nature as a concrete particular.[5] Aristotle himself is a source of some of this confusion. Notoriously, he seems to have a different conception of "substance" in his *Categories* than in his later *Metaphysics*. Specifically, in *Categories*, a substance belongs to a category composed, roughly, of those things that exist in ontological independence of other things of the same sort.[6] This notion is generally called *primary substance* or *first substance* and refers to individuals. The Aristotelian ontology sees first substances as hylomorphic compositions—composites of form and matter. A substance

---

[4] John Marenbon, *Boethius* (New York: Oxford University Press, 2003), 71.

[5] Swinburne, *The Christian God*, 212–15.

[6] For discussion and defense of this reading of Aristotle in the *Categories*, see Joshua Hoffman and Gary Rosenkrantz, *Substance: Its Nature and Existence* (New York: Routledge, 1997).

is made up of various sorts of constituents: for example, its nature (or essence), which constitutes the substance as a member of a particular natural kind; its accidental properties, which inhere in the substance but do not exist independently of it; and its stuff or matter. In *Metaphysics*, however, Aristotle introduces another concept of substance, namely, that which different individual members of a natural kind share in common.[7] This notion is generally called *second substance* and refers to a universal, a nature. Aristotle uses the word *ousia* for both. While the two concepts are clear and distinct, failure to use the term *ousia* unambiguously— especially in translating from Greek to Latin and back—contributed in no small way to the growing confusion in the theological formulations. For example, Cyril of Alexandria can speak of Christ having two natures (using *physis* in the sense of second substance) and one nature (using *physis* in the sense of first substance) in the very same paragraph.[8]

Fourth, the *contemporary lack* of theological and philosophical context renders terminological considerations quite problematic. In our day, terminology is often used with little understanding of nuances of meaning. *Substance*, to most modern ears, connotes "stuff"—the chemistry—rather than "thing." Thus, as William Alston points out, many contemporary theologians reject substance language when speaking of the Trinity simply because they understand *substance* to be an inert, static object. But that is a gross misunderstanding of the philosophical usage of *substance*.[9] Similarly, in criticizing modern theologians who claim that the medieval notion of personhood has been superceded in modern thought, Alfred J. Freddoso concludes that "those who make assertions like this have a disappointingly superficial and unduly selective acquaintance with the voluminous recent philosophical literature on substance, personhood and personal identity."[10]

For these reasons, simply consulting the vocabulary of the ecumenical councils will not be adequate to dispel all Christological confusion or defeat the charge of incoherence. In fact, many of these same consid-

[7] See Michael J. Loux, "Ousia: A Prolegomenon to Metaphysics Z and H," *HPQ* 2 (1985): 241–66.
[8] See p. 99.
[9] William P. Alston, "Substance and the Trinity," in Stephen T. Davis, Daniel Kendall, and Gerald O'Collins, eds., *The Trinity* (New York: Oxford University Press, 1999), 187–88.
[10] Alfred J. Freddoso, "Human Nature, Potency, and the Incarnation," *FP* 3 (1986): 29.

erations make it impossible to use strictly biblical terminology, confining our discussion to terms such as *soul* or *spirit*. Simply reflecting on the arguments within biblical anthropology, in which both dichotomists and trichotomists marshal biblical support for their respective positions, should caution us to the truth that, for the most part, biblical authors did not employ their vocabulary as technical terms with univocal meanings.

Historical Development

It is standard wisdom that the Chalcedonian Definition left undefined the crucial terms "substance" (*ousia*), "nature" (*physis*) and "person" (*hypostasis*).[11] Sarah Coakley notes, "If anything is 'defined' in the 'Definition' it is not these key terms. To be sure, these terms had a pre-history, but it was an ambiguous one and the 'Definition' does not clear up the ambiguity."[12] Richard Norris claimed that Chalcedon did nothing more than set regulatory linguistic boundaries.[13] Certainly it did more than that, but as Coakley observes, "The major achievement of Chalcedon is its 'regulatory' vocabulary, on which semantic grid the events of salvation are now plotted . . . The 'rules' of predication are now that duality resides in the *physis* and unity in the *hypostasis*."[14]

While some of the ambiguity resulting from the lack of clear definitions of the terms *physis* and *hypostasis* may have been intentional, some also resulted from the shifting metaphysical background in the Eastern portion of the church. There Neoplatonism, which would remain dominant in the West for several centuries longer, was being supplanted by a renewed form of Aristotelianism.

On an Aristotelian ontology, it is easy to slide from the notion of a nature in the abstract to the notion of an individual nature which is a

---

[11] See Richard A. Norris, "Chalcedon Revisited: A Historical and Theological Reflection," in B. Nassif, ed., *New Perspectives on Historical Theology* (Grand Rapids: Eerdmans, 1996), 140–58; John Macquarrie, *Christology Revisited* (Harrisburg, PA: Trinity Press International, 1998), 45–48.

[12] Sarah Coakley, "What Does Chalcedon Solve and What Does It Not? Some Reflections in the Status and Meaning of the Chalcedonian 'Definition,'" in Davis, *The Incarnation*, 148.

[13] Norris, "Chalcedon Revisited," 141–42.

[14] Coakley, "What Does Chalcedon Solve," 148–9. Note, however, Donald Fairbairn's chapter in this volume, in which he argues—compellingly, in my opinion—that Chalcedon should be seen as doing more than merely regulating the rules of predication.

constituent of a particular individual. And just this happened in discussions of Christ's human nature. A Neoplatonist would say that Christ's human nature is a universal, identical to the human nature exemplified by every other human, while an Aristotelian would say that Christ's human nature was a particular, a substance composed of form (an intellective soul) and matter (a human body).

The ambiguity between the Neoplatonist and the Aristotelian notions of "substance" shows up right in the Chalcedonian Definition itself. When the Definition proclaims that our Lord Jesus Christ is "consubstantial with the Father according to his deity and consubstantial with us according to his humanity," it is clear that there is an equivocation in the key term *consubstantial*. For to say that Christ is of the same substance as the Father is to say that Christ is of the same *first substance*, namely, the one entity that is the tripersonal God. But to say that he is of the same substance as us is to say that he is of the same *second substance*, namely, that he like us exemplifies human nature.

The ambiguity of the Chalcedonian Definition opened the door to the Eutychian and Monothelite controversies of the sixth and seventh centuries. The Eutychians thought that understanding the human nature of Christ as an individual nature entailed that the Logos assumed a human person—a view they considered outright Nestorianism. Consequently, the Eutychians rejected the two-nature language of Chalcedon and held that Christ had just one nature, a sort of hybrid of the divine and the human. The fifth council (Constantinople II, 553) settled the issue with respect to Christ's natures, condemning the Eutychian views as heretical.

Both theological concerns (avoiding Nestorianism) and political concerns (unifying a fractious church) contributed to the popularity of monothelitism in the seventh century. This view was not so clearly heretical. Adolf Harnack observed, "The doctrine of one will equally with that of two wills would have been in harmony with the decisions of the Fourth and Fifth Councils."[15]

But politics and theology have always been a combustible mix. What one side saw as a reasonable via media looked to the other side like apostasy, and the sincere theologians seem to have used the political powers

---

[15] Adolf von Harnack, *History of Dogma*, 3rd ed., trans Neil Buchanan (Boston: Little, Brown, 1898), 4:254.

of emperors, patriarchs, and bishops about as much as they in turn were used by the powers, and the voices in the controversy continued their crescendo.

A compromise solution was attempted in the *Ecthesis*, written by Patriarch Sergius of Constantinople, endorsed by Pope Honorius I, and promulgated by the Emperor Heraclitus in 638. The *Ecthesis* affirmed two natures but one *energeia*, or action. The central declaration of the *Ecthesis* maintained:

> Because the expression one energy, although some of the Fathers use it, yet soundeth strange to the ears of some, and disquiets them . . . and since in the same way many take offense at the expression, two energies, since it is not used by any of the holy Fathers (on account of the fact that) we should then be obliged as a consequence to teach two mutually contradictory wills, as if God the Logos, aiming at our salvation, was willing to endure suffering, but His manhood had opposed itself to this His will, which is impious and foreign to the Christian dogma—when even the wicked Nestorius, although he, dividing the Incarnation and introducing two Sons, did not venture to maintain two wills of the same, but, on the contrary taught the similar willing of the two persons assumed by him; how can, then, the orthodox, who worship only one Son and Lord, admit in Him two, and those mutually opposed wills?[16]

The compromise was unstable, and debate shifted to the issue of will rather than action. The Chalcedonian tradition was not clear on this; it simply had not come up. Both sides desired to avoid Nestorianism, on the one hand, and Eutychianism on the other. Colorful figures such as Pyrrhus and Maximus the Confessor debated the opposing sides, and Emperor Constans II replaced the *Ecthesis* with the *Typos*, which simply banned discussion of either the monothelite or the dyothelite formulas. Finally, Constans' successor, Emperor Constantine IV (668–85),

---

[16] *The Disputation with Pyrrhus of Our Father Among the Saints Maximus the Confessor*, trans. Joseph P. Farrell (South Canaan, PA: St. Tikhon's Seminary Press, n.d.), 3. I am indebted to John McKinley for this reference.

convened the sixth ecumenical council in 680 (the third to be held at Constantinople) to settle the issue. Political considerations, while not absent from previous councils, figured large in the maneuvering and debating both before and while the delegates gathered.[17]

The opinion that prevailed at Constantinople was that a will properly belongs to a nature. Since Chalcedon made clear that Jesus had two natures, it followed that he had two wills. To deny this was essentially to deny the incarnation. In support of this line of reasoning, the bishops of the sixth council, following the soteriological maxim of Gregory of Nazianzus, "The unassumed is unhealed,"[18] argued that Christ must have a human will, or else our wills could not be redeemed. To safeguard against the impious suggestion that Jesus might have been internally conflicted by his two wills, the council explained that the human will was always subordinate to the divine will.

The council affirmed as well the idea that in Jesus there were two *energeia*, and drew some further distinctions that need not concern us here. The main point is clear enough: The dyothelites (two wills) prevailed, and the monothelites (one will) were anathematized as heretics. What is far less clear is whether earlier church fathers would have been so quick to accept the reified natures, each complete with its own proper will and working, that the sixth council affirmed.

To summarize, the era of the ecumenical councils of the church produced, in the end, an understanding of the incarnation against the background of an ontology according to which the human nature of Christ was an individualized nature, a particular, constituted by a human body and intellective soul, which included a human will. This nature was assumed by the Logos, the second person of the Trinity, who being divine also had a divine nature. By the sixth ecumenical council (681), the Chalcedonian Definition had been dogmatically asserted to entail that Christ had two wills.[19]

---

[17] John Meyendorff, *Imperial Unity and Christian Divisions: The Church 450–680 A.D.* (Crestwood, NY: St. Vladimir's Seminary Press, 1989), 341–65.

[18] Gregory of Nazianzus, "To Cledonius the Priest Against Apollinarius," in Edward R. Hardy, ed., *Christology of the Later Fathers*, LCC (Philadelphia: Westminster Press, 1954), 218.

[19] The dyothelite model of the sixth council was more fully developed by John of Damascus (676?–754?); see Brian Daley, "Nature and the 'Mode of Union'," in Davis, *The*

We noted, though, that the patristic and conciliar periods were times of theological turmoil, terminological confusion, and changing metaphysical backgrounds. The Christological understanding forged at Constantinople III, which passed into the medieval Western church as the definitive interpretation of Chalcedon, does not represent the unambiguous teaching of all the fathers and early theologians.

Medieval Philosophical Theology

From the eighth century on, the tendency in the Western church was towards increased metaphysical sophistication, offering ever more refined analyses of the one person/two natures formula. This was fueled in part by the rising challenge of sophisticated Islamic philosophy, and in part by a rediscovery and adaptation of Aristotle into what had been a Neoplatonic philosophical background to Christian theology.

The Dyothelite Model

Marilyn Adams recounts the considerable attention devoted by medieval philosophical theologians to the question of what sort of human nature Christ had.[20] The obscure-sounding scholastic topic was not entirely without merit. For it was agreed that the Logos assumed just enough of what we are to save us (recall Nazianzus's maxim), but no more than was fitting for a divine person.

The concern to define precisely what sort of human nature the Logos assumed was closely related to a second concern, namely, the need to avoid a return of Nestorianism. Boethius's famous definition of a person as an "individual substance of a rational nature,"[21] together with the growing consensus that Christ's human nature was a substance, led directly to a problem: if an individual substance of a rational nature constituted a person in the case of every other human person, and if the Logos

---

Incarnation, 190–93.

[20] Marilyn McCord Adams, *What Sort of Human Nature? Medieval Philosophy and the Systematics of Christology: The Aquinas Lecture, 1999* (Milwaukee: Marquette University Press, 1999).

[21] Boethius *Contra Eutyches and Nestorius* 3. Boethius gives this basic definition in discussing problems inherent in translating *ousia* and *hypostasis* from Greek to Latin. His definition was virtually unquestioned in medieval scholasticism. See Richard Cross, *The Metaphysics of the Incarnation* (Oxford: Oxford University Press, 2002), 239–41.

assumed such an individual substantial nature, how was it that the Logos did not assume a human person? That is, how could Nestorianism be avoided?

The medieval philosophical theologians came up with an ingenious solution. The Christologies developed, for example, by Thomas Aquinas, John Duns Scotus, and William of Ockham, employed the technical concept of a *suppositum*, an independently existing, ultimate bearer or sustainer of properties, which is not itself born or sustained by anything else. A *suppositum* is thus similar to Aristotle's first substance, but in the unique case of the incarnation, there exists a substance which is not a *suppositum*: Christ's individual human nature (a substance) is sustained by the Logos as the *suppositum*—the ultimate bearer of properties.[22]

Space considerations force me to leave detailed exposition of medieval sources to others.[23] The upshot of scholastic thought was a model of the hypostatic union that incorporated a view of human personhood that I will label as HP for convenience. HP involves the following disjunctive principle of human personhood:

> HP: An individual human nature N is such that for any time *t* at which N exists, either:
>
> (i) N is a human person; or
> (ii) N is sustained by a divine person.

In (i), the individual human nature is itself the *suppositum*, while in (ii) it is the Logos (or, if another divine person possibly could become incarnate, that person) which is the *suppositum*. Note that, given the metaphysical understanding of individual human natures as particulars (substances) which are human persons, it follows that individual human natures have wills. So to say that Christ had a human nature as well as a divine nature was to say, in full agreement with the sixth council, that he

---

[22] This account, or something quite similar, has been defended in recent years by a number of writers, for example, Alfred J. Freddoso, "Logic, Ontology and Ockham's Christology" *NS* 57 (1983): 293–330, as well as his "Human Nature"; Thomas P. Flint, "The Possibilities of Incarnation: Some Radical Molinist Suggestions," *RS* 37 (2001): 307–20, and Flint, "A Death He Freely Accepted: Molinist Reflections on the Incarnation," *FP* 18 (2001): 3–20; Eleonore Stump, "Aquinas' Metaphysics of the Incarnation," in Davis, *The Incarnation*; and Cross, *The Metaphysics of the Incarnation*.

[23] See Freddoso, "Human Nature." For an historical survey of the medieval metaphysical development of the incarnation, see Cross, *Metaphysics of the Incarnation*, 239–45.

had two wills. This medieval dyothelite model of the incarnation became standard among most Roman Catholic theologians. This model also lies behind the Christology of the Reformers, who devoted little attention to the metaphysics of scholastic Christology, being preoccupied with soteriological and ecclesiological issues, which they viewed as far more pressing.

Difficulties with the Dyothelite Model

There is no question that (given a certain metaphysical background) this understanding is faithful to the Chalcedonian Definition as well as to the Christological pronouncements of the ecumenical councils. But the medieval model, relying on HP, has seemed highly problematic to many contemporary philosophical theologians.

The medieval model is open to at least four objections. First, these distinctions would never have occurred to anybody who was not trying to account for the incarnation, so the account seems rather ad hoc, and philosophers dislike ad hoc-ishness. However, I do not think that is a fatal flaw. Philosophical theologians in the Christian tradition have always recognized that not all truths of God are accessible by natural reason; some must be accepted on the basis of revelation. That alone introduces seemingly ad hoc elements.[24] Since the hypostatic union is *sui generis*, we must expect a certain amount of uniqueness in developing an account of it.

Second, insofar as it includes HP, the medieval model says that N (an individual human nature) is a human person in every case except when N is sustained by a divine person.[25] Putting it a bit differently, if CHN is Christ's human nature, then CHN is not a person. But every other individual human nature N *is* a person. This leaves the philosophical theologian with the task of specifying just what it is that is lacking when CHN

---

[24] Where *ad hoc* in this sense means something like "not motivated by deliverances of reason alone, but introduced solely to solve a particular problem."

[25] Freddoso notes that medieval theologians were careful not to affirm that Christ was a human person, but said rather that he was a person who is a human being (or man), or that he was a divine person who assumed a human nature. For to say that A is a human person would be to say that A is itself a *suppositum*, and so to say that Christ was a human person would be to fall into Nestorianism. Freddoso, "Human Nature," 29–30. Reluctance to say that Christ is a human person was not shared by the theologians of the Patristic period; examples abound. The linguistic precision of the medieval theologians was one of the strengths of scholasticism.

is sustained by a divine person that keeps it from being also a human person. Duns Scotus, that "subtle doctor," explained this lack in terms of a "twofold negation,"[26] which seems to commit him to an ontology that includes negative properties—a controversial position which finds very little sympathy among contemporary ontologists. Still, the claim that CHN is sustained by a divine person without thereby also being a human person could be defended as simply a miraculous act of God. So Freddoso, in explaining Duns Scotus's account, observes sympathetically: "In the Incarnation God simply brings it about by a special act that a certain individual human nature, exactly similar to every other in its ontological constitution and intrinsic inclinations, fails to satisfy the metaphysical conditions required for it to be a human person."[27] As with *ad hoc*-ishness, appeals to miracles are not out of bounds for a Christian philosophical theologian. But larger difficulties await.

The third objection to the medieval model arises when we ask whether, possibly, the Logos could have assumed any human nature whatsoever, or whether, necessarily, he could assume only the one that he in fact did assume. Most of the medieval theologians argued that the incarnation itself was a contingent event: it is possible that the Logos would not have become incarnate. Most of them thought, further, that it was a contingent matter that the Logos assumed the particular human nature (CHN) that he did in fact assume.[28] In our day, theologians and philosophers such as Millard Erickson and Thomas Flint agree.[29]

But if CHN is only contingently assumed by the Logos, then two rather unsavory possibilities arise.[30] First, the Logos could possibly assume *any* human nature. So there is a possible world in which that

---

[26] See ibid., 32–33 for details.

[27] Ibid., 33. In the end, Freddoso rejects the Scotan account.

[28] Duns Scotus and Ockham apparently held this view, although Aquinas held that the union was neither accidental nor essential, but a *sui generis* modality, "substantial" union. See Freddoso, "Human Nature," 29–31; Christopher Hughes, *On a Complex Theory of a Simple God* (Ithaca, NY: Cornell University Press, 1989), 244–66.

[29] Millard J. Erickson, *The Word Became Flesh: A Contemporary Incarnational Christology* (Grand Rapids: Baker, 1991), 561–64; Flint, "Possibilities," 307. While Erickson and Flint come at this conclusion from very different perspectives, both see it as a possible way towards a solution to the question of Christ's impeccability.

[30] Objections along these lines have been raised by Freddoso, "Human Nature," and William Lane Craig, "Flint's Radical Molinist Christology Not Radical Enough," *FP* 32 (2006): 55–64.

individual human nature DHN (DeWeese's human nature), which is identical to me in the actual world, is instead the human nature of Christ. This is not to say that I would be God, since on being assumed, DHN would cease to be sustained by me and would be sustained by the Logos, and so DHN would no longer be identical to me (nor, indeed, identical to any person). But identity is a necessary property (anything is necessarily identical to itself), so this conclusion seems impossible: if DHN is identical to me, it is always identical to me as long as—and in any possible world in which—it exists.

But let us suppose that the Logos, should he become incarnate, can only assume CHN and not DHN or the individual human nature of any other already-existing human. But the assumption of CHN by the Logos is only contingent, raising the question (here lurks the second unsavory possibility) of whether the Logos could "decouple" from CHN, leaving behind a merely human person. Scotus and Ockham believe the answer is yes; Erickson and Flint accept something like this.[31] Erickson writes:

> If Jesus were to have sinned, his deity could not have been involved. Unless we are to adopt some form of Nestorianism, the conclusion seems to be that the incarnation would have terminated short of the actual sin. At the very brink of the decision to sin, where that decision had not yet taken place, but the Father knew it was about to be made, the Second Person of the Trinity would have left the human nature of Jesus . . . Had the Logos departed, Jesus would not have died. That would have been the case only if the person had been merely divine, only the Logos, as various forms of Apollinarianism required. Rather, Jesus would have survived, but would have "slumped" to mere humanity, and sinful humanity at that.[32]

---

[31] Freddoso, "Human Nature," 31–35; Erickson, *The Word Became Flesh*, 561–64; Flint, "Possibilities," 307–8. I should note that Flint's view is much more nuanced, involving as it does backtracking counterfactuals, but I will pass over those complications. Aquinas apparently believed that this was metaphysically impossible, as does Freddoso: "Human Nature," 46–47.

[32] Erickson, *The Word Became Flesh*, 563–64.

On its face, this strains credulity. For we are asked to accept the following:

1. At time t_1, CHN is hypostatically united to the Logos in the single person of Christ.
2. At t_2 (later than t_1) the Logos "decouples" from CHN.
3. At t_2, CHN becomes an individual human person (by HP).

We are asked to accept the possibility that a human person—presumably a first-century Jewish male (call him Jacob)—could suddenly come into existence, neither by direct creation (as Adam and Eve) nor by virgin birth (Jesus). The questions raised are momentous: What memories would Jacob have? Would a second virgin birth, a second incarnation, be necessary? What would come of the previously true (and perhaps salvific) beliefs of the disciples ("You are the Messiah, the Son of the Living God" [Matt 16:16])? Not to mention the declarations of the Father ("This is my Son, the Beloved, with whom I am well pleased" [Matt 3:17]; "Listen to him" [Matt 17:5])!

But such idle speculations are unnecessary. If statements (1)–(3) were accepted, then it would be the case that at t_2 CHN acquired the property of *being identical to Jacob*, a property which CHN lacked an instant earlier. But since identity is a necessary property, it is impossible for CHN to acquire this property, and the envisioned scenario is impossible. Similarly, the scenario implies that at t_2 CHN acquired the property *being a person*, which (on pain of Nestorianism) CHN lacked at t_1. But a strong case can be made that *being a person* is not a property which a thing can possess contingently, and if so, then again the scenario is impossible.[33] Hence it seems most reasonable to conclude that the Logos, should he become incarnate, *necessarily* assumes CHN (rather than some other particular human nature), and so standard interpretations of the dyothelite model are seriously flawed. It may still be, though, that the dyothelite model is correct and it is the interpretations which have somehow gone astray. But that brings us to the final difficulty for the model.

---

[33] Freddoso, "Human Nature," 34–38; Craig, "Not Radical Enough," 60–61.

Perhaps most troubling of all is the fourth objection; it is not clear that the dyothelite model actually succeeds in avoiding something that looks suspiciously like Nestorianism. Suppose we grant that the technical metaphysical notion of a *suppositum* can be pressed into service in a minimally ad hoc and suitably qualified sense. Further, suppose that we can assuage concerns about the status of CHN in cases where it is not sustained by the Logos. Even so, does the dyothelite model really explain the Chalcedonian Definition, with a *single* person sustaining two natures?

I believe that the quasi-Nestorian aspects of the dyothelite model can be seen most clearly when we consider its implication that Christ had two minds and two wills.[34] Jesuit scholar Gerald O'Collins recognizes that the sixth council's decree makes it necessary to discuss "issues about the two minds and two wills that are the *necessary corollary* of Christ's two natures recognized by the Council of Chalcedon."[35] Elsewhere O'Collins states, "Since consciousness is on the side of nature and not of person, Chalcedon's doctrine supports [the] distinction between Christ's human and divine consciousnesses."[36] Now, I am assuming the truthfulness of the Chalcedonian Definition of "one person, two natures," so whatever belongs to persons, Christ had one of, and whatever belongs to natures, he had two of. The issue, though, is this: does a consciousness or a mind or a will belong to a person or to a nature? I cannot claim to have a single, conclusive, compelling argument against the dyothelite model's locating wills and minds in natures, but three lines of argument call into question its adequacy.

First, the view that a person could have two minds (two wills, two consciousnesses) is, on its face, implausible. We surely have prima facie justification to believe that whenever we encounter a mind (of a suitable complexity which would rule out animal minds), we encounter a person. On the medieval model, we are asked to imagine two minds but only one person.

---

[34] Perhaps the most rigorous defense of a two-minds interpretation is Thomas V. Morris, *The Logic of God Incarnate* (Ithaca, NY: Cornell University Press, 1986).

[35] Gerald O'Collins, *Incarnation*, NCTS (New York: Continuum, 2002), 87 (emphasis added).

[36] Gerald O'Collins, *Interpreting Jesus* (London: Chapman, 1983), 190.

The implausibility only increases when one looks to proponents of the medieval model for explication. Thomas Morris, for example, calls our attention to certain examples: "There are cases of brain hemisphere commisurotomy, multiple personality, and even hypnosis, in which we are confronted by what seems to be in some significant sense a single individual human being, one person, but one person with apparently two or more distinct streams or ranges of consciousness, distinct domains of experience."[37]

Now, I think it is clear that none of these analogies—commisurotomies, dissociative disorders, or hypnotic states—represent two minds; all involve a single improperly functioning mind. But surely, if the best analogies for a model of the incarnation rely on abnormal psychology, something must be amiss with the model. A. T. Hanson comments dryly, "It looks as if it could be explained, or at least understood, on the basis of some sort of psychological analogy—though the analogy with schizophrenia is by no means encouraging."[38] Similarly, John Macquarrie writes, "Two wills in one person would be a pathological condition, and this was surely not what the church wanted to say about Jesus Christ. Willing belongs to the self or personal center, and although Chalcedon spoke of two natures, it acknowledged one person, and therefore a unitary willing. No doubt human nature has a plurality of desires, and these may conflict with one another, but this is something different from willing."[39] I have already granted that we cannot expect to fit the miracle of the incarnation neatly into our "normal" categories. Still, it seems desirable to avoid any conceptual model of the incarnation that attributes to Jesus a condition that we would consider pathological in any other person, unless such a model were forced upon us.

---

[37] Morris, *The Logic of God Incarnate,* 105. Swinburne cites others in this century who have appealed to Freudian models of a divided mind in *The Christian God,* 202, n. 11. Trenton Merricks invokes hemisphere commisurotomy as a model for the social Trinity: "Split Brains and the Godhead," in Thomas Crisp, Matthew Davidson, and David Vander Laan, eds., *Knowledge and Reality: Essays in Honor of Alvin Plantinga on His Seventieth Birthday* (Dordrecht: Kluwer Academic Publishers, 2006).

[38] A. T. Hanson, "Two Consciousnesses: The Modern Version of Chalcedon," *SJT* 37 (1984): 474.

[39] John Macquarrie, *Jesus Christ in Modern Thought* (London: SCM, 1990), 166–67. See Richard Sturch, *The Word and the Christ: An Essay in Analytic Christology* (Oxford: Oxford University Press, 1991), 139–40, for additional objections along these lines.

As I said, whenever we encounter a mind of a suitable complexity, we have prima facie justification to believe we have encountered a person. So it is not surprising that defenders of the dyothelite view are at pains to show that Christ's human will did not conflict with his divine will. For example, Gregory of Nazianzus had written before Chalcedon, "For [Christ's] human will cannot be opposed to God, seeing that it is altogether taken into God."[40] But then, did Christ ever decide to act *as a man*? Or was his human will always regulated by his divine will, so that every decision Jesus made was a decision of his divine will? If the "'subjection' of the human will to the divine is then naturally interpreted as any human desires always being kept in place by stronger divine desires,"[41] one cannot help wondering whether the infinite difference between human and divine desires within one person would not render the power of the human desires vanishingly small.

On the dyothelite model, not only does Christ's human will threaten to disappear, but Christ's entire human mind as well. Gregory of Nazianzus claimed, "It is clear to every one that he [Christ] knows as God and knows not as man."[42] And R. P. C. Hanson observes: "The human mind was so much overshadowed or absorbed by the divine that though it was there it made no difference. The chief reason why any of the ancients wanted to acknowledge a human mind in Christ was that it could sluice off the human passions which can only with danger (they thought) be ascribed to the Godhead."[43]

The unintended result of this line of thinking is that Christ's human will/mind/consciousness becomes little more than a theoretical entity with no observable consequences in the life of Christ. Christ's exemplary role as a perfect man simply evaporates.

On a two-minds view, what happens when the two minds of Christ encounter one another? Karl Rahner writes, "Now it may and indeed must of course be said that the doctrine of the unconfused and unchanged real human nature implies, as the struggle against monothelitism after

---

[40] Gregory of Nazianzus, "Fourth Theological Oration," in Hardy, *Christology of the Later Fathers*, 185.

[41] Swinburne, *The Christian God*, 198–99.

[42] Gregory of Nazianzus, "Fourth Theological Oration," 188.

[43] Cited by A. T. Hanson, "Two Consciousnesses," 476.

the rejection of monophysitism shows, that the 'human nature' of the Logos possesses a genuine, spontaneous, free, spiritual, active centre, a human selfconsciousness, which as creaturely faces the eternal Word in a genuinely human attitude of adoration, obedience, a most radical sense of creaturehood."[44] It is difficult to overstate the oddness of this picture, in which CHN, which is not a person, consciously recognizes and worships its divine personal *suppositum*, the Logos. While not referring directly to Rahner, Donald MacLeod is most emphatic in rejecting this view: "His human nature certainly did not exist in an I-Thou relationship to his divine nature: such an understanding would plunge us into the most unambiguous Nestorianism."[45]

Worse, if the two-minds view entails (as it apparently does) two self-consciousnesses, then the following is not only a possibility, but must have in fact been the normal case: CHN is conscious of being a "self" and of having experience E, say, being tempted in the wilderness.[46] The Logos is conscious of being a "self" and of having experience F, say, of creating the world. Not surprisingly, CHN is not conscious of F as his own experience. But, on a two-minds view, neither is the Logos conscious of experience E *as his own experience* (although, being omniscient, the Logos knows that CHN had the experience E). And this is the point, I believe, where the quasi-Nestorian aspects of the medieval model are felt most acutely.

Indeed, is it even coherent to speak of CHN as having self-consciousness if it is not a "self"—that is, a person? Considerations such as this motivate Sturch's insistence on a single "ego," "I," "self" or "central self," and it seems to me that this line of reasoning is correct.

---

[44] Karl Rahner, "Current Problems in Christology," in *Theological Investigations*, trans. Cornelius Ernst (Baltimore: Helicon, 1961), 157–58; original German *Schriften sur Theologie*, I (Zurich and Cologne: Benziger Verlag, 1954).

[45] Donald Macleod, *The Person of Christ*, CCT (Downers Grove, IL: InterVarsity Press, 1998), 201. Macleod here is not targeting Rahner explicitly, but a hypothetical view which, it seems, Rahner exemplifies. Rahner once remarked, "Perhaps it is possible to be an orthodox Nestorian or an orthodox Monophysite. If this were the case, I would prefer to be an orthodox Nestorian." *Karl Rahner in Dialogue: Conversations and Interviews 1965–82*, ed. P. Imhof and H. Biallowons (New York: Crossroad, 1986), 127.

[46] This example is chosen deliberately, for the reason that the two-minds/two-consciousnesses view is frequently invoked by its proponents to explain how Jesus (CHN) could be genuinely tempted, while the Logos, being God, could never be tempted.

As Morris develops his account, he shies away from its obvious quasi-Nestorian aspects, conceding that Jesus did not have "a personal set of cognitive and causal powers distinct from [those] of God the Son."[47] But then what remains of the two-minds account?

Before moving on to an alternative proposal, I should note that some defenders of the two-minds account have employed reduplicative propositions in its defense. A reduplicative proposition is a conjunctive proposition of the form "x is F *qua* M and x is not F *qua* N." *Qua* means "as" or "in the capacity of." So, one could say something like, "Christ experienced E *qua* man, and did not experience F *qua* man." But this will not do for explaining the experiences of Christ, for experience is irreducibly first-person, and the defender must give an account of the same report in terms of the first-person indexical "I." That is, there must have been an "I" that experienced E, and an "I" that experienced F. Now if the defender proposes that Christ could say, "I experienced E as a man, but I did not experience F as a man (but rather as divine)," then the defender has tacitly posited a second-order center of experience (I will resist calling it a superego). But then the defender is no longer offering a two-minds account.[48]

A Contemporary Model

Theologians as well as philosophers have expressed misgivings about the two-minds/two wills implications of the dyothelite decree of the sixth council (Constantinople III). A. H. Strong writes:

> This possession of two natures does not involve a
> double personality in the God-man, for the reason that
> the Logos takes into union with himself, not an individual

---

[47] Morris, *The Logic of God Incarnate*, 161.

[48] Eleonore Stump makes the "qua move" in "Aquinas' Metaphysics of the Incarnation." Peter van Inwagen analyzes reduplicative propositions in terms of his very controversial thesis of relative identity in "Not by Confusion of Substance, but by Unity of Person," in Alan G. Padgett, ed., *Reason and the Christian Religion: Essays in Honor of Richard Swinburne* (Oxford: Clarendon, 1994). Thomas Senor, "Incarnation, Timelessness, and Leibniz's Law Problems," in Gregory E. Ganssle and David M. Woodruff, eds., *God and Time: Essays on the Divine Nature* (New York: Oxford University Press, 2002), 231, analyzes the semantics of reduplicative propositions and concludes they can not help in explicating seemingly contradictory features of the incarnation.

man with already developed personality, but human nature, which has had no separate existence before its union with the divine. Christ's human nature is impersonal, in the sense that it attains self-consciousness and self-determination only in the personality of the God-man. Here it is important to mark the distinction between nature and person. Nature is substance possessed in common [i.e. Aristotle's second substance]; . . . Person is nature separately subsisting, with powers of consciousness and will . . . *For this reason, Christ has not two consciousnesses and two wills, but a single consciousness and a single will.*[49]

J. O. Buswell Jr., unwilling to dismiss entirely the council's decree but at the same time rather skeptical of it, says this:

I cannot deny that the wording of the decision of the [sixth] council seems to imply that a "will" is a substantive entity, like a hand or a foot. Yet I do not believe that such an opinion can be dogmatically asserted as the actual meaning of the council. We are familiar with the tendency of human expressions, not only toward literal reification or hypostatization, the tendency to regard an abstraction as a substantive entity; but we are also familiar with the tendency of language toward *metaphorical* reification. I cannot prove that the implications of the wording of the third council of Constantinople were merely metaphorical and not literal, though in my opinion a case could be made for such a conclusion.[50]

Gordon Lewis and Bruce Demarest simply dismiss the sixth council's declaration: "The Third council of Constantinople (681), undoubtedly falsely, asserted that there are two wills in Jesus Christ and that the human will is subordinate to the divine."[51]

---

[49] Augustus Hopkins Strong, *Systematic Theology* (Philadelphia: Judson Press, 1907), 694–95 (emphasis added).
[50] James Oliver Buswell Jr., *Systematic Theology* (Grand Rapids: Zondervan, 1962), 2:53–54.
[51] Gordon R. Lewis and Bruce A. Demarest, *Integrative Theology* (Grand Rapids: Zondervan, 1990), 2:317.

As already noted, the Chalcedonian Definition says that Jesus is one person with two natures, leaving those crucial terms undefined. Where Chalcedon feared to tread, there is room for constructive philosophical theology. Millard Erickson noted in his work on the Trinity: "At this point, it appears unlikely that a great deal more will be contributed to the doctrine of the Trinity from the biblical studies, where probably most of the relevant biblical passages have been well examined. What is more likely, however, is that more progress will be made in understanding the conceptual factors in the doctrine of triunity . . . The growing number of philosophers giving serious attention to philosophical issues related to Christian theology provide a valuable resource for theology."[52] I suspect Erickson would agree that this is true for Christology also. Indeed, the most thoroughly developed attempts to construct a contemporary model that avoids the problems associated with the dyothelite model have come from theologically trained philosophers.[53]

Clarifying Terms: Persons and Natures

In explicating the contemporary monothelite model, I will begin with definitions. Failure to pay attention to definitions leads to imprecision and misunderstanding. I am not claiming that these definitions are the only legitimate definitions for the concepts involved, nor that they are necessarily superior to the definitions of the concepts held by the later councils and the medieval philosophical theologians. These definitions do, however, explicate how the concepts are understood by many contemporary Christian philosophical theologians.

1. *Persons.* It is common—but, I believe, mistaken nonetheless—to claim that *persona* as used by the Latin fathers, or *prosopon* and *hypostasis* as used by the Greek fathers, meant something quite different from our modern notion of "person."[54] It begs the question simply to claim that

---

[52] Millard F. Erickson, *God in Three Persons: A Contemporary Interpretation of the Trinity* (Grand Rapids: Baker, 1995), 343–44.

[53] For example, Richard Sturch, *The Word and the Christ*, and William Lane Craig, "The Incarnation," in Moreland and Craig, *Philosophical Foundations*, 597–613.

[54] See discussions in Sarah Coakley, "'Persons' in the 'Social' Doctrine of the Trinity: A Critique of Current Analytic Discussion," in Davis, Kendall, and O'Collins, eds., *The Trinity*, 126–30. Richard Müller, *Dictionary of Latin and Greek Theological Terms* (Grand Rapids: Baker, 1985), 223–27, succinctly summarizes the changing usage of the terms.

the fathers did not understand themselves and each other much as we understand ourselves, subsisting independently of each other even while relating to each other. They surely would have regarded themselves, and each other, as conscious, beminded, morally responsible agents. And so Boethius's famous definition certainly reflects the theological as well as the mundane usage. Stating it a bit more carefully:

> A *person* is an individual with an appropriately complex and structured set of mental properties, faculties (a natural grouping of capacities) and higher order capacities, unified by internal relations.

That is to say, a person is an individual, a particular that has its own properties but is not "had by" something else.

The structured set of mental properties or capacities (of an appropriate complexity so as to rule out animals) essential to personhood includes at least the following:

> (a) Consciousness (including sensation, thought, belief, desire and volition);
> (b) Self-consciousness (awareness of self as a unified subject, and second-order awareness of one's first-order mental states); and
> (c) Relationality (capacity for relationships with other persons).

Let us consider these properties or capacities in order.

(a) Consciousness. At least five kinds of conscious states exist.[55] A *sensation* is a state of awareness, e.g., a conscious experience of sound or pain. Some sensations are perceptual experiences of things outside me like a tree. Consequently, the capacity of sensation entails the capacity of gaining information concerning the external world. Others are experiential states within me like pains. Emotions are a subclass of sensations. A *thought* is a mental content that can be expressed in an entire sentence. Some thoughts logically imply other thoughts, while other thoughts don't entail, but merely provide evidence for, other thoughts.

---

[55] For the development and defense of this classification of mental properties, see Richard Swinburne, *The Evolution of the Soul*, rev. ed. (Oxford: Clarendon, 1997), part 1.

The capacity for thought is thus a necessary condition for rationality. A *belief* is a person's view, accepted to varying degrees of strength, of how things really are. The content of a belief is a proposition, and beliefs can be true or false depending on the truth value of the propositional content of the belief. A *desire* is a certain felt inclination to do, have, or experience certain things. *Volition* is the capacity of choice, an exercise of power, an endeavoring to act, usually for the sake of some purpose. Further, this volitional capacity must be free in some sense (libertarian or compatibilist freedom), for intuitions run very deep that an entity all of whose behavior is causally determined does not qualify as a person, whatever other attributes it might have.

(b) Self-consciousness. Self-consciousness is the irreducible, first-person, introspective awareness of one's self as a conscious subject. It is also the second-order awareness of first-order mental states. The first is an awareness of "I," while the second is an awareness of being aware.[56]

It is in virtue of the capacities of consciousness and self-consciousness that persons are morally responsible agents.

(c) Relationality. Persons have the capacity to relate to other things, notably other persons, by communicating relatively complex content (thoughts, beliefs, emotions, etc.) by various means, including but not limited to language. In the light of biblical revelation as well as empirical observation, I take it that this capacity to relate to other persons is different in kind, and not merely in degree, from humans' capacity to relate to animals, or animals' ability to relate to other members of their species. That is, without minimizing the depth of relationship one can establish with a dog, for example, I would insist that the human capacity to enter into relationships with other persons—human, angelic or divine—is a unique feature of what it is to be a person. The nature of the perichoretic relationship among the divine persons of the Trinity reflects their relationality.

It is important to note that these mental properties and powers may be either actual or potential; what is necessary for personhood is the *capacity* for such properties and powers, and the capacities are grounded in that very person, not in existent properties of the biological organism

---

[56] J. P. Moreland, "A Defense of a Substance Dualist View of the Soul," in J. P. Moreland and David M. Ciocchi, eds., *Christian Perspectives on Being Human* (Grand Rapids: Baker, 1993), 68.

that is the person's body. An individual person possesses all these faculties/capacities, or the higher-order capacity to develop them, whether that person is a fetus, asleep, in a coma, or suffering severe dementia.

The definition says that these mental properties are unified by internal relations: a word of explanation of the concept of internal relations is in order. A relation is *external* to something if that relation does not enter into the very nature of that thing, while a relation is *internal* if it does enter into the thing's nature. So, for example, *being located north of San Diego* is an external relation in which I stand to San Diego; that could well change, but I would still be me if I travel south of San Diego. However, *being the oldest son of Joseph and Doris DeWeese* is an internal relation in which I stand to my parents; I would not be the person I am if I did not stand in that relation to my parents.[57] More generally, if *a* stands in R to *b* and R is internal to *a*, then anything that does not stand in R to *b* cannot be identical to *a*.

Applying this to the definition, the unity of the mental properties of a person derives from their being internally related to the person, so that the thoughts, experiences, reasonings, etc. that a person has, as well as her higher-order capacities, are *hers* and not another's. While I might, for example, entertain the same proposition as she does, or experience the same symphony or roller-coaster ride, it is wrong to say I am thinking *her* thoughts or having *her* experiences. And even though God infallibly knows what she is thinking and experiencing, God knows those thoughts and experiences *as hers* (object—third person) and not as his (subject—first person).

The definition thus gives us the unity of the experiencing subject as essential to personhood.

In the literature of philosophy and philosophical theology, what I have here called a "person" is often referred to as a "soul." But I want to avoid confusion that might stem from the various biblical uses of *nephesh* and *psyche*, so I shall retain the term *person*.[58] It should be clear

---

[57] By "person that I am," I mean the individual substance that is my person, not the personality, experiences, memories, etc., which I have had in virtue of growing up in the home of Joseph and Doris DeWeese.

[58] Robert Saucy summarizes the biblical uses of *soul*: "As breathing is the mark of life, so 'soul' refers to the creature enlivened by the breath of life or the spirit. The great emphasis in *soul* is thus upon man as a living being. As such it is used in relation to man's appetites,

that *person* refers to something immaterial. Human persons normally have bodies and function holistically as a body-soul unity, but to claim that embodiment is essential to being human persons, or to equate (human) personhood to emergent properties of a body or brain, or to argue that human persons are wholly constituted by their bodies, is in my view a grave philosophical and theological error.

2. *Natures.* As noted above, some philosophers, especially in the Aristotelian tradition, speak of individual natures or essences. But that has led to the problems we have examined. Noting the confusion in Christological developments between the fourth and sixth councils, Swinburne comments, "This whole mess has been produced by forgetting that human nature, and certainly Christ's human nature, is a universal; what individuates him is something else."[59] Fairbairn states it as a fundamental Christological axiom: one must not treat a nature as if it were a person.[60] What is relevant to the development of a contemporary model is a kind-nature, or nature as a universal:

> A *nature* is a complex property that includes all properties essential to an individual's being a member of a kind; the set of properties which are necessarily coinstantiated in any individual of that kind.

---

yearnings, and desires, whether they be those of the body (e.g., Deut 23:24 NASB margin; Ps 107:9 NASB; Prov 25:25) or those of the inner person (e.g., Exod 15:9 NASB margin; Prov 21:10 NASB; Jer 12:7 NASB). It is also linked in this sense with man's longing for God and his word (e.g., Pss 42:1,2; 63:1; 119:20). As evidenced in these references to human passions and longings, *soul* has the characteristic of all the aspects of human personality, that is, thought, emotion, volition.

"Soul is also used for the life of an individual . . . In such uses it refers not to life in the abstract, but the living self in all of its dynamic. Since this life is manifest most clearly in the personal characteristics of the inner person, soul sometimes is used along with body ("flesh") to represent the whole person . . .

"In sum, then, *soul* in its most comprehensive sense stands for the entire person—the human being is a living soul. As the uses above indicate, *soul* may be used for various aspects of the person, even the person who survives the death of this body. But even in these uses, there is the underlying thought that these actions or characteristics of the soul are those of the whole person." Robert Saucy, "Theology of Human Nature," in Moreland and Ciocchi, *Christian Perspectives on Being Human*, 38–41.

[59] Swinburne, *The Christian God*, 215.

[60] Fairbairn, "The One Person Who Is Jesus Christ," chapter 3 in this volume, pp. 81,108.

Nature in this sense is the abstract "whatness" of a kind, e.g. the "dogginess" of my dog Rusty, or the "humanity" of my wife Barbara. Generally we may take *nature* and *essence* as interchangeable terms. A nature is an abstract thing, and must be instantiated in, exemplified by, or "had" by a particular. For example, Rusty instantiates the nature "dogginess." Natures as such do not have concrete existence on their own apart from individuals.

Any actual person, then, is an individual *together with a nature*; there are no "denatured persons." The nature determines what *kind* of person it is. It is logically possible that personhood be instantiated in various kinds, e.g. divine persons, angelic persons, human persons, Martian or Klingon persons, and so on. *Divine person*, *human person*, and *angelic person* are thus species of the genus *Person*.

Now if this is correct, then since mental properties inhere in persons and not natures, it follows that the mind and will are faculties or capacities of persons and not of natures. Persons are conscious, natures are not; persons have the capacity of making choices and exercising active power, natures do not. So persons have minds and wills, natures do not. Being abstract, natures cannot think, cannot desire, and cannot exercise active power. But the nature determines what kind of mind or will it is—divine, angelic, human, and so forth.

Several additional comments on natures in general are necessary. First, as Thomas Morris notes,[61] we must distinguish *common* (even *universal*) properties of a kind from *essential* properties—the nature—of a kind. For example, it is a common property (indeed, at this point in time, a universal property) of all humans that they have lived part of their lives on Earth. But should humanity eventually establish a colony on Mars, say, it is conceivable that a human could live her entire life without setting foot on Earth. So "having lived part of one's life on Earth" is not an *essential* property of humanness, although it is a common property of all humans.

Second, again following Morris's lead, it is crucial to distinguish properties which constitute *mere* kind-membership from *full* kind-membership. For example, a brick instantiates the nature of—has all the properties

---

[61] Morris, *The Logic of God Incarnate*, 62–70.

essential to—a material object, such as extension, mass, spatio-temporal location, etc. It is *fully* a material object. But although a dolphin is also *fully* a material object, in virtue of instantiating the nature of a material object, a dolphin is not *merely* a material object, since it also instantiates the nature of a living organism.

So while a property such as "undergoes progressive development in physical and mental powers and capacities" is a *common* human property, it is not *essential* (or else Adam would not have been human). And while "having a disposition to sin" may be a *common* property of humans (except for Christ), it is not an *essential* property (at least, not if the doctrine of the incarnation is true).

Third, natures come in various levels of specificity. To use the example just noted, a dolphin can have the nature of a material object, the nature of an animal, the nature of a mammal, and the nature of the family *Delphinidae*. Indeed, in general, a single substance can have more than one nature. It is customary, however, to speak of natural kinds as the lowest-level (*infimae*) species, so a dolphin is a member of the natural kind *Delphinidae*, but mammal, animal and material object are not natural kinds.

I will not attempt to specify the set of properties that constitute divine and human natures; the literature is already overcrowded with such discussions.[62] However, let me simply note that inability precisely to define human or divine nature in no way entails that there is no such thing, or that we cannot meaningfully speak of such natures.[63] Nor will I attempt to demonstrate that there is no intrinsic incompatibility such that a person with a fully divine nature could not at the same time exemplify a fully human nature; much has been written in defense of that claim also.[64]

---

[62] On the divine nature, see, for example, Edward R. Wierenga, *The Nature of God: An Inquiry into the Divine Attributes* (Ithaca, NY: Cornell University Press, 1989), or Joshua Hoffman and Gary S. Rosenkrantz, *The Divine Attributes* (Oxford: Blackwell, 2002). On human nature, see, for example, Moreland and Ciocchi, *Christian Perspectives on Being Human*, or Leslie Stevenson and David L. Haberman, *Ten Theories of Human Nature*, 3rd ed. (New York: Oxford University Press, 1998). Robert Pasnau, *Thomas Aquinas on Human Nature* (New York: Cambridge University Press, 2002), is of relevant historical interest, and includes significant interaction with contemporary analytical perspectives.

[63] See Sturch, *The Word and the Christ*, 135, for further defense of this claim.

[64] See Morris, *The Logic of God Incarnate, passim.*

The concepts of person and nature outlined above, which are common in contemporary ontology,[65] allow for construction of a model of the incarnation that avoids some of the problems which attend the dyothelite model constructed using medieval metaphysics.

A Contemporary Model of the Incarnation

One Person, Two Natures: The Model Stated

The second person of the Trinity, the divine Logos, is eternally a person with a divine nature. Indeed, the person of the Logos essentially (necessarily) instantiates the divine nature, while the instantiation by the Logos of human nature is contingent—that is, the Logos would still be the second person of the Trinity apart from the incarnation. At the incarnation, the set of properties that define human nature are assumed by the Logos and thus are exemplified by a divine person. So in a very unambiguous sense, Jesus is *fully* (but not *merely*) human. At the moment he assumed human nature, the Logos also assumed a human body. A. H. Strong comments: "The Logos did not take into union with himself an already developed human person, such as James, Peter, or John, but human nature before it had become personal or was capable of receiving a name. Christ's human nature realized its personality only in union with the divine. At Jesus' conception the two natures vitally united to form one person with a single consciousness and will. Jesus' consciousness and will were . . . always theanthropic—an activity of the one personality which unites in itself the human and the divine."[66]

Since a person has a mind and a will, and a nature does not, Christ had one mind and one will, which belong to his divine person. The model is thus, strictly and literally, monothelite, although given the different metaphysical understandings of personhood and nature that were current at the time of the sixth council, it is not at all clear that this proposed contemporary model entails the view that was condemned in 681. Perhaps it could be called "neomonothelite" to emphasize the changed metaphysical

---

[65] Not to mention classical theology. See, for example, Martin Chemnitz, *The Two Natures in Christ*, trans. J. A. O. Preuss (St. Louis: Concordia, 1971; original Latin edition 1578), 29–34. See also Strong, *Systematic Theology*, 692–97.

[66] Ibid., 679, 695.

presuppositions; but "neo" as a prefix to the name of a traditional heresy does not constitute a really helpful label.

During the earthly ministry of the incarnation, the Logos voluntarily restricted the exercise of his personhood capacities to the range of thoughts, sensations, volitions, perceptions, etc., that can be exercised by a person operating within the normal limitations of human nature, including being embodied as an organism of the species *Homo sapiens.* But since humans were created in the image and likeness of God, such a limitation is not incompatible with human nature being assumed by a divine person. Thomas Morris, in fact, holds something very similar:

> "[Jesus] was not a being endowed with a set of personal cognitive and causal powers distinct from the cognitive and causal powers of God the Son. For Jesus was the same person as God the Son. Thus, the personal cognitive and causal powers operative in the case of Jesus' earthly mind were just none other than the cognitive and causal powers of God the Son. The results of their operation through the human body, under the constraints proper to the conditions of a fully human existence, were just such as to give rise to a human mind, an earthly noetic structure distinct from the properly divine noetic structure involved with the unconstrained exercise of divine powers."[67]

(As indicated above, I think Morris is wrong in the claim that the constraints voluntarily assumed by our Lord when he took on the form of a servant "gave rise" to a second mind. Rather, I would say that the voluntarily constrained divine mind, restricted to operating through a human nature and a human body, just was a human mind.[68])

This model does not follow the radical nineteenth-century kenotic theologians such as Thomasius, Ebrard, or Forsyth in claiming that in assuming human nature the Logos necessarily lost certain divine attributes.[69]

---

[67] Morris, *The Logic of God Incarnate,* 161–62.

[68] This approach still lets us understand how to reconcile the impeccability of Christ with the reality of his temptation along lines suggested by Morris. Space does not allow me to pursue the issue here.

[69] For more on radical kenoticism, see Erickson, *The Word Became Flesh,* 78–86; Moreland and Craig, *Philosophical Foundations,* 604–5; Sturch, *The Word and the Christ,* "Excursus

Radical kenoticism in this sense is fatally flawed both philosophically and theologically. Philosophically, if the Logos possesses divine nature essentially, then he could not give up divine attributes and be the same individual. Theologically, Jesus must be divine to accomplish redemption, and he is so confessed by all the orthodox creeds and councils.

Rather, the contemporary model explains the "self-emptying" (Phil 2:5) as Christ's voluntary self-limitation to exercise his personhood through his human nature, gaining information about the world through the perceptual faculties of his human body, learning and storing memories through the instrumentality of his human brain, living a perfect human life by his perfect obedience and complete dependence on the Holy Spirit.

Certainly it becomes difficult to press an explanation of the relationship of the divine and the human in Christ much further, but this difficulty is shared equally, as we have seen, by the dyothelite model. On the contemporary model, we could still meaningfully speak about the "human mind" of Christ, but we would not be referring to a faculty or entity, and we would no longer be tempted to think of it as another person. The "human mind" of Christ refers to the mode of operation of the mind of the Logos functioning within the constraints of (voluntarily limited by) Jesus' human nature and the organs of a human body. At the same time, the mind of the Logos, functioning gloriously and perfectly according to the divine nature, never sleeps, never ceases to be omniscient. But rather than constituting two minds, we should understand the human mind as sort of a limited subset of the divine mind. We could say, with Craig, that the divine mind is "largely subliminal," or with Morris, that the divine mind is analogous to the unconscious, or with Sturch, that "the 'self' who undergoes the joys and pains of Jesus of Nazareth, who *is* Jesus of Nazareth, is also the 'self' of God the Son."[70]

A Crucial Objection: Is This Heresy?

If the medieval model veers close to Nestorianism, perhaps the contemporary model veers too close to Apollinarianism. Both Sturch and

---

III: *Kenosis*." See also Klaus Issler's discussion of kenoticism on p. 200.

[70] Craig, "The Incarnation," 610; Morris, *The Logic of God Incarnate*, 105; Sturch, *The Word and the Christ*, 130.

Craig have attempted to deflect the charge of Apollinarianism in their presentations of a contemporary model.[71] How real is the danger that the contemporary model represents an objectionable quasi-Apollinarianism?

Put simply, Apollinarius was a trichotimist who believed that a human was composed of a body, an animal soul, and a rational soul. In his model of the incarnation, the rational soul of Jesus was simply not present but was replaced with the Logos. Of Christ, he wrote, "He is not a man, though like a man; for He is not consubstantial with man in the most important element [viz., a rational soul]." Christ is something of a *tertium quid*, "a mean between God and man, neither wholly man nor wholly God, but a combination of God and man."[72] As the resulting being was neither fully God nor fully man, Apollinarius's model was rightly condemned as deficient. Apollinarianism was rejected by the church because it was thought to undo the logic of salvation by asserting that Jesus Christ's human nature was missing the most important thing required to make someone human.

Is the contemporary model guilty of a quasi-Apollinarianism, denying that Christ had a human soul or spirit?[73] Well, it is not guilty in any immediately obvious way. First, the contemporary model presents a Christ who is fully human and fully God, one person in two natures; it surely is not presenting the hypostatic union as a *tertium quid*. Second, as noted above, the terms "soul" and "spirit" do not have univocal technical meanings in Scripture such that their use in a particular way can be made a mark of orthodoxy. Third, the claim that "Christ had a human soul" can be understood two ways. On one reading, we would take it as asserting that Christ possessed a thing that was a human soul (in virtue of the thing that is a human soul being necessarily a part of what composes human nature). This is how the claim is understood on the medieval dyothelite model. But on the second reading, the claim asserts that Christ's soul was

---

[71] Sturch, *The Word and the Christ*, 130–31; Craig, "The Incarnation," 599, 608. Perhaps unfortunately, Craig refers to his model as "broadly Apollinarian (once rehabilitated to meet the standards of Orthodoxy)," in "Not Radical Enough," 62 n. 16; or as a "reformulation (or rehabilitation!) of Apollinarius' insight," in "Incarnation," 609. Such allusions are unfortunate, inviting all those who rightly wish to avoid the heresy of Apollinarianism to reject the view wholesale.

[72] Cited by Macleod, *The Person of Christ*, 159.

[73] I thank Robert Saucy, Alan Gomes, and the late Stanley Grenz, who voiced such objections to me, and forced me to think more deeply about these issues.

human (in virtue of the soulish aspects of the person of Christ functioning according to his human nature). So Christ's soul was *fully* human even though not *merely* human. Fourth, the contemporary model proposed here seeks to do better justice than the medieval dyothelite model (and its modern defenders) to the guiding insight of Cyril of Alexandria, which is that the personal agent at work in the incarnation is the eternal Logos. Stepping away from two-minds Christology is stepping back towards the patristic consensus as articulated by Cyril and Chalcedon: anti-Arian, anti-Apollinarian, anti-Nestorian, and anti-Eutychian.

So the contemporary model seems to be safe from charges that it is simply a retooled Apollinarianism. Yet it remains suspect because the model is clearly monothelite (positing only one will in the incarnate Christ), and monothelitism was condemned by the sixth council. Now, it certainly should give an Evangelical pause when a proposed theological model departs from positions endorsed by the seven ecumenical councils. But such departure is not necessarily fatal. For example, very few Evangelicals would accept the decree of the seventh council (Nicaea II, 787). Convened in response to the iconoclastic controversy,[74] the seventh council decreed that images must be placed in all churches and are to be venerated (but not worshipped). Perhaps more striking, the Nicene Creed, developed by the first ecumenical council (Nicaea I, 325) and amplified by the second council (Constantinople I, 381), reads in part, "We acknowledge one baptism for the remission of sins." While this creed was endorsed by all subsequent councils, the particular way it uses the words of Acts 2:38 here indicates a theology of baptism that Protestant Evangelicals do not think passes the test of being truly scriptural. The point is this: while most Evangelicals should and do regard the deliverances of the ecumenical councils as weighty in defining the orthodox faith, they would agree that the councils cannot be accepted uncritically but must themselves be judged by the authority of Scripture.

Finally, what of Gregory of Nazianzus' maxim that the unassumed is unhealed? If Christ did not assume a human soul, then our human souls

---

[74] *Iconoclasm* means "image breaking." The Iconoclast movement of the eighth and ninth centuries sought to remove images (icons) from churches and so to eliminate the practice of venerating or worshipping such images. The Iconoclasts not only destroyed icons but burned some churches and monasteries and tortured and killed a number of monks, primarily in the eastern part of the empire. The seventh council declared iconoclasm a heresy.

cannot be redeemed—or so critics of the contemporary model argue. In response, we should note that the maxim is a slogan; its meaning must be carefully explicated. While Gregory used the slogan in opposing Apollinarianism, and it was later invoked against monothelitism, we have seen how that opposition is grounded in the view that wills belong to natures and so Christ must have had two wills (dyothelitism). Gregory's maxim presupposes that a nature (with all it contains, lacking nothing) is joined to the Logos, but that a person is emphatically not taken into union with the Logos. The objection we are considering to the contemporary monothelite model applies the maxim to the human soul. But a defender of the contemporary model would simply deny that a soul is something a person *has*; rather, a soul is what a person *is*. In another context Robert Saucy (who himself defends a dyothelite model) writes that "*soul* in its most comprehensive sense stands for the entire person—the human being is a living soul."[75] The contemporary model understands soul in this sense, so Christ did indeed "have" a fully human soul simply because he was fully—though not merely—a complete human person.[76]

Some Implications of the Contemporary Model

Theological

The contemporary model has trinitarian implications. Christians have always believed that God has a unitary will. The medieval philosophical theologians took this to mean that the will of the Father was numerically identical to the will of the Son, which itself was numerically identical to the will of the Spirit. They were not saying that the trinitarian persons always desired the identical thing, nor that they always willed the same object or event. There was, in a strict and literal sense, only one will in the Godhead. For example, one of the arguments for dyothelitism offered by Pope Agatho in his letter to the sixth council claims that wills must

---

[75] Saucy, "Theology of Human Nature," 41.

[76] Indeed, I believe this model is the only way to make sense of the *enhypostatia* doctrine, which comes from Leontius of Byzantium. According to this doctrine, the human nature of Christ is incomplete, needing its own hypostasis to be a person. The hypostasis of the human nature is the Logos himself, so the human nature of Christ is enhypostatic. On (many interpretations of) the medieval model, the human nature of Christ is possibly anhypostatic, that is, as we saw above, it possibly exists on its own apart from the Logos.

go with natures on the basis of a Trinitarian analogy: "For if anybody should mean a personal will, when in the holy Trinity there are said to be three Persons, it would be necessary that there should be asserted three personal wills, and three personal operations (which is absurd and truly profane). Since, as the truth of the Christian faith holds, the will is natural, where the one nature of the holy and inseparable Trinity is spoken of, it must be consistently understood that there is one natural will, and one natural operation."[77]

That has the consequence that what the Father wills, the Son and the Spirit also will, and so on. That presents no problem if *will* means "desire." But if it means "exercise of active power," as it must if there is strictly one will, problems arise. The contemporary model solves the problems, for it allows that the three persons of the Trinity desire the same thing, but at the same time also allows for the three persons to exercise their individual active power. On the understanding represented by Agatho's statement, there is one will in the Trinity and two in Jesus Christ. On the contemporary model, there are three wills (i.e., three faculties of volition) in the Trinity and one in Jesus Christ.

This leads to a more satisfying interpretation of the scene in the garden of Gethsemane. When Jesus prays, "My Father, if it is possible, may this cup be taken from me; nevertheless, not as I will, but as you will" (Matt 26:39), we can understand it in a very straightforward way—the one personal will of Christ who, with human nature and a human body was operating as a fully human person, desired the cup of suffering, death, and separation from the Father, to be taken from him. But Christ submitted his (personal) will to the divine will of the Father. On the dyothelite model, we would have to gloss the passage something like this: "The human will of Christ's human nature desired that the cup pass, but his divine will (which was numerically identical with the Father's will), did not, and it is the divine will which controls Jesus' decision-making, so there is no possibility that the human desires will be acted upon. While normally the divine will in Christ so overpowers his human will that the human will is invisible, on this one occasion we are privileged to see it."

---

[77] Henry R. Percival, ed., *The Seven Ecumenical Councils*, vol. 14, NPNF[2], 332–33. I thank John McKinley for calling my attention to this reference.

The advantages of simplicity favor the contemporary model. As Craig says: "[Christ's prayers in the garden] do not contemplate a struggle of Jesus' human will with his divine will (he is not, after all, talking to himself!), but have reference to the interaction between Jesus' will ('my will') and the Father's will ('yours'). Possessing a typical human consciousness, Jesus had to struggle against fear, weakness and temptation in order to align his will with that of his heavenly Father. The will of the Logos had in virtue of the Incarnation become the will of the man Jesus of Nazareth."[78]

A second theological advantage is this. The contemporary model allows us to take at face value statements of Jesus such as when he said to the leper who asked for healing, "I am willing" (Mark 1:41). The human being standing there was willing; we don't need to posit a divine will which was willing and with which the human will concurred (as it always did). And when Jesus says, "Not my will but yours be done," he is by the exercise of his own active power submitting his natural desire to avoid the coming agony to the desire of the Father, and the coming exercise of the Father's active power.

Practical

There is also a great practical advantage to this theological understanding. Analogous to Nazianzus' maxim, "The unassumed is not healed," perhaps a second maxim should guide Christology: "The unexemplified is not an example." That is, to whatever degree Jesus fails to exemplify the qualities of human personhood, to that degree he fails to be our example. But, of course, Scripture holds him up as our example. We should fix our eyes on him so we do not lose heart (Heb 12:2–3). He is our brother who shared our humanity, who suffered when he was tempted (Heb 2:12–18), and was tempted in every way just as we are (Heb 4:16). And at least once, Jesus himself said that he set us an example (John 13:6).

Here is the relevance of this second Christological principle. If Jesus really had two minds and two wills, then the exemplary nature of his perfect obedience, prayer life, resisting temptation, suffering, and so on,

---

[78] Craig, "Incarnation," in Moreland and Craig, *Philosophical Foundations*, 611.

become highly problematic. But according to the contemporary model, Jesus truly is our example of a perfect human individual.[79]

Conclusion

A case can be made that the contemporary model is philosophically superior to the medieval dyothelite model, and further, that it is equal if not superior in interpreting the biblical data. Moreover, it is superior in generating new positive implications, especially in showing the relevance of Christ as our example in spiritual formation. For these reasons, the contemporary model deserves serious consideration. It should not be forgotten, however, that this is a model, a conceptual scheme attempting to show, consonant with contemporary metaphysics, that the Chalcedonian Definition is logically coherent, and indeed plausible. It should not be understood as claiming to be the only true account of the hypostatic union.

At the end of the day, whether a Christian philosopher or theologian holds to some version of the medieval dyothelite model or of the contemporary model, we can rejoice that we are not called to believe an impossibility, and that there is no incoherence lying at the heart of our faith. The result in our lives should be deeper doxology as we celebrate God's grace and love poured out on us in Jesus Christ.[80]

Resources for Further Reading

Craig, William Lane. "The Incarnation." Chap. 30 in *Philosophical Foundations for a Christian Worldview*, ed. J. P. Moreland and William Lane Craig. Downers Grove, IL: InterVarsity, 2003. Intermediate. A very helpful sketch of the development of Christology and different understandings of the hypostatic union, with a proposal for a contemporary model.

---

[79] For a thorough exploration of the notion of Christ as our example, see Klaus Issler's chap. 6.

[80] My thanks for stimulating comments to audiences at sessions of the Evangelical Theological Society Annual Meetings in 2002 and 2003 where very early versions of these ideas were presented. Special thanks for helpful and challenging comments to Bill Craig, Alan Gomes, Klaus Issler, J. P. Moreland, Fred Sanders, Robert Saucy and Bruce A. Ware.

Cross, Richard. *The Metaphysics of the Incarnation.* New York: Oxford University Press, 2002. Advanced. A thorough exposition of the metaphysics of medieval Christologies, with a focus on Aquinas and Duns Scotus.

Davis, Stephen T., Daniel Kendall, and Gerald O'Collins, eds. *The Incarnation: An Interdisciplinary Symposium on the Incarnation of the Son of God.* New York: Oxford University Press, 2002. Advanced. A very helpful anthology of papers from an interdisciplinary symposium, bringing together in one volume papers by biblical, patristic, medieval and modern theologians and philosophers, as well as papers dealing with aesthetics, ethics, and homiletics.

Erickson, Millard J. *The Word Became Flesh: A Contemporary Incarnational Christology.* Grand Rapids: Baker, 1991. Intermediate. Perhaps the best, most comprehensive Christology available from an Evangelical theologian. Erickson does unwittingly oscillate between implications of the medieval and the contemporary models as discussed in this article.

Hardy, Edward R., ed. *Christology of the Later Fathers.* LCC. Philadelphia: Westminster Press, 1954. A very helpful collection in one volume of the Christological writings of Athanasius, Gregory of Nazianzus and Gregory of Nyssa, as well as several other significant documents such as the Tome of Leo.

Study Questions

1. Explain the definitions of *person* and *nature*.
2. Explain the two models of incarnation and how they each interpret Matthew 26:39.
3. Describe how each model explains the essential unity of Jesus' person and nature.
4. Explain the objections for each model, and how each model responds to these objections.

Part 2

THE WORK OF
CHRIST

5

CHRIST'S ATONEMENT

A Work of the Trinity

Bruce A. Ware

Chapter Summary

Anselm's important question, *Cur Deus Homo?* (Why the God-Man?), needs to be examined afresh in light of current trends in trinitarian and Christological studies, which minimize the immanent Trinity and the preexistence of the Son of God, respectively. This chapter will argue, in part, that the "success" of the atonement depends on the identity of Christ as the theanthropic person, the One who is both fully God and fully man in the incarnation. But adding to the importance of seeing the atonement as the accomplishment of the God-man is the realization that the atonement's accomplishment depends just as much on the work of the Father and the Spirit in conjunction with the Son. So, in addition to Anselm's question, we must pose the question, *Cur Pater Spiritusque?* (Why the Father and the Spirit?). That is, this chapter will also seek to lay out a rationale for understanding the atonement as the work of the triune God such that without the Trinity there could be no atonement and hence no salvation. Seeing this, we realize how dependent we are on the truths defended at Nicaea (AD 325) and Chalcedon (AD 451), where the doctrines of the Trinity and then the hypostatic union were brought to orthodox clarity. Not only is the whole of salvation the work of the triune God, but it is the particular burden of this chapter to demonstrate that the atonement in and of itself can only rightly be comprehended as the work of the Father and the Spirit in conjunction with the God-man, Jesus Christ of Nazareth.

Axioms for Christological Study

1. Jesus Christ cannot be understood in his person or his work without the Trinity. Without the Father and the Spirit, Jesus would not be who he is and could not have done what he did.
2. The person and work of Christ are based not merely on his being divine, but on his Sonship both in eternity and in history.
3. The identity of Jesus as Savior is inextricably tied to his being the Spirit-anointed Messiah, whose very person requires the indwelling and empowering Spirit for him to be who he is and to accomplish what he has come to do.

KEY TERMS

atonement	immanent Trinity	economic Trinity
eternal relation structure	eternal authority structure	eternal submission
egalitarianism	Spirit-anointed	Messiah

Latin terms	*Cur Deus Homo?*	*Cur Deus Trinus?* *qua*
Greek term	*taxis*	

In the eleventh century, Anselm asked, "*Cur Deus Homo?*" i.e., Why did God become man? In contemplating the doctrine of the incarnation and the Chalcedonian affirmation that in Christ the divine nature and a human nature are fully united but not confused in the one person, Jesus Christ of Nazareth, Anselm sought to give an explanation of why this hypostatic union of the divine *ousia* and the human *ousia* was in fact necessary for our salvation. One might think of Anselm's purpose, then, in these terms: he sought to articulate just why Christ must be both God and man in order for this Christ, the Messiah, to be a Savior and for his atoning death to be efficacious. Anselm expresses the heart of his answer to this question in one place this way, saying that "it is necessary that a God-Man should pay" for sin, since, "no one can pay except God, and no one ought to pay except man."[1]

In more recent years of this twenty-first century, I have been led to contemplate a similar kind of question, but this in regard to the doctrine of the Trinity and its relationship both to Christ as the atoning Savior and to the efficacy of his atoning death. Rather than *Cur Deus Homo*? our question here is *Cur Deus Trinus*? i.e., Why must God be three in one for salvation to be effected? Thus, the overall question that frames this chapter is this: Must God be triune for the Messiah to be our atoning Savior and for his atoning death to be efficacious? That is, is it necessary that the God who saves be the trinitarian deity of the Christian faith? Or, yet differently, is there a necessary relationship in Christian theology between the doctrine of the Trinity and the doctrine of the atonement? *Cur Deus Trinus*? Must God be triune for Christ's identity and his atoning death to be what they are?

This chapter will argue that the trinitarian personhood of God is necessary in both respects. The argument will be made primarily from biblical teaching that demonstrates the necessity of trinitarian relations for comprehending rightly both Christ's identity as the atoning Savior and for his accomplishing the atoning work he came to do. Some other recent works have discussed the nature of the Trinity and the atonement,[2] but what often seems lacking or given insufficient attention in these discussions is careful reflection on Scripture's own teaching that should inform, first and foremost, how we understand both the Trinity and the relationship of the Trinity to Christ's work of atonement. In what follows, then,

---

[1] Anselm, *Cur Deus Homo* 2.6.

[2] See, e.g., Robert Sherman, *King, Priest, and Prophet: A Trinitarian Theology of Atonement* (New York: T&T Clark, 2004); Georg Pfleiderer, "The Atonement," in Paul Louis Metzger, ed., *Trinitarian Soundings in Systematic Theology* (New York: T&T Clark, 2005), 127–38; and Ronald F. Thiemann, "Beyond Exclusivism and Absolutism: A Trinitarian Theology of the Cross," in Miroslav Volf and Michael Welker, eds., *God's Life in Trinity* (Minneapolis: Fortress, 2006), 118–29.

we first will focus attention on the relationship of the Trinity to the identity of Christ as the atoning Savior, and in the following section consider
the relation of the Trinity to his atoning work.

The Trinity and the Identity of Christ as the Atoning Savior

The identity of Jesus as Messiah and Savior is tied, both historically
and of necessity, to his relationships with the Father and Spirit respectively. Put differently, if you imagine for a moment removing the Father
and the Spirit from the historical person Jesus Christ of Nazareth, you
realize that this Jesus the Christ could not be—i.e., he could not exist
and be who he is—in their absence. Indeed, the identity of Christ as
atoning Savior depends on the reality of the Trinity. Consider with me
the relationship of the Christ as Savior to the Father and to the Spirit,
each in turn.

The Father and the Identity of Jesus

To announce the bottom line at the top, the identity of Jesus as Savior
is inextricably tied to his being the Son of the Father, sent by the Father
to accomplish the Father's will. In other words, who Jesus is and what
he came to accomplish have everything to do with his Sonship, both in
the immanent Trinity and in the economic Trinity, or more simply, both
in eternity and in history.

From the beginning, the church has understood the names Father
and Son for these respective persons of the Trinity to be appellations of
their eternal personhood and relationship, respectively, not merely con-
ventions suitable for the incarnation. If the Father sends his Son into
the world (John 3:17) and if the Father creates and reveals and redeems
through his Son (Heb 1:1–3), then these names refer not to some ad hoc
arrangement for the incarnation but to an eternal relationship in which
the Father is the eternal Father of the Son, and the Son is the eternal Son
of the Father. Now, what is in these names? Geoffrey Wainwright muses
over the fact that "'Father' was the name that the second person in his
human existence considered most appropriate as an address to the first
person." But why is this? To this question, Wainwright can only say that
"there must be . . . something about human fatherhood that makes Father

a suitable way for Jesus to designate the one who sent him. In trinitarian terms, the crucial point is that Father was the address Jesus characteristically used in this connection."[3] However, just what the "something" is, Wainwright does not tell us.

But is it not obvious? Jesus said often throughout his ministry that he came down from heaven to do the will of his Father (John 6:38). Indeed, the Father installed his Son as King on Mount Zion to reign over the nations (Ps 2:6–9), and in the end it will be the Father who puts all things in subjection to his Son (1 Cor 15:27–28). Without question, a central part of the notion of "father" is that of fatherly authority. Certainly this is not all there is to being a father, but while there is more, there certainly is not less or other. The masculine terminology used of God throughout Scripture conveys, within the patriarchal cultures of Israel and the early church, the obvious point that God, portrayed in masculine ways, had authority over his people. Father, King, and Lord communicate, by their masculine gender referencing, a rightful authority that was to be respected and followed. And the father-son relationship in particular evidences, among other things, the authority of the father over the son. Malachi 1:6, for example, indicates just this connection between father and authority: "'A son honors his father, and servants their master. If then I am a father, where is the honor due me? And if I am a master, where is the respect due me?' says the LORD of hosts." God as Father is rightfully deserving of his children's honor, respect, and obedience. To fail to see this is to miss one of the primary reasons God chose the name Father to name himself. If the Father is the eternal Father of the Son, and if the Son is the eternal Son of the Father, this marks their relationship as one in which an inherent and eternal authority and submission structure exists. The Son *qua* eternal Son heeds the voice and command and will of his eternal Father.

One implication of the submission of the Son *qua* eternal Son to the Father *qua* eternal Father should be noted. Those who deny any eternal submission of the Son to the Father simply have no grounding for answering the question why it was the Son and not the Father or Spirit who was sent to become incarnate. And even more basic is the question why the eternal names for Father and Son would be exactly *these* names.

---

[3] Geoffrey Wainwright, "The Doctrine of the Trinity: Where the Church Stands or Falls," *Interpretation* 45 (1991): 120.

John Thompson has indicated a trend in much modern trinitarian discussion to separate Christology from trinitarian formulations. He writes that "Christology and the Trinity were virtually divorced. It was both stated and assumed that any one of the three persons could become incarnate . . . There was thus only an accidental relation between the economy of revelation and redemption and the eternal triune being of God."[4] It appears that contemporary egalitarianism is vulnerable also to this criticism. Since, in the egalitarians' understanding, nothing in God grounds the Son being the Son of the Father, and since every aspect of the Son's earthly submission to the Father is divorced altogether from any eternal relation that exists between the Father and Son, there simply is no reason why the Father should send the Son. In Thompson's words, it appears that the egalitarian view would permit "any one of the three persons" to become incarnate. Yet we have scriptural revelation that clearly says that the Son came down out of heaven to do the will of his Father. This sending is not ad hoc. In eternity, the Father commissioned the Son who then willingly laid aside the glory he had with the Father to come and purchase our pardon and renewal. Such glory is diminished if there is no eternal Father-Son relation on the basis of which the Father wills to send, the Son submits and comes, and the Spirit willingly empowers.

Consider more specifically some of the biblical teaching supporting this contention. Psalm 2 records the raging of the nations against "the Lord and his anointed" (Ps 2:2). The very reference to "his anointed" indicates already the supreme position that this Lord has over the one he anoints for the work to be described. As we read on, far from trembling at the rebellious counsel of the kings of the earth, God rather laughs from his exalted place in the heavens (Ps 2:4). Of God it is said, "Then he will speak to them in his wrath, and terrify them in his fury, saying, 'I have set my king on Zion, my holy hill'" (Ps 2:5–6). Notice that God asserts his rightful jurisdiction over the nations of the world, and he also affirms his authority over the very king whom he sets over the nations. The point, then, is clear. God's supremacy is both over the nations themselves and over this king whom he places over the nations.

---

[4] John Thompson, *Modern Trinitarian Perspectives* (New York: Oxford University Press, 1994), 22.

And who is this king whom God sets over the kings of the nations? He is none other than his own Son. We read further in Psalm 2:7–9: "I will tell of the decree of the LORD: He said to me, 'You are my son; today I have begotten you. Ask of me, and I will make the nations your heritage, and the ends of the earth your possession. You shall break them with a rod of iron, and dash them in pieces like a potter's vessel.'"

The citation of Psalm 2:7 in Acts and Hebrews makes clear that the reference here is to one who is the eternal Son of God and will become the incarnate Son, whom the Father places over the nations. God the Father subjects the nations to his own rulership by sending his Anointed, God the Son, to come as the incarnate Son and King to reign over the world. And from Revelation 19 we learn that the incarnate but now crucified and risen Son, the "Word of God" (v. 13) and the "King of kings and Lord of lords" (v. 16) will indeed bring forth the wrath of God Almighty on the nations who stand against him. Although the fulfillment of this text is clearly through the incarnate Son who will come to live, die, be raised, and, in the end, be exalted over all in fulfillment of the Father's will, still Psalm 2 records, also clearly, the preincarnate will of this Father to anoint and install this particular one, his own Son, to be this king. Here, then, is evidence that the Father's role is supreme over the Son as it is supreme over all things, for it is the Father who anoints the Son, who puts the Son in his place as king over the nations, and through his Son brings all things into subjection under his Son's feet.

So, it is not merely that Jesus is a Son, per se, but that he is the Son of *this* Father—this Father who himself uniquely is King and Redeemer, and who decrees to exercise both his salvation of and triumph over the nations through none other than his Son. We express no disrespect for the Son when we observe that it is absolutely true that Jesus the Christ could not be who he is, nor could his mission be what it was, apart from his being the Son of the Father, begotten by the Father, and commissioned by the Father for his mission. We have no atoning Savior who is not the Son of *this* Father.

Consider Daniel 7:13–14, another passage which indicates that the identity of the Messiah is tied directly to the Father: "I saw in the night visions, and behold, with the clouds of heaven there came one like a son of man, and he came to the Ancient of Days and was presented before him. And to him was given dominion and glory and a kingdom, that all peoples, nations, and languages should serve him; his dominion is an everlasting dominion, which shall not pass away, and his kingdom shall not be destroyed" (ESV).

Note that the language of "given" in verse 14 indicates that the Son's identity as the coming King of kings and Lord of lords depends on his being Son of this Ancient One (more literally, "Ancient of Days"). That is, while it is true that the Christ, the Messiah, who comes to conquer all and establish his dominion over all, is the one who fulfills what this text announces, it is also true that this only happens because the Ancient of Days (surely the Father) gives to him the right and responsibility to carry out this mission.

As these texts imply, it was the will of the Father in eternity past to send the Son into the world to be Savior and King. The historical Sonship of the Messiah, then, reflects the eternal relationship of the Sonship of the second person of the Trinity with his Father. Here, as elsewhere, the immanent Trinity takes priority over and explains the economic Trinity, Karl Rahner's maxim notwithstanding.[5] The identity of Jesus as atoning and conquering Savior is inexplicable without reference to his being the eternal Son of the eternal Father, now begotten as the Christ, the incarnate Son of his Father.

New Testament teaching, and particularly the teaching of Jesus himself, confirms that his identity as Son and Savior is dependent on his being sent by the Father. First Corinthians 11:3 offers a truth-claim about the relationship between the Father and Son that reflects an eternal verity.[6] That God is the head of Christ is not suggested by the apostle Paul

---

[5] Karl Rahner, *The Trinity* (New York: Herder, 1970), 22, has famously stated, "The 'economic' Trinity is the 'immanent' Trinity, and the 'immanent' Trinity is the 'economic' Trinity." Most interpreters of Rahner have understood him to mean that we only know the immanent Trinity through the experience of God in the economy of his revelation, thus reducing the immanent to the economic Trinity. For insightful discussion of Rahner, see Paul Molnar, *Divine Freedom and the Doctrine of The Immanent Trinity* (Edinburgh: T&T Clark, 2002), 83–124, 167–96; Stanley Grenz, *Rediscovering the Triune God: The Trinity in Contemporary Theology* (Minneapolis: Augsburg Fortress, 2004), 55–71; and Fred Sanders, *The Image of the Immanent Trinity: Rahner's Rule and the Theological Interpretation of Scripture* (New York: Peter Lang, 2004).

[6] For helpful discussion of the interpretation of *kephale* ("head") and its bearing on this text, see Wayne Grudem, *Evangelical Feminism and Biblical Truth* (Sisters, OR: Multnomah,

to be an ad hoc relationship for Christ's mission during the incarnation. It is rather stated as a standing truth regarding this relationship. God is the head of Christ, and placing this at the end of verse 3 likely indicates that the grounding for the other two instances of headship is found in this one. The Father has authority over the Son. There is a relationship of authority and submission in the very Godhead on the basis of which the other authority-submission relationships of Christ and man, and man and woman, depend.[7]

John's Gospel mentions forty times that Jesus was sent by the Father to accomplish his mission. Christopher Cowan demonstrates that the "sending" language in John indicates centrally, though not exclusively, the concept of Jesus as the agent of another (viz., his Father) who carries out the will of the Sender in obedience as the Sent One.[8] This being the case, it is noteworthy that a number of the instances of the Father's sending of the Son indicate that the sending took place in regard to the preincarnate Son. John 3:16–17 reads, "For God so loved the world that he gave his only Son, so that everyone who believes in him may not perish but may have eternal life. Indeed, God did not send the Son into the world to condemn the world, but in order that the world might be saved through him." That the Father sent the Son into the world indicates the sending took place prior to the incarnation itself. The Son of eternity past, then, obeyed the Father in coming into the world, since he was sent by the Father so to come. In John 6:38, Jesus says, "For I have come down from heaven, not to do my own will, but the will of him who sent me." These words could not be clearer that the obedience to the will of the Father took place in eternity past as the preincarnate Son came from heaven at the will of the Father. Again, in John 8:42 Jesus said, "I did not come on my own, but he [i.e., the Father] sent me." By the Father's initiative and will, then, the Son came. How could it be clearer that the Son obeyed the will of the Father and carried out his plan and purpose by coming into the world? Or again Jesus said, "Can you say that the one

---

2004), 568–94.

[7] In other words, it does seem clear that Paul's central point in 1 Corinthians 11:3 is that the *taxis* of God's headship over his Son accounts for the presence of *taxis* in man's relationship with Christ and the woman's relationship with man.

[8] Christopher Cowan, "The Father and Son in the Fourth Gospel: Johannine Subordination Revisited," *JETS* 49 (2006): 115–35.

whom the Father has sanctified and sent into the world is blaspheming because I said, 'I am God's Son'?" (John 10:36). Clearly, the Father both consecrated the Son for the very mission he planned for him, and then he sent the Son into the world to fulfill what he had designed. For this to be meaningful, we must understand both the consecration and sending of the Son as happening prior to the incarnation and thus in the design and purpose of God in eternity past.

The Synoptic Gospels likewise confirm, albeit with less detail, what we see regularly in John's Gospel, viz., that the eternal Son is under the authority of his Father. Commenting particularly on the significance of the order of the divine names in Matthew 28:19, Simon Gathercole writes:

> We have already seen how in Mark 13.32 Jesus stands between God and the angels in a heavenly hierarchy; in Matt. 28.19, however, we have a *divine* hierarchy of Father, Son, and Spirit: all three persons participate in the divine name invoked in baptism.
>
> Already within the context of earliest Christianity, there is significance in the *order* of the names, however. Very common in the synoptics is the implication of the Father's authority over the Son and the corresponding obedience of the Son to the Father. All things are given to the Son by his Father (Matt. 11.27 par. Luke 10.22; Matt. 28.18), and he continues to depend on the Father in prayer (e.g. Mark 1.35). Perhaps most clearly of all, the Son is frequently described as *sent* by the Father: once or twice in Mark, twice in Matthew, four times in Luke. Sending clearly presupposes an authority of the sender over the envoy.
>
> In terms of the Son's authority over the Spirit, in John and Acts it is evident that the Son sends the Spirit (John 15.26; cf. 14.26; Acts 2.33). Jesus' sending of the Spirit at Pentecost would have been understood as the fulfillment of John the Baptist's promise (common to all four Gospels) that Jesus would baptize with the Holy Spirit.

This itself presupposes divine identity: as Jenson rightly
notes, "No prophet as such can do this. To give the Spirit
is to act from the position of God." But if the Son is the
one who *sends* the Spirit, then this again would presuppose
a relationship of hierarchy within a Jewish context. As a
result, it can be concluded that the order Father-Son-Spirit
in Matt. 28.19 is not incidental; rather, it is born out of the
early Christian thinking that the Father has authority over
the Son, who in turn has authority over the Spirit.[9]

Regarding the Father's sending of the Son, as found particularly in
the Synoptics, Gathercole also comments on the significance of Luke
7:8, which provides a helpful illustration of the authority and submission inherent in such sending: "For I also am a man set under authority,
with soldiers under me; I say to one, 'Go,' and he goes; and to another,
'Come,' and he comes . . ."[10] Indeed, the order of the divine names in
Matthew 28:19 and the language of the sending of the Son, both in the
Synoptics and in John, indicate the eternal *taxis* among the members of
the Trinity.

Consider also Peter's claim: "He was destined before the foundation of the world, but was revealed at the end of the ages for your sake.
Through him you have come to trust in God, who raised him from the
dead and gave him glory, so that your faith and hope are set on God"
(1 Pet 1:20–21). The key phrase, of course, is Peter's reference to Christ
having been "destined" by the Father before the foundation of the world.
What the NRSV translates here as "destined" is literally "foreknown,"
but foreknowledge here does not mean merely knowing ahead of time
what is going to happen. Of course God has foreknowledge in that sense.
But more than that, to foreknow is to choose one for some certain purpose,[11] to know in the sense of favoring this particular one upon whom

---

[9] Simon J. Gathercole, *The Pre-existent Son: Recovering the Christologies of Matthew,
Mark, and Luke* (Grand Rapids: Eerdmans, 2006), 72–73. Gathercole's quotation of
Jenson is from R. W. Jenson, *Systematic Theology*, vol. 1, *The Triune God* (Oxford: Oxford
University Press, 1997), 88.

[10] Gathercole, *Pre-existent Son*, 72. In a footnote, Gathercole expresses gratitude to Audrey
Dawson for suggesting this example.

[11] See, e.g., Thomas R. Schreiner, *1, 2 Peter, Jude*, NAC 37 (Nashville: B&H, 2003),
87–88. Schreiner comments, "In the Greek text of v. 19 the word 'Christ' appears last,

you choose to bestow some privileged service or calling. Thus, God had established his Son as the one who would bring everything into subjection under his feet, his Son as the one who would be raised above all of creation and given the name that is above every name. His Son would be given glory (1:21) through his suffering, death, and subsequent resurrection and exaltation. But when did the Father make this prior decision to choose his Son for this favored of all callings? "Before the foundation of the world" is the answer given by Peter. This requires, then, an authority-submission relationship in eternity past, one in which the Father chooses and sends, and one in which the Son submits and comes.

New Testament teachings on Christ as the Creator also confirm this same authority and submission structure between the Father and Son. Although Christ is portrayed as the Creator, nonetheless he creates under the authority of the Father. In Colossians Paul expresses thanks "to the Father" specifically in 1:12, who has "rescued us from the power of darkness and transferred us into the kingdom of his beloved Son" (1:13). With this stress on the Father's work, now he speaks of creation being done "in" Christ, indicating that the Son does what he does as the agent of the Father. First Corinthians 8:6 confirms this understanding, for here we read of "one God, the Father, from whom are all things and for whom we exist, and one Lord, Jesus Christ, through whom are all things and through whom we exist." The Father creates by or through the agency of the Son. As such, Genesis 1 is echoed in John 1 insofar as the God who speaks and brings creation into existence (Gen 1) does so through his Word (John 1:3). So by him, the eternal Word, all things are created. The Son as Creator of the universe does so as the instrument and agent of the Father's will and work.

Consider two confirmatory statements of the Son's eternal identity as the Son of the Father, both from Fathers of the early church. First, in his *Treatise on the Trinity*, Hilary of Poitiers writes:

> That the Son is not on a level with the Father and is not
> equal to Him is chiefly shown in the fact that He was sub-
> jected to Him to render obedience, in that the Lord rained

---

separated from the term 'blood' by five words. The text was likely written in this way so that it would be clear that the Christ was the subject of the participle commencing v. 20. The Christ 'was chosen before the creation of the world'" (87).

from the Lord and that the Father did not, as Photinus
and Sabellius say, rain from Himself; in that He then sat
down at the right hand of God when it was told Him to
seat Himself; in that He is sent, in that He receives, in
that He submits in all things to the will of Him who sent
Him. But the subordination of filial love is not a diminution of essence, nor does pious duty cause a degeneration
of nature, since in spite of the fact that both the Unborn
Father is God and the Only-begotten Son of God is God,
God is nevertheless One, and the subjection and dignity of
the Son are both taught in that by being called Son He is
made subject to that name which because it implies that
God is His Father is yet a name which denotes His nature.
Having a name which belongs to Him whose Son He is,
He is subject to the Father both in service and name; yet
in such a way that the subordination of His name bears
witness to the true character of His natural and exactly
similar essence.[12]

How important it is to affirm with Hilary that "subordination of filial
love is not a diminution of essence, nor does pious duty cause a degeneration of nature," since God is one. As such, "the subjection and dignity
of the Son are both taught" in his being called Son. Indeed, the Son is
fully God, and yet as Son of the Father, he is subject to the Father. His
identity as the Son who comes to redeem is one inseparable, then, from
the Father who sends him.

Second, hear how Augustine discusses both the essential equality of
the Father and Son, and the eternal procession of the Son from the Father,
which is the reason for the Father's sending of the Son who was always,
in eternity past, the one to obey and carry out the will of the Father:

If however the reason why the Son is said to have been
sent by the Father is simply that the one is the Father and
the other the Son then there is nothing at all to stop us
believing that the Son is equal to the Father and consubstantial and co-eternal, and yet that the Son is sent by the

---

[12] Hilary of Poitiers, *Treatise on the Trinity*, NPNF[2], 9:18.

Father. Not because one is greater and the other less, but because one is the Father and the other the Son; one is the begetter, the other begotten; the first is the one from whom the sent one is; the other is the one who is from the sender. For the Son is from the Father, not the Father from the Son. In the light of this we can now perceive that the Son is not just said to have been sent because the Word became flesh, but that he was sent in order for the Word to become flesh, and by his bodily presence to do all that was written. That is, we should understand that it was not just the man who the Word became that was sent, but that the Word was sent to become man. For he was not sent in virtue of some disparity of power or substance or anything in him that was not equal to the Father, but in virtue of the Son being from the Father, not the Father being from the Son.[13]

While the Son was fully God—"consubstantial and co-eternal" with the Father—yet he was sent, as Augustine says, "in order for the Word to become flesh."[14] This indicates the *taxis*, the order, in the Trinity prior

---

[13] Augustine, *The Trinity* 5.27. Edmund Hill, *The Works of St. Augustine*, vol. 5 (New York: New City Press, 1991).

[14] In two places in his recent book (Kevin Giles, *Jesus and the Father: Modern Evangelicals Reinvent the Doctrine of the Trinity* [Grand Rapids: Zondervan, 2006], 191–92, 229–30), Giles takes issue with my treatment of Augustine here. Both discussions by Giles refer to the same previously published chapter (Bruce A. Ware, "Tampering with the Trinity," in Wayne Grudem, ed., *Biblical Foundations for Manhood and Womanhood* [Wheaton: Crossway, 2002], 246). The second discussion by Giles (229–30) repeats in shorter form nearly verbatim the identical objection he raised earlier (191–92) to my understanding of Augustine. Unfortunately, the readers of Giles' book, in both passages where he discusses my quotation and treatment of Augustine, have been sadly misinformed. For some inexplicable reason, in both discussions of my treatment of Augustine, Giles provides for the reader only the first portion of the longer quote from Augustine that I have provided in my previous published chapter (and even here he puts ellipses in the place of the phrase, "and yet that the Son is sent by the Father," where Augustine indicates he is making two points about the Father-Son relation, not just one). And of course, in that first portion, Augustine truly does affirm clearly and boldly that the Father and the Son are consubstantial and coeternal. But in the same block quote reproduced in my chapter, immediately following where Giles has quit quoting, Augustine continues as follows:

> In the light of this we can now perceive that the Son is not just said to have been sent because the Word became flesh, but that he was sent in order for the Word to become flesh, and by his bodily presence to do all that was written. That is, we should understand that it was not just the man who the Word became that was sent, but that the Word was sent to become man. For he was not sent in virtue

to the incarnation, which *taxis* is manifest as he becomes incarnate and obeys the will of the Father. Apart from Jesus' relationship to his Father, his identity as Savior sent into the world is inexplicable.

And of course, this very reality of being in submission to the Father marks the Son's relationship with the Father for all of eternity future. Recall the remarkable words of 1 Corinthians 15:25–28:

> For he must reign until he has put all his enemies under his feet. The last enemy to be destroyed is death. For "God has put all things in subjection under his feet." But when it says, "All things are put in subjection," it is plain that this does not include the one who put all things in subjection under him. When all things are subjected to him, then the Son himself will also be subjected to the one who put all things in subjection under him, so that God may be all in all.

Regarding this text, the late Colin Gunton has commented that this description of the Son's future subjection to the Father has "implications for what we may say about the being of God eternally, and would seem to suggest a subordination of *taxis*—of ordering within the divine life—but not one of deity or regard. It is as truly divine to be the obedient self-giving Son as it is to be the Father who sends and the Spirit who renews and perfects."[15] We are enabled to see here something of what

---

of some disparity of power or substance or anything in him that was not equal to the Father, but in virtue of the Son being from the Father, not the Father being from the Son.

So, what I wrote earlier of Augustine's view in fact is born out by the longer and complete quotation that readers would have been able to see if Giles had simply continued the quotation of Augustine fully. Yes indeed, the Father and Son are fully and completely equal in essence (stressed by Augustine in the first part of his longer statement, the portion quoted by Giles), while the Son as from the Father is under the authority of his Father, having come to earth to become incarnate precisely because he was sent from his Father to become a man (stressed by Augustine's double statement of this understanding in the second part of his longer statement, the portion omitted by Giles). I cannot say why Professor Giles omitted the very portion of the quotation that supported my claim that Augustine affirms the preincarnate authority of the Father over the Son. But whatever the reason, the fact remains that Augustine affirms both the essential equality of the Father and the Son along with the preincarnate functional submission of the Son to the Father. Giles' own discussion, by its attenuated quotation of Augustine, turns out to be the treatment of Augustine, which in fact denies what Augustine affirms.

[15] Colin E. Gunton, *The Promise of Trinitarian Theology*, 2nd ed. (Edinburgh: T&T Clark,

constitutes the beauty, the wisdom, and the goodness of the relations among the trinitarian persons when we see the Son at work accomplishing the will of the Father. It is the nature of God both to exert authority and to obey in submission. And since this is the eternal nature of God, we may know that it is beautiful and it is good, and because of this, we are prompted to marvel a bit more at the glory that is our triune God. Indeed, then, the Son's identity is wrapped up essentially with his being the Son in submission to this Father.

Finally, listen afresh to the interchange Jesus had with his disciples at Caesarea Philippi:

> Now when Jesus came into the district of Caesarea Philippi, he asked his disciples, "Who do people say that the Son of Man is?" And they said, "Some say John the Baptist, but others Elijah, and still others Jeremiah or one of the prophets." He said to them, "But who do you say that I am?" Simon Peter answered, "You are the Messiah, the Son of the living God." And Jesus answered him, "Blessed are you, Simon son of Jonah! For flesh and blood has not revealed this to you, but my Father in heaven." (Matt 16:13–17)

There can be no doubt that the very identity of the Son who comes as the atoning Savior is his identity as the Son of the Father who sent him into the world to accomplish the mission the Father designed for him to do. The identity of Jesus, the Christ, then, is impossible to comprehend or account for apart from his relationship with the Father.

The Spirit and the Identity of Jesus

To announce the bottom line at the top, the identity of Jesus as Savior is inextricably tied to his being the Spirit-anointed Messiah whose very person requires the indwelling and empowering Spirit for him to be who he is and to accomplish what he has come to do. Consider some of the biblical teaching supporting this contention.

1991, 1997), 197.

The angel said to her, "Do not be afraid, Mary, for you have found favor with God. And now, you will conceive in your womb and bear a son, and you will name him Jesus. He will be great, and will be called the Son of the Most High, and the Lord God will give to him the throne of his ancestor David. He will reign over the house of Jacob forever, and of his kingdom there will be no end." Mary said to the angel, "How can this be, since I am a virgin?" The angel said to her, "The Holy Spirit will come upon you, and the power of the Most High will overshadow you; therefore the child to be born will be holy; he will be called Son of God." (Luke 1:30–35)

"I myself did not know him; but I came baptizing with water for this reason, that he might be revealed to Israel." And John testified, "I saw the Spirit descending from heaven like a dove, and it remained on him. I myself did not know him, but the one who sent me to baptize with water said to me, 'He on whom you see the Spirit descend and remain is the one who baptizes with the Holy Spirit.' And I myself have seen and have testified that this is the Son of God." (John 1:31–34)

When he came to Nazareth, where he had been brought up, he went to the synagogue on the sabbath day, as was his custom. He stood up to read, and the scroll of the prophet Isaiah was given to him. He unrolled the scroll and found the place where it was written: "The Spirit of the Lord is upon me, because he has anointed me to bring good news to the poor. He has sent me to proclaim release to the captives and recovery of sight to the blind, to let the oppressed go free, to proclaim the year of the Lord's favor." And he rolled up the scroll, gave it back to the attendant, and sat down. The eyes of all in the synagogue were fixed on him. Then he began to say to them, "Today this scripture has been fulfilled in your hearing." (Luke 4:16–21)

"But if it is by the Spirit of God that I cast out demons,
then the kingdom of God has come to you." (Matt 12:28)

"You know . . . how God anointed Jesus of Nazareth
with the Holy Spirit and with power; how he went about
doing good and healing all who were oppressed by the
devil, for God was with him." (Acts 10:36–38)

Jesus is none other than the Spirit-anointed Messiah. In the Gospels,
his very conception as the God-man is supernaturally accomplished by
the power of the Spirit (Luke 1:35). And his life is lived and his mission
accomplished through the leading and empowerment of the Spirit (Luke
4:1,14). If he casts out demons by the Spirit of God, then we know that
the kingdom of God has come (Matt 12:28). None other than a Messiah
who brings with him the Spirit is the true Messiah long ago foretold
(e.g., Isa 11:1–9; 42:1–9; 61:1–3). When he comes into Nazareth and
announces his true identity to the townspeople of his upbringing, he se-
lects from the prophet Isaiah, not chapter 53 but chapter 61. The Spirit of
the Lord upon him demonstrates his authentic messianic identity. And,
as the Spirit-anointed Messiah, he will then live his life and carry out his
mission in the power of this Spirit (Acts 10:38). As Bobrinskoy writes,
"Henceforth, Jesus will live our entire human existence with its anxiet-
ies, its temptations, its struggles, its sufferings and its joys. But it is in the
Spirit that He will live His humanity as the Son of God in an unceasing,
free obedience to the Father."[16]

The very identity of Jesus as the Christ is inexplicable apart from his
relationship with both the Father and the Spirit. The Father is the Father
of the Son, and as such he commissions and sends his Son into the world
to be and do what he calls him to. The Son, though, cannot be who he is
apart from the anointing of the Spirit who brings him into being in the
virgin conception within Mary, and then abides with him as the necessary presence and power of his messianic identity and ability.[17] *Cur Deus*

---

[16] Boris Bobrinskoy, *The Mystery of the Trinity: Trinitarian Experience and Vision in the
Biblical and Patristic Tradition* (Crestwood, NY: St Vladimir's Seminary Press, 1999),
88–89.

[17] See Gerald F. Hawthorne, *The Presence and the Power: The Significance of the Holy
Spirit in the Life and Ministry of Jesus* (Dallas: Word, 1991); and James M. Hamilton, *God's
Indwelling Presence: The Holy Spirit in the Old and New Testaments*, in the NACSBT 1

Trinus? Must God be triune for Christ to be our atoning Savior? Yes indeed. The Trinity is necessary for the identity of Christ as Savior, and we will explore in the next section the necessity of the Trinity also to the efficacy of his atoning death.

The Trinity and the Efficacy of Christ's Atoning Death

We have seen that the identity of Jesus as Messiah and Savior is tied, both historically and of necessity, to his relationships with the Father and Spirit, respectively. In addition, it is clear upon reflection that the efficacy of his atoning death is tied, both historically and of necessity, to the work of the Father and the Spirit, along with and through the Son, to effect our salvation. Just how is salvation dependent upon the saving God being triune? Consider the work of the Father, and of the Spirit, respectively, in relation to the efficacy of Christ's atoning work.

The Efficacy of Christ's Atonement and the Father

To announce the bottom line at the top, the efficacy of Christ's atoning work is inextricably tied to his accomplishing the work that the Father sent him to do, a work designed by the Father and carried out through the obedience and faithfulness of the Son. But when you ask, just whose work ultimately is this work of salvation? or who designed the plan of salvation that is carried out historically in and through the cross and resurrection of Christ? the answer from Scripture is plainly that the Father is the grand architect, the wise designer, of our salvation, brought into actuality by the Son he commissioned and sent. Consider some of the evidence of the Father's role as grand architect and wise designer of the salvation wrought in Christ.

Consider Paul's teaching that the Father, before the foundation of the world, has chosen us in Christ (Eph 1:4) and predestined us to adoption through Christ (Eph 1:5). Since the Father is specified by Paul as the one who chose us in eternity past, we must take seriously that it is his choice in particular, and hence the authority by which we are placed in Christ rests with the Father. Surely this shows both the Father's supreme position of authority over all, but it also shows that the Son's work fulfills

---

(Nashville, TN: B&H, 2006).

what the Father has willed. Echoes of "not my will but yours be done" can be heard in the very electing will of the Father. It is his will that the Son accomplishes, and his will to which the Son submits. Furthermore, among the blessings for which we praise the Father is the blessing of providing his Son to redeem us from our sin (Eph 1:7). Indeed, the Father is praised for redeeming us through his Son (cf., Isa 53:10; John 1:29; Acts 2:23; Rom 8:32), and for this reason, the Father is deserving of all praise for the lavish display of his glorious grace (Eph 1:6–8,12,14). And among the blessings enumerated in Ephesians 1, a very telling statement comes beginning in verse 9. Ephesians 1:9–12 says:

> he has made known to us the mystery of his will, according
> to his good pleasure that he set forth in Christ, as a plan for
> the fullness of time, to gather up all things in him, things in
> heaven and things on earth. In Christ we have also obtained
> an inheritance, having been destined according to the pur-
> pose of him who accomplishes all things according to his
> counsel and will, so that we, who were the first to set our
> hope on Christ, might live for the praise of his glory.

Paul describes the whole revelation of our salvation as an outwork-ing, by Christ, of the plan and purpose of the Father. The plan, purpose, intention, mysterious will, and good pleasure of God the Father are all being accomplished by Christ the beloved Son, "according to the pur-pose of him," the Father, "who accomplishes all things according to his counsel and will."

Similarly, notice how in Colossians 1:12–14 Paul says that he is

> giving thanks to the Father who has enabled you to share
> in the inheritance of the saints in the light. He has rescued
> us from the power of darkness and transferred us into the
> kingdom of his beloved Son, in whom we have redemp-
> tion, the forgiveness of sins.

Of course, Paul continues the same line of thought indicating that cre-ation (Col 1:16) and ultimate reconciliation (Col 1:20) is done "by" or "in" or "through" the Son as he carries out the will of the Father. It is clear, then, that the Father is said to have worked through the Son in creation, redemption, and ultimate reconciliation of all things to himself. Both creation and redemption, works accomplished by the Son, are ultimately and rightly seen as works of the Father that are done through the agency of his eternal Son according to the design and the will of the Father.

Along with the clear indications that the work of the Son is designed by the Father, we also have an abundance of statements from the Son himself that he was not here to do his own will, or accomplish his own work, but to fulfill the will and work of his Father. Of the many texts we could consider, look carefully at John 8:26–29:

> "I have much to say about you and much to condemn;
> but the one who sent me is true, and I declare to the world
> what I have heard from him." They did not understand that
> he was speaking to them about the Father. So Jesus said,
> "When you have lifted up the Son of Man, then you will
> realize that I am he, and that I do nothing on my own, but
> I speak these things as the Father instructed me. And the
> one who sent me is with me; he has not left me alone, for
> I always do what is pleasing to him."

There is not a hint in Jesus' self-understanding or teaching elsewhere that differs with the themes announced here. From beginning to end, he came to do the will of his Father. All the way to the garden of Gethsemane, when in agony he cried "not my will but yours be done," he accomplished, in every word spoken, every action performed, every attitude and motive of heart, always and only the will of the Father.

Indeed, it is only because of his absolute obedience that it can be said, as Paul declares in 2 Corinthians 5:21, "For our sake he made him to be sin who knew no sin, so that in him we might become the righteousness of God." Or, as stated in Philippians 2:8, Christ "became obedient to the point of death—even death on a cross." So verse 9: "Therefore God also highly exalted him . . ." We conclude, then, that the efficacy of the atoning work of Christ is dependent upon the Father's design of our redemption, his commissioning of his Son to come and accomplish the salvation he planned, and on the Son obeying, every moment of every day of his life, always and only the will of his Father. Indeed, the efficacy of the atoning work of Christ is impossible without Christ's relationship to the Father.

One further point must be seen and stressed if we are to understand the necessary relationship of the Father to the efficacy of Christ's atoning death. It is only by the work of the Father that the Father's own justice against our sin, in Christ, is met. That is, Christ's death could not have atoned for sin had not the Father judged our sin in his Son. This, I take it, is the heart of what Romans 3:23–26 is about:

> since all have sinned and fall short of the glory of God; they are now justified by his grace as a gift, through the redemption that is in Christ Jesus, whom God put forward as a sacrifice of atonement by his blood, effective through faith. He did this to show his righteousness, because in his divine forbearance he had passed over the sins previously committed; it was to prove at the present time that he himself is righteous and that he justifies the one who has faith in Jesus.

The Father displayed Christ as the satisfaction for sin in his blood, to be received by faith. The imputation of our sin to Christ (2 Cor 5:21), and the judgment of our sin in Christ (Rom 3:25) were the work of the Father, without which the death of Christ could not have accomplished the atoning benefit that it has, through faith in him.[18]

It is worth contemplating a bit further the passion of the Christ as he submitted willingly to the tortuous trial and painful death on the cross. Clearly the agony he experienced was real, and it was severe. As will be explored more fully below, his experience of agony did not begin on the cross; in the garden, praying for the Father to remove the cup, Jesus knew precisely what would be coming. But then on the cross itself, his cry, "My God, my God, why have you forsaken me?" (Matt 27:46), has intrigued thoughtful Christians over the centuries. Just what does

---

[18] Recent years have witnessed an increasing debate on the nature of the atonement, and in particular, much reconsideration is underway of the atonement as most fundamentally one of penal substitution. This debate is one of the most significant of our day, since the very heart of the gospel itself is at stake. On this subject, I would recommend to readers the recent four-views book that provides some of the major proposals being made by Evangelicals (James K. Beilby and Paul R. Eddy, eds., *The Nature of the Atonement: Four Views* [Downers Grove, IL: InterVarsity, 2006]). I especially commend to readers the very fine chapter defending penal substitution: Thomas R. Schreiner, "Penal Substitution View," 67–98.

this mean? What happened to Jesus and his relationship with the Father at this moment? Surely Jesus cannot have meant that the Father disapproved of his Son or of his work, since he was accomplishing precisely what the Father sent him to do. So the forsaking of the Son by the Father must have in view precisely and strictly the sin he now bore for our salvation. Recall Paul's affirmation that God made Christ, who knew no sin, "to be sin for us" (2 Cor 5:21). As the Father charged (imputed) our sin to his Son, and then viewed his Son as bearer of "the sin of the world" (John 1:29), the Father's wrath now would be directed at his Son *qua* sin-bearer, causing him to suffer the penalty and succumb to the death that sinners, instead, deserved.

Even while the Father vented his wrath on his sin-bearing Son, we should not see this as any real fracturing of the Father-Son relationship. Consider at least these three factors. First, Jesus' quotation of Psalm 22:1 brings to mind the whole of this psalm. While it begins, to be sure, with an expression of abandonment, it soon turns to expressions of hope that the God, who forsook his own, will once again come to his aid and vindicate him in the sight of all the peoples (Ps 22:19–31). Indeed, Jesus knows the painful truth of the Father's judgment of him as the bearer of sin, but he also knows the Father's commitment to him as the ultimate and triumphant conqueror and King over all. In that sense, never is there a breach in the relationship the Son has with the Father, or the Father with the Son, since all that transpires on the cross fulfills the Father's plan, by the Son's willing obedience, which looks beyond the cross to the victory and triumph to be attained.

Second, even while suffering on the cross for our sin, Jesus prayed to the Father, and his doing so indicates both the purity of the Son *qua* Son himself as well as the closest of personal relationships imaginable that he continues to have with the Father. "Father," he cried, "forgive them; for they do not know what they are doing" (Luke 23:34). Clearly the forsaking of Matthew 27:46 must take into account also the prayer of Luke 23:34. Forsaken as sin-bearer, he was accepted and loved as precious Son.

Third, no such breach in the Father-Son relationship can have occurred, for the seventh and final saying of Jesus on the cross is precisely to this same Father who is judging sin in his Son. Jesus' final exclamation, "Father, into your hands I commend my spirit" (Luke 23:46), makes clear that even while he is suffering and about to die, the Son trusts fully in his Father and looks to him for strength and hope.

All this is to say that Jesus bore our sin in his body on the cross, to the great pleasure of his Father and in fulfillment of the Father's will. That this involved both the imputation of our sin to the sinless Son, and the executing of the Father's wrath against his Son as the sin-bearer, does not change the fact that the Son did what he did fully and entirely in accord with the Father's own will and purpose. But further, he performed this great work, along with all else that he did throughout the whole of his life, also in the power of the Spirit, and it is to this theme that we now turn.

The Efficacy of Christ's Atonement and the Spirit

To announce the bottom line at the top, the efficacy of Christ's atoning work is inextricably tied to his being the Spirit-anointed Messiah, whose very obedience, miracles, and fulfillment of the Father's will require the indwelling and empowering Spirit for him to accomplish what he came to do. Consider some of the biblical teaching supporting this contention.[19]

Jesus lived his life as a full human in submission to the Spirit. This is a theme that is anticipated in Old Testament prophecies and is shown to be true in the Gospel accounts of Jesus' life and ministry; but it is a theme far too little appreciated by those of us in Evangelical churches. For many of us, the correct answer to the question, "How did Jesus live his life of full obedience to the Father?" is, "Jesus was God in human flesh, and as God he lived his life of sinless obedience, out of the power of his divine nature." While it is absolutely true that Jesus is both fully God and fully man, this answer does not reflect what the Scriptures teach us when we think carefully about what they say.

Consider, for example, Isaiah's prophetic teaching about the coming Spirit-anointed Messiah that we find in Isaiah 11:1–2:

---

[19] See chapter 6 for Klaus Issler's discussion of the theme of Jesus' humanity and the necessity of the Spirit's empowerment of Jesus for him to be who he was and accomplish what he came to do.

> A shoot shall come out from the stump of Jesse,
> and a branch shall grow out of his roots.
> The spirit of the Lord shall rest on him,
> the spirit of wisdom and understanding,
> the spirit of counsel and might,
> the spirit of knowledge and the fear of the Lord.

Does it not seem odd that if Jesus (the coming "shoot from the stump of Jesse") lived his life of obedience by the power of his divine nature, that we would read that when he comes "the Spirit of the LORD shall rest upon him?" After all, what can the Spirit of God add to the divine nature of Jesus? The answer, of course, is "nothing." Jesus' divine nature is omnipotent, omniscient, and in every way infinite and eternal in the fullness of perfection. Furthermore, Jesus' divine nature is the same divine nature as the divine nature of the Spirit and of the Father. So why should Jesus be given the Spirit?

But this is not the only question that Isaiah 11:1–2 raises. Think further about what is said particularly in verse 2: the Spirit who will rest on Jesus will be the Spirit of wisdom, understanding, counsel, might, knowledge, and the fear of the Lord. Does this not indicate that the wisdom that Jesus will exhibit in his earthly ministry as the Son of David, from the stump of Jesse, will be wisdom wrought in him by the Spirit? Are not the understanding, the counsel, the might, the knowledge, and the fear of the Lord that Jesus manifests in his life and teaching the qualities elicited through him by the Spirit? In fact, Isaiah 11:2 is strikingly similar to the "fruit of the Spirit" described in Galatians 5:22–23 as "love, joy, peace, patience, kindness, generosity, faithfulness, gentleness, and self-control." These qualities of the Spirit himself are born in and through our lives, worked out in and through our very character and actions. So too with Jesus, the Spirit of the Lord will work in and through him the very character qualities and capacities that characterize the Spirit at work in and through him.

Consider further that one of the first things we read about Jesus' public ministry is that he followed the lead of the Spirit and lived in the power of the Spirit. Luke tells us that after his baptism, "Jesus, full of the Holy Spirit, returned from the Jordan and was led by the Spirit in the wilderness, where for forty days he was tempted by the devil" (Luke 4:1–2a). Why mention the Spirit in such ways unless the very places that Jesus would go, and his very empowerment for obedience, were linked to the Spirit being in him and working through him? In his temptations, Jesus prevailed over the deceitful schemes of the devil, and we read further, "Then Jesus, filled with the power of the Spirit, returned to Galilee . . ." (Luke 4:14). It seems clear that Luke wants us to know that Jesus is living his life by the power of the Spirit, obeying the Father, and resisting temptation, as the Spirit works in him.

Among the first places Jesus went in Galilee was his home town, Nazareth, where he entered the synagogue on the Sabbath and read Scripture for them in their hearing. When handed the book of Isaiah, he "found the place where it was written,"

> The Spirit of the Lord is upon me,
> because he has anointed me to bring good news to the
>   poor.
> He has sent me to proclaim release to the captives
> and recovery of sight to the blind,
> to let the oppressed go free,
> to proclaim the year of the Lord's favor.
>   (Luke 4:18–19, quoting from Isa 61:1–2).

When Jesus had finished reading, he handed the book back to the attendant, sat down, and said, "Today this Scripture has been fulfilled in your hearing" (Luke 4:21). It is astonishing that Jesus not only knew that he was the Spirit-anointed Messiah, but that the fact of his being Spirit-anointed was so crucial that he selected this text to read and announce its fulfillment.

There is much more from Scripture that could be considered showing that Jesus lived his life, carried out his mission, performed his miracles, and in every way obeyed the Father—all by the power of the Spirit. Perhaps one further text will help bring home the significance of this perspective of Jesus' life and ministry. When Peter preached the gospel to Cornelius, he started with a careful summary of Jesus' life and ministry. Peter spoke of "how God anointed Jesus of Nazareth with the Holy Spirit and with power; how he went about doing good and healing all who were oppressed by the devil, for God was with him" (Acts 10:38). Peter does not say that Jesus went about doing good and healing all who were oppressed, for he relied on the power of his own divine nature (which, of course, Jesus had!). Peter instead appeals to Jesus' Spirit anointing as the basis on which Jesus lived his life, performed his miracles, and completed the mission given him by the Father. And Peter's reference to Jesus being anointed "with the Holy Spirit and with power" is an unmistakable parallel to what Jesus had said to Peter (and the other disciples): "you will receive power when the Holy Spirit has come upon you" (Acts 1:8). The point is this: just as Jesus lived his (fully human) life in the power of the Holy Spirit, his disciples at Pentecost, would likewise receive the Holy Spirit and his power, by which they would live their lives and carry out the calling given them. Although Jesus was fully God, as a man he chose to rely not on his own divine nature but to rely on the power of the Spirit. In this way, he lived his life as an example for us (1 Pet 2:21–22) and fulfilled the perfect human obedience that Adam failed to accomplish.

Yes, Jesus lived his life in the power of the Spirit; for Jesus came as the second Adam, the seed of Abraham, the son of David—a human being who needed supernatural enablement to live the human life of obedience and sacrifice that the Father had ordained for him to carry out. In short, the "human Jesus" needed the Spirit in ways that the "divine Jesus" simply did not and could not. But since Jesus came as "one of us," as it were, as a full human being who lived our life and died in our place, he came in need of the Spirit of God to empower his life, ministry, obedience, miracles, and all that he did in obedience to the Father.

Jesus lived as a fully human being, in reliance on the Holy Spirit; yet Jesus, the second person of the Trinity, submitted himself fully to the Spirit, whom he later said would "glorify me." As a man, Jesus submitted to the Spirit. In rank within the Trinity, Jesus had authority over the Spirit, yet for the sake of the mission he humbled himself. In taking on our human flesh, he submitted to the very one over whom he has rightful authority.

This explains some aspects of Jesus' life that otherwise are inexplicable. It explains, for example, how it is, as we read in Luke 2:40,52, that

Jesus grew in wisdom. How can this be? He certainly cannot grow in wisdom in his divine nature, so what must this mean? Perhaps we can think of it this way: in the consciousness of the God-man, the person Jesus Christ of Nazareth, he accepted the limitations of what it is to be a human in order to grow in understanding, to grow in wisdom, as the Spirit in him would help him see things more clearly, understand God's Word with greater clarity and greater forcefulness as he grew older. Like other babies he did not know everything at birth but had to grow in his understanding and in wisdom as he aged and matured. We should not think of Jesus lying in the manger in Bethlehem looking up at the stars of the heavens and contemplating the physics of the universe he had created! Rather, that baby in a manger, though he uniquely was the God-man, had accepted the confines of human limitations in order to live as one of us.

In accepting these human limitations, Jesus did not discard or give up any attributes of deity, however. Absolutely not! To think so is to deny the fully deity of Christ and to entertain a view judged by the church as a heresy. Rather, while Jesus was fully God, and as such retained all the infinite and eternal attributes possessed by his divine nature, he accepted the limitation or restriction of the expression of certain of his divine attributes in order to live fully as a man. After all, Jesus could not have experienced life as we know it, or lived life as authentically human if, for example, he was omniscient in his own consciousness as the person, Jesus Christ of Nazareth. While Jesus as God continued to possess the attribute of omniscience, he accepted the limitation of not having access to this infinite knowledge so that he could live as we live and grow in wisdom and understanding, through the hard work of learning, by the power of the Spirit. This explains, then, what Jesus says concerning the hour of the second coming, which "no one knows, neither the angels in heaven, nor the Son, but only the Father" (Mark 13:32). Arius, of course, thought that this text supported his contention, against Nicaea, that Jesus was not God. The problem with Arius' view, simply put, is that so much evidence stands against him on this issue. Scripture is replete with teaching supporting the full deity of the Son, and thankfully the bishops at Nicaea (AD 325) were decisive in their judgment against Arianism. Yet this text does say that the Son does not know something that the Father knows.

How are we to understand this statement by Christ, since we accept that he was in nature fully God?

It seems that the answer must be that Jesus Christ, as a man, accepted the limitations of his human existence, including the limited knowledge that goes with living as a finite human being. In his divine nature, he retained omniscience, but in the consciousness of Jesus, the God-man, he accepted a restricted knowledge so he would have to trust his Father. He had to live by faith. He had to grow. He had to study. He had to, as Hebrews puts it, be "made perfect [i.e., mature]" (Heb 5:9). He grew in these ways through the things he suffered and through the things that he learned. Hebrews also teaches that "he learned obedience through what he suffered" (Heb 5:8). That is, Jesus learned little by little throughout life to obey increasingly difficult demands of his Father until he would become ready for the ultimate demand of going to the cross, which even at that point was obviously excruciatingly difficult. How else do we explain Jesus in the garden sweating, as it were, drops of blood, three times crying out to the Father, "Father, if you be willing, let this cup pass from me?" To fail to see how enormously difficult this act of obedience was for Jesus is to miss the obvious! How excruciatingly painful was this obedience! How did he arrive at the place where, at this time, he was able to obey, even though his obedience was so very hard? He was prepared to accept this, the greatest of all challenges, because of tests of faith along the way. He learned obedience not by being disobedient and moving from disobedience to obedience, but rather by being obedient in yet more difficult tasks, demands, and challenges until the ultimate test had come. As a man, Jesus submitted to the Spirit, grew in wisdom, learned to obey the Father in increasingly difficult ways; and in all he did and said, he lived his life in the power of the Spirit.

How was Jesus, in the end, able to accept the will of the Father "for the joy that was set before him," and endure "the cross, disregarding its shame," and sit down at the right hand of the throne of his Father (Heb 12:2)? The writer of Hebrews had already answered this earlier. Hebrews 9:14 says, "How much more will the blood of Christ, who through the eternal Spirit offered himself without blemish to God, purify our conscience from dead works to worship the living God!" Yes, Jesus lived his life and performed his miracles and fulfilled the will of his Father, all through the empowerment of the Spirit. Hawthorne is correct when he writes, "It was as the Bearer of the Spirit that he consciously stood as the champion of God in the battle with Satan."[20]

Of course, the application of the work of Christ to sinners' lives, causing them to be born again and be remade in the image of Christ is also the work of the Spirit. For example, consider that regeneration to newness of life takes place by the Spirit. Recall Jesus' conversation with Nicodemus:

> Jesus answered him, "Very truly, I tell you, no one can see the kingdom of God without being born [again]." Nicodemus said to him, "How can anyone be born after having grown old? Can one enter a second time into the mother's womb and be born?" Jesus answered, "Very truly, I tell you, no one can enter the kingdom of God without being born of water and Spirit. What is born of the flesh is flesh, and what is born of the Spirit is spirit. Do not be astonished that I said to you, 'You must be born [again].' The wind blows where it chooses, and you hear the sound of it, but you do not know where it comes from or where it goes. So it is with everyone who is born of the Spirit." (John 3:3–8)[21]

Regeneration, or being born again, can only happen as the Spirit of God works in one's heart so as to bring about new life. This is the Spirit's work to awaken a dead heart (Ezek 36:26–27; Eph 2:1) and to open blind eyes (Acts 26:18; 2 Cor 4:4) so that a person now sees the glory of Christ (2 Cor 4:6) and responds positively to God, loving what he formerly hated and turning now to the light that he had previously despised (John 3:20–21). Because the condition we all are in apart from this work of the Spirit is one of rebellion to God, we must be made new in order to turn to God in trust and hope. Paul makes clear just how

---

[20] Hawthorne, *Presence and the Power*, 172.

[21] I am quoting the NRSV here as throughout the present book, but have opted for "born again" where NRSV gives "born from above." The Greek term here could mean either, but the context ("can one enter a second time into the mother's womb?") seems to give preference to the translation "born again" (as in KJV, NASB, ESV, HCSB, and others).

firmly set we are against God in our sin. He writes, "To set the mind on the flesh is death, but to set the mind on the Spirit is life and peace. For this reason the mind that is set on the flesh is hostile to God; it does not submit to God's law—indeed it cannot, and those who are in the flesh cannot please God" (Rom 8:6–8). As a result of our sinful rebellion and hostility to the true and living God, we cannot put faith in Christ Jesus, and we cannot love God.

Paul points out the same inability to trust Christ elsewhere, but he uses a different analogy to express the same basic insight. To the Corinthians he writes, "The god of this world has blinded the minds of the unbelievers, to keep them from seeing the light of the gospel of the glory of Christ, who is the image of God" (2 Cor 4:4). Unbelievers, then, cannot see the glory of Christ, much less believe in him. To do so requires the work of the Spirit in their hearts to open blind eyes and awaken dead hearts so as to believe in Christ (2 Cor 4:6). This is why the New Testament authors are so jealous that God receive all the glory in our salvation. In our sin we simply cannot take credit for coming to Christ since we were hostile to God (Rom 8:6–8), we were blind and unable to see the glory of Christ (2 Cor 4:4), and we were dead in our trespasses and sins (Eph 2:1). No wonder Paul exclaims, "For by grace you have been saved through faith, and this is not your own doing; it is the gift of God—not the result of works, so that no one may boast" (Eph 2:8–9). Our regeneration and conversion, moving us to repent of sin and trust in Christ, are the work of the Spirit. The Spirit must awaken our hearts to see the beauty of Christ, fall before him, and put our hope and trust in him. God gets all the glory in our conversion. And how is Jesus glorified in this? The Spirit awakens our dead hearts and opens our blind eyes to see Jesus! Amazingly, when the Spirit works in our hearts to bring us salvation, his central purpose is to show us the beauty and glory of Jesus, not himself. Although the Spirit plays this crucial role in our salvation, his goal is to open our eyes to behold the wonder and glory of Christ.

Conclusion

The very identity of Christ as the one and only Savior and the full efficacy of the atoning work of Christ, then, are inexplicable apart from his relationship with both the Father and the Spirit. The Father is the Father of the Son, and as such he commissions and sends his Son into the world to be and do what he calls him to. The design of salvation is the Father's, and the justice brought to bear against our sin was executed by the Father. The Son, however, could not accomplish the obedience and perform the works that he did apart from the anointing of the Spirit who abides with him as the necessary presence and power of his messianic identity and ability. *Cur Deus Trinus?* Must God be triune for Christ to be a Savior? Indeed, the Trinity is necessary for the identity of Christ as the atoning Savior, and the Trinity is necessary also to the efficacy of his atoning death. The God of salvation, then, can be none other than the triune God of the Bible.[22]

For Further Reading

Hawthorne, Gerald F. *The Presence and the Power: The Significance of the Holy Spirit in the Life and Ministry of Jesus.* Dallas: Word, 1991. This classic treatment of the Holy Spirit in the life and ministry of Jesus is almost one-of-a-kind, both in the specific theme it covers and in its overall argumentation and development. It is one of the most insightful treatments one could consider on how Jesus lived the life he did and accomplished the work the Father sent him to do.

Hamilton, James M. *God's Indwelling Presence: The Holy Spirit in the Old and New Testaments.* NACSBT 1. Nashville, TN: B&H, 2006. Hamilton develops the work of the Spirit throughout the Bible, and his treatment of the Spirit in the life and ministry of Jesus parallels to a significant degree the argument and position of Hawthorne.

Stott, John R. W. *The Cross of Christ.* Downers Grove: InterVarsity, 1986. This volume continues to be, in this author's judgment, the finest treatment of Christ's atoning sacrifice available. Stott's discussion of the Son's fulfillment of the Father's purpose and plan is central to his thesis, though more emphasis might have been placed on the role of the Spirit in accomplishing the atonement.

---

[22] Portions of this chapter have appeared previously in the author's *Father, Son, and Holy Spirit: Relationships, Roles, and Relevance* (Wheaton, IL: Crossway, 2005).

Ware, Bruce A. *Father, Son, and Holy Spirit: Relationships, Roles, and Relevance.* Wheaton, IL: Crossway, 2005. Much of the specific development of relationships among the Trinity expressed in this chapter is given fuller treatment in this short volume.

Study Questions

1. What biblical evidence is offered to support these claims:
    a. The identity of Jesus the Son is specifically related to God the Father.
    b. The Son has an eternal relation of submission to the Father.
2. How does the author argue that the Son required the indwelling and empowering Spirit for him to be who he is and to accomplish his work?
3. What is the proof that our salvation—and specifically the efficacy of Jesus' atoning death—is tied both historically and of necessity to the work of the Father and the Spirit, along with and through the Son?

6

JESUS' EXAMPLE
Prototype of the Dependent, Spirit-Filled Life

Klaus Issler

Chapter Summary

Our Lord Jesus Christ, in his common life with us, gave believers of all time a *genuine model* for how to live the Christian life beyond the limitations of an average human life. I argue specifically that Jesus Christ's supernaturally oriented life on this earth resulted from his predominant dependence on the divine resources of the Father and of the Holy Spirit, while employing his own divine powers infrequently, if at all. Without an appreciation of the dependence Jesus exercised in the Father and in the Holy Spirit, it is not possible to understand how Jesus can be our genuine example—this is a critical missing ingredient for a robust *imitatio Christi*.

Axioms for Christological Study

1. Jesus is an example for all Christians.
2. What is unexemplified in Jesus' life cannot be an example for Christians.
3. Much of Jesus' mission on Earth was unique to him as the Messiah-King, yet what Christians can share in common with Jesus is the *manner* in which he lived and in which he carried out his mission.

Klaus Issler

KEY TERMS

imitation	example	emptied himself
veiling or concealment	occasionally dependent	predominantly dependent
exclusively dependent		

Latin terms	*imitatio Christi*	*conformitas*

Greek terms	*kenosis*	*mimeomai*
	akoloutheo	*pistis Christou*
	archegos	

. . . how God anointed Jesus of Nazareth with the Holy Spirit and with power; how he went about doing good and healing all who were oppressed by the devil, for God was with him.

—Acts 10:38

The Son is the prototype of those "who are led by the Spirit of God" (Rom 8:14) . . . It is the Spirit that gives Jesus his human equipoise, for considering the gigantic dimensions of what he says and does, such equipoise would be impossible apart from the Spirit.

—Hans Urs von Balthasar

We esteem Olympic athletes who reach their goal after struggling against severe obstacles. Is Jesus such a hero to Christians? Did Jesus genuinely struggle against the challenges of life just like us? Or, while he lived on Earth and engaged in ministry to others, did Jesus have access to something extra that is unique to him and unavailable to believers?

In this chapter, I examine the biblical teaching of Jesus' authentic human experience in relation to the scriptural theme that Jesus is our example for living the Christian life. I argue specifically that Jesus Christ's supernaturally oriented life on this earth resulted from his predominant dependence on the divine resources of the Father and the Holy Spirit, while living fully in his humanity, employing his own divine powers

---

[1] The epigraph from this chapter is drawn from Hans Urs von Balthasar, *Prayer* (San Francisco: Ignatius, 1979), 163.

190

infrequently, if at all. This claim is not a novel one. Thomas Oden, a theologian who specializes in advocating the consensus views of the Christian theological tradition, argues that "as a man, Jesus walked day by day in radical dependence upon God the Spirit, prayed, and spoke by the power of the Spirit. In portraying Jesus as constantly dependent upon the Spirit, the Gospels were not challenging or questioning his deity or divine Sonship. Rather, as eternal Son the theandric person already was truly God, while as a man, Jesus was truly human, bone of our bone, flesh of our flesh, seed of Abraham, whose humanity was continually replenished by the Spirit (Luke 4:14; Heb 2:14–17)."[2]

R. A. Torrey (1856–1928), likewise attempting to articulate only *What the Bible Teaches*, taught that Jesus "lived, thought, worked, taught, conquered sin and won victories for God in the power of that same Spirit whom we all may have."[3] In this chapter I articulate a more nuanced statement of this claim, bringing together the various lines of scriptural evidence.

First, this chapter will introduce the *imitatio Christi* theme and present the dependency thesis. Support for the proposal comes from two lines of evidence: (1) that Jesus depended on the Father (e.g., John 14:10–11) as a human who himself expressed faith in God (e.g., Heb 12:2), and (2) that Jesus depended on the Holy Spirit (e.g., Acts 10:38). Later, we will address some potential problems. Finally, after discussing Jesus' childhood, we will explore a few implications for his childhood, using the proposal as a working hypothesis.

If a convergence of this evidence supports a pervasive theme of dependency in Jesus' life and ministry, then we may infer that Jesus depended to a greater degree on the Father and the Spirit and much less upon his own divine power. The degree to which Jesus depended on the Father and the Spirit, instead of his own divine power, is the degree to which Jesus can be our genuine example.

The thrust of the project is to draw out implications of an orthodox Christology for practical Christian living. Our purpose is not to diminish

---

[2] Thomas Oden, *Systematic Theology*, vol. 3, *Life in the Spirit* (1992; repr., Peabody, MA: Prince, 1998), 47; for a more extensive comment see Michael Wilkins, *Matthew*, NIVAC (Grand Rapids: Zondervan, 2004), 162–65.

[3] R. A. Torrey, *What the Bible Teaches* (Old Tappan, NJ: Fleming Revell, 1898), 289.

the doctrine of Christ's deity but rather to enrich our doctrine of sanctification and Christian living. By refining our understanding of Jesus Christ we can benefit from the Bible's teaching that Jesus is our genuine example. Yet as we delve into this mystery—to honor our Lord's full humanity—we must do so cautiously so as not to diminish his full deity.[4]

At a general level it is difficult to deny Jesus' humanity at the obvious points: he was embodied[5] (e.g., he was thirsty, Matt 25:35; hungry, Matt 4:2; weary, John 4:6; and he died, John 19:30–34). He experienced a full range of emotions (e.g., weeping, Luke 19:41; compassion, Mark 6:34; righteous anger, Mark 3:5; frustration, Matt 17:17; and being troubled in spirit, Matt 26:37). Many who encountered him, especially the religious leaders, regarded Jesus as nothing more than human, not as some kind of alien or superhero from outer space. To paraphrase the Nazareth folk with whom he grew up, "It's just Jesus, no one special" (Mark 6:3). Furthermore, Jesus was tempted (Matt 4:1–11)—a characteristic which Scripture denies of God (Jas 1:13)—yet without sinning (Heb 4:15).

Orthodoxy affirms that Jesus' humanity was a critical factor for our salvation. Erickson notes: "If . . . Jesus was not really one of us, humanity has not been united with deity, and we cannot be saved. For the validity of the work accomplished in Christ's death, or at least its applicability to us as human beings, depends upon the reality of his humanity, just as the efficacy of it depends upon the genuineness of his deity."[6] Regarding God's design of human nature, Bernard Ramm notes, "In the very act of the creation the possibility of a future incarnation was made possible. If humankind is produced in the image of God then there is some of that image in God. Hence God can become incarnate."[7]

Furthermore, Paul's comparison between Adam and Christ bears testimony to the humanity of Jesus (Rom 5:12–21; 1 Cor 15:20–22 and

---

[4] The study works with the canonical New Testament texts and within the basic boundary conditions for orthodox theological inquiry as set down by the Chalcedonian Definition (AD 451).

[5] I use the past tense, although Jesus still lives today with both divine and human natures.

[6] Millard Erickson, *Christian Theology* (Grand Rapids: Baker, 1985), 706.

[7] Bernard Ramm, *An Evangelical Christology* (Nashville: Thomas Nelson, 1985), 53. Furthermore, Ramm explains, "In the humanity of Jesus Christ God has revealed what it is to be a true person. Hence a Christian anthropology can be constructed only from a Christology," 77.

45–49).[8] Through his experiences and suffering as a human, Jesus became our sympathetic high priest (Heb 2:10–17; 4:15–16; 5:8–10), one who now intercedes for us (Rom 8:34). Thus, Jesus is like us.

In becoming incarnate, our Lord Jesus Christ as one person is both fully divine and fully human. Although this study emphasizes what is commonly shared between Jesus Christ and all believers, there is no denial that Jesus is also unique and different from us; he is not *merely* human. For purposes of analysis in studying Jesus, three layers of focus are possible: studying Jesus as divine, as divine-human, and as human (see Table 6.1). The first two layers of analysis focus on aspects unique to Jesus. The final layer focuses exclusively on Jesus' humanity, what he shares in common with us, the primary emphasis of this chapter.

Table 6.1 Three Levels of Analysis in Christology

	Level of Analysis	Descriptive Biblical Terms
Unique	1. Jesus as Divine	The Son (Matt 11:27; 28:19) The Word (John 1:1) (Second Person of the Trinity)
	2. Jesus as Divine-Human	The Word became flesh (John 1:14) Messiah/Christ (John 4:25–26) King (John 18:33–37; Rev 17:14) Prophet (Acts 3:22; Luke 13:33; Deut 18:15) Savior (Mark 10:45; Rom 3:21–26) High Priest (Heb 7:17) Mediator (1 Tim 2:5; Heb 8:6)
Common	3. Jesus as Human	Last Adam (Rom 5:14; 1 Cor 15:45) Our Brother (Heb 2:11) Our Example (1 Pet 2:21)

As the unique "mediator between God and humankind" (1 Tim 2:5), Jesus can "show us the Father" (John 14:8–10) and also show us how to

---

[8] Did Jesus fulfill a moral obligation by defeating Satan in his humanity as the Second Adam, since the First Adam surrendered his rightful role (e.g., Heb 2:14–15)?

live as humans by setting us "an example, that you also should do as I have done to you" (John 13:15). In his atoning work for us Jesus became our Savior, the unique mediator between God and humankind (1 Tim 2:5). Luke Johnson notes, "Jesus is not the mediator on the basis of his teachings or deeds, or even as an object of belief, but on the basis of his very humanity: Jesus is the representative human before the one God."[9]

The Imitation of Jesus Christ (*imitatio Christi*)

The example of Jesus Christ has been an important and continuing theme throughout Church history, as evident in the popularity of two classic devotional books: *The Imitation of Christ* by Thomas à Kempis (1380–1471) and *In His Steps* by Charles Sheldon (1857–1946).[10] This theme is currently evident in the abbreviation WWJD: "What would Jesus do?" Standard orthodox systematic texts frequently employ the term "Christlikeness" or "likeness to Christ" for the expectation that believers acquire the virtues displayed by Jesus.[11] In Christian ethics Jesus is presented as the ethical standard. For example, Richard Hays notes, "If God really did raise Jesus from the dead, everything that Jesus taught and exemplified is vindicated by a God more powerful than death. He must therefore be seen as the bearer of the truth and the definitive paradigm for obedience to God . . . For the church, it is perhaps important to know that the obedience of faith was lived out in history by the flesh-and-blood man Jesus, for his example teaches us that to trust in the power of God over history is not to trust in vain."[12]

---

[9] Luke T. Johnson, *Letters to Paul's Delegates* (Harrisburg, PA: Trinity, 1996), 131, emphasis added.

[10] Thomas à Kempis, *The Imitation of Christ*, trans. Leo Sherley-Price (London: Penguin, 1952). Charles Sheldon, *In His Steps* (1897; repr. Grand Rapids: Revell/Chosen, 1984).

[11] See, for example, Millard Erickson, *Christian Theology* (Grand Rapids: Baker, 1985), 970, and Wayne Grudem, *Systematic Theology* (Grand Rapids: Zondervan, 1994), 542.

[12] Richard Hays. *The Moral Vision of the New Testament* (San Francisco: HarperSan Francisco, 1996), 166–67. Linda Zagzebski has proposed a virtue ethics model in which the incarnation is a central feature: "The Incarnation and Virtue Ethics," in *The Incarnation*, ed. Stephen T. Davis, Daniel Kendall, and Gerald O'Collins (Oxford: Oxford University Press, 2002), 313–31. One distinctive feature of Christianity in contrast to all other religions or ideologies is that in Jesus Christ we actually have a perfect ethical human exemplar, a claim no other religion or ideology can make.

Within spiritual formation, Dallas Willard claims that Jesus Christ demonstrates how believers can live the Christian life. "Jesus came among us to show and teach the life for which we were made . . . Indeed, by taking the title Son of man, he staked his claim to be all that the human being was originally supposed to be—and surely much more. Colloquially we might describe him as humanity's 'fair-haired boy,' the one who expresses its deepest nature and on whom its hopes rest."[13]

Biblical Basis for Imitating Jesus

The biblical evidence that believers should imitate the example of Jesus is culled from various approaches.[14] First, the main New Testament passages explicitly teaching the imitation of Jesus Christ are these:

1. from Jesus' own lips in John 13:15,[15]
2. from Paul in Philippians 2:4–11 (see further comments below),
3. from Peter in 1 Peter 2:21–23, and
4. from the author of Hebrews 12:1–6.

Second, various commands to believers identify Jesus' life and specific character traits as the standard to follow, using the connectives "just as/as" (e.g., *hōsper, kathōs*) or "also/too" (Matt 20:28;[16] John 13:14,15,34; 15:12; Rom 6:11; 15:3,7; 2 Cor 1:5; Eph 5:2,25,29; Heb 4:15; 1 Pet 4:1; 1 John 2:6; 3:3,16; see also Eph 4:32; Col 3:13; 1 Tim 1:16). Additionally, a few passages indicate a mutuality of shared experience—suffering is mentioned most often—between Jesus Christ and

---

[13] Dallas Willard, *The Divine Conspiracy* (San Francisco: HarperSan Francisco, 1998), 27.

[14] Some of the major studies of this theme in English include E. J. Tinsley, *The Imitation of God in Christ* (London: SCM, 1960) and Tinsley, "Some Principles for Reconstructing a Doctrine of the Imitation of Christ," *SJT* 1 (1972): 45–57; Kevin Giles, "'*Imitatio Christi*' in the New Testament," *RTR* 38 (1979): 65–73; Gerald F. Hawthorne, "The Imitation of Christ: Discipleship in Philippians," in Richard Longenecker, ed., *Patterns of Discipleship in the New Testament* (Grand Rapids: Eerdmans, 1966), 63–79; and Marguerite Shuster, "The Use and Misuse of the Idea of the Imitation of Christ," *Ex Auditu* 14 (1998): 70–81.

[15] Matthew 11:29 (*manthanō*, "learn from Me") could fit here.

[16] In discussing the parallel verse in Mark 10:45, R. T. France states, "But we must not forget that this crucial verse, however great its soteriological implications, occurs in the context as a model for Jesus' disciples to follow. . . . They, too, must serve rather than be served" (*The Gospel of Mark*, NIGTC [Grand Rapids: Eerdmans, 2002], 421).

believers (John 17:14,16; 20:21; Rom 8:17,29; 2 Cor 8:9; 10:1; Phil 3:10–11; Col 1:24; 1 John 1:7; 3:3).

Third, Paul urged believers to imitate his own example (1 Cor 4:16; 11:1; Phil 3:17; 1 Thess 1:6; 2 Thess 3:7–9; and 1 Tim 1:16) just as he imitated the example of Jesus (1 Cor 11:1; cp. 1 Thess 1:6). Peter exhorted elders to serve as examples (1 Pet 5:3), alluding implicitly to Jesus' teaching that he was an example of servanthood (e.g., Matt 20:25–28; Luke 22:27; John 13:15).

Concerns about Imitating Jesus

Some scholars are not convinced that the New Testament writers actually present Jesus' life on Earth as an example for believers and argue that instead of imitation the New Testament always stresses allegiance and obedience to the *risen* Lord. For example, Wilhelm Michaelis claimed of the verb "to imitate": "There is thus no thought of an imitation, whether outward or inward, of the earthly life of Jesus in either individual features or total impress. The call for an *imitatio Christi* finds no support in the statements of Paul."[17] Others claim that Jesus' command to follow him (e.g., John 8:12; 10:27) cannot be a call to imitation, but rather a call to be a loyal disciple of the Lord Jesus. An alleged distinction must be made between the word "to follow" (*akoloutheo*), which occurs only in the Gospels and Acts, and "to imitate" (*mimeomai*), occurring only in the Epistles. Yet Kevin Giles notes, "The contrast between the Gospels and the Epistles in relation to imitating Christ is therefore, in essence, not one of emphasis or theme but only one of terminology."[18]

Some reluctance regarding the imitation of Christ among Protestants may stem from Martin Luther's own suspicion of the concept, particularly that it may imply works and moral endeavor rather than God's grace. Rather than *imitatio,* Luther preferred to speak of *conformitas* to Christ,

---

[17] Wilhelm Michaelis, "*mimeomai*," *TDNT*, 4:672. In a footnote, Michaelis quotes Martin Dibelius, "The qualities to be imitated are not the virtues of a human person but the properties of the divine person."

[18] Kevin Giles, "*Imitatio Christi*," 69. Based on his reading of the two standard German monographs on the subject, Giles explains that "H. D. Betz [*Nachfolge und Nachahmung Jesu Christi im Neuen Testament*, Tübingen: Mohr Siebeck, 1967] and A. Schulz [*Nachfolgen und Nachahmen*. Munich: Koesel-Verlag, 1962] carefully study these two motifs and after having analyzed each independently come to the conclusion that in substance the meaning of both is the same" (69, note 22).

a process of conformation to Christ through the work of the Spirit. Yet, Tinsley notes, imitation must remain as a legitimate theological concept: "In a fully developed theology of the Christian life as imitation of Christ both the terms *conformitas* and *imitatio* would need to be used. The imitative life of the Christian involves both God's activity, through the Spirit, in conforming man to his image in Christ (*conformitas*), and man's focusing of his moral and spiritual attention on the exemplary, Christ (*imitatio*)."[19]

Marguerite Shuster raises legitimate concerns about studying Jesus as our example: "My fundamental point is that what we need, and what the New Testament offers us, is first and foremost, not an example, but a Savior. My major caveat with respect to imitation themes is that they tend to obscure that fundamental point."[20] Any exclusive focus on the example of Jesus effectively truncates the genuine gospel. Sanctification must never be reduced to our own moral effort. It is a process in which God the Spirit works, and in which we cooperate, attending to what is in our power to do, sustained by God's power (e.g., Eph 4:17–24; Phil 2:12–13). Yet once Jesus is affirmed as our Savior and our high priest, can Jesus also serve as our example to imitate?

We must approach this exemplar teaching with humility, even though it seems audacious that we can follow Jesus' example. As Shuster notes, "Even the thought that we could actually do as Jesus would do is a rather heady idea . . . we shall surely fail utterly at our best efforts to follow in Jesus' footsteps except insofar as the Spirit enables us."[21] Despite various concerns, Shuster affirms that the New Testament presents Jesus as our example. "It would seem evident that, even if some qualifications may sometimes be required, the thought of Jesus as model is not lacking in the New Testament, and insofar as it is present, surely it commends

---

[19] E. J. Tinsley, "Some Principles," 45. For further study of Luther's understanding of *imitatio* and *conformitas*, see Dietmar Lage, *Martin Luther's Christology and Ethics* (New York: Edwin Mellen, 1990).

[20] Shuster, "Use and Misuse," 74. Yet focusing on Jesus as a moral exemplar need not lead us doctrinally astray to affirm a moral influence atonement theory. For a survey of moral example atonement theories, see Alister McGrath, *Christian Theology* (Oxford: Blackwell, 1997), 407–12.

[21] Shuster, "Use and Misuse," 76–77.

itself to us . . . the exemplary strain does exist and should not just be ignored."[22]

Special Case of Philippians 2

One final qualification is based on the interpretation of the classic passage of Philippians 2:5–11, centered on the exhortation, "Let the same mind be in you that was in Christ Jesus." Is this a text about imitating Christ? In his often-cited study, Ralph Martin claims that the focus of Paul's exhortation appears in the last three verses emphasizing the exaltation of Christ. Thus Jesus' earthly life is *not* the central feature of this passage: "The Apostolic summons is not: Follow Jesus by doing as He did—an impossible feat in any case, for who can be a 'second Christ' who quits His heavenly glory and dies in shame and is taken up into the throne of the universe? The appeal and injunction to the Philippians in their pride and selfishness are rather: Become in your conduct and church relationships the type of persons who, by that kenosis, death and exaltation of the Lord of glory, have a place in His body, the Church."[23] Martin seems to confuse the tasks of Jesus' vocation, which are unique, with the manner in which he lived to carry out his vocation. We do not emulate his mission, and callings will vary among us, but we can emulate Jesus' manner of living.

Yet other New Testament scholars affirm the traditional view that Paul uses the example of the earthly Jesus as an encouragement to follow in his footsteps.[24] Moreover, Joseph Hellerman has argued that Paul intentionally turns upside down the normal Roman honor motif in Philippi, which highlighted an upward movement toward success.

> I maintain that Paul, in his portrayal of Jesus in [Philippians 2] verses 6–8, has taken Rome's *cursus*

---

[22] Ibid., 73, 77. Two other helpful points raised by Shuster regard (1) the misuse of the concept of imitation, particularly the selectivity of what is considered for imitation and what is ignored, and (2) that we exclude from consideration the distinctive cultural forms of that day that Jesus practiced (p. 74).

[23] Ralph Martin, *A Hymn of Christ: Philippians 2:5–11 in Recent Interpretation and in the Setting of Early Christian Worship* (Downers Grove, IL: InterVarsity, 1997), 290–91.

[24] See Morna Hooker, "Philippians 2:6–11," in *Jesus und Paulus (Festschrift for W. G. Kummel),* ed. E. E. Ellis and E. Grasser (Tübingen: Mohr-Siebeck, 1975), 151–64; and Gerald Hawthorne, "The Imitation of Christ," 63–79.

ideology and turned it on its head, so to speak, as he presents Christ descending a *cursus pudorum* ("a succession or race of ignominies") from equality with God, to the status of a slave, to the physical and social death of public crucifixion . . . The presentation, I suggest, was intended by Paul . . . to encourage persons in the church who possessed some degree of honor or status in the broader social world of the colony to utilize their status, after the analogy of Jesus, in the service of others.[25]

Thus, Philippians 2:5–11 offers a strong case for Jesus as our example. Jesus' human life accomplished much more than being our example, yet his example for believers cannot be ignored.

Jesus' Divine Dependency

Having affirmed the biblical support for Jesus as our example, let us explore how that is possible since Jesus has two natures. In this section I present the problem, identify some options, and then defend my proposal that Jesus predominantly lived a dependent, Spirit-filled life on this earth as our example.

The Problem and Possible Options

In studying Jesus' state of humiliation on this earth (i.e., his unglorified human nature), we must account for the *apparent* incompatibility between his human nature (e.g., human "weaknesses" of temptability, weariness, death), and his divine nature (especially the three "omni" attributes).[26] For example, Leon Morris notes that in his humanity Jesus was to some extent ignorant. "Ignorance is an inevitable accompaniment of the only human life that we know . . . Sometimes one meets people who overlook this aspect of Jesus' life. They picture him going on a serene way, knowing the thoughts of everyone about him, knowing the

---

[25] Joseph H. Hellerman, *Reconstructing Honor in Roman Philippi: Carmen Christi as Cursus Pudorum*, SNTSMS 132 (Cambridge: Cambridge University Press, 2005), 1–2.
[26] E.g., Scripture gives evidence of Jesus' ignorance (e.g., Matt 24:36 = Mark 13:32), yet God is omniscient; Jesus is physically weary (John 19:17, carried cross for a while; then Simon had to carry it for Jesus, Mark 15:21), yet God is omnipotent; Jesus was subject to temptation (Heb 2:18; 4:15) yet God cannot be tempted; and he died, yet God cannot die.

outcome of every course of action in which he or they were engaging. If this was the manner of it, then the life Jesus lived was not a human life, even human life at its highest level."[27]

How, then, was it possible for Jesus to express human powers in light of his divine powers, since the use of certain divine attributes would seem to override the use of corresponding human attributes? The orthodox explanation is that, during Jesus' state of humiliation, the incarnation involved not only the *addition* of human nature but also some form of *veiling or concealment* of his divine glory (e.g., John 17:5). John Calvin notes that Jesus "took the image of a servant, and content with such lowness, allowed his divinity to be hidden by a 'veil of flesh.'"[28]

The concept of veiling is developed in several key passages (e.g., John 17:5; 2 Cor 8:9; Eph 4:10; Phil 2:7; Heb 5:7–9). According to Ben Witherington, the verb "emptied himself" [*ekenōsen*[29]] in Philippians 2:7 "must have some content to it, and it is not adequate to say Christ did not subtract anything since in fact he added a human nature. The latter is true enough, but the text says that he did empty himself or strip himself. What it does not tell us explicitly is of what he emptied himself. The contrast between verses 6b and 7a is very suggestive; that is, Christ set aside his rightful divine prerogatives or status. This does not mean he set aside his divine nature, but it does indicate some sort of self-limitation, some sort

---

[27] Leon Morris, *The Lord from Heaven* (London: InterVarsity, 1958), 46–47. Note that in Mark 11:13 Jesus saw the fig tree in leaf, walked up to the fig tree, and then was surprised to learn no figs were available.

[28] John Calvin, *Institutes of the Christian Religion*, ed. John T. McNeil, trans. Ford Lewis Battles, LCC (Philadelphia: Westminster, 1960), 1:476 (*Institutes* 2.13.2).

[29] The term *kenōsis* has often been associated with theological proposals describing the hypostatic union during the time of Jesus' state of humiliation. Unfortunately, the biblical term itself became associated with radical proposals in which Jesus divested himself of some or all of his divine attributes. Grudem admits that the word can be used in a weaker sense not referring to the radical kenotic theories but meaning "simply that Jesus gave up his glory and privilege for a time while he was on earth. (This is essentially the view we have advocated in this text)" (*Systematic Theology* [Grand Rapids: Zondervan, 1994], 551, n. 28). Yet Grudem prefers to avoid the term due to potential confusion. William Lane Craig, "The Incarnation" (chap. 30 in *Philosophical Foundations for a Christian*, ed. J. P. Moreland and William Lane Craig [Downers Grove, IL: InterVarsity, 2003]) is in basic agreement with Grudem, yet Millard Erickson is willing to use the term: the "view we have been introducing is a species of kenotic theology" (551) or, specifically a "kenosis by addition" (*The Word Became Flesh* [Grand Rapids: Baker, 1991], 555).

For a summary of major criticisms of kenotic theories see Donald Macleod, *The Person of Christ* (Downers Grove, IL: InterVarsity, 1998), 209–12.

of setting aside of divine rights or privileges."[30] Although Jesus was God, he veiled his deity, permitting himself to experience a normal human life with its attendant weaknesses (Heb 2:17).

Some prefer to leave the mystery of the incarnation as is, not explaining but simply reasserting the two natures. For example, some rely on a reduplicative strategy as the sole means of explaining the apparent incompatibility of the two natures.[31] They argue, for example, that Jesus *as God* is omniscient, but that Jesus *as man* is not; that Jesus *as God* is upholding the universe with his omnipotence, but Jesus *as man* can get weary.[32] Yet others think it worthwhile to explain the matter further, although at some point we must all bow to this divine mystery.

What is at issue is the overpowering nature of the three "omni" attributes—omnipotence, omnipresence, and omniscience—in relation to the corresponding and finite human attributes. To clarify differences among incarnational views, A. H. Strong outlined five general categories (with his own view, identified as the True View, "midway between two pairs of erroneous views"):

(1) Gess: The Logos gave up all divine attributes;

(2) Thomasius: The Logos gave up relative attributes only;

(3) True View: The Logos gave up the independent exercise of divine attributes;

(4) Old Orthodoxy: Christ gave up the use of divine attributes;

(5) Anselm: Christ acted as if he did not possess divine attributes.[33]

Contemporary orthodox views would fit within the third and fourth categories, yet these particular groupings are too broad.

---

[30] Ben Witherington, *Friendship and Finances in Philippi* (Valley Forge, PA: Trinity Press International, 1994), 66.

[31] See p. 166. Among New Testament scholars, I. Howard Marshall notes the apparent inconsistency and leaves it there: "There might seem to be some tension between the concept of Jesus as a person who needs the Spirit to accomplish his mission (like a human agent of God) and as the Son of God who has all the insight and power that he needs for his task." *New Testament Theology* (Downers Grove, IL: InterVarsity, 2004), 199.

[32] Thomas Morris notes, "Some traditional theologians may have been guilty of this sort of strategy, relying too heavily on a mere distinction between the two natures and on a reduplicative form of statement about Christ—Christ *as God* had this property, *as man* its complement—in the attempt to avoid contradiction." *The Logic of God Incarnate* (1986; repr., Eugene, OR: Wipf & Stock, 2001), 38. But ultimately for Morris this strategy is not convincing (cf. 48–55).

[33] Augustus H. Strong, *Systematic Theology* (Philadelphia: Judson, 1907), 704.

Perhaps a focus on one divine attribute, *omnipotence*, offers a way to explore further both the apparent incompatibility of Jesus' divine and human attributes and the role of the Father and of the Holy Spirit in Jesus' life and ministry. By what supernatural or divine power did Jesus live his life on Earth? Jesus had access to two possible sources of divine power: either (1) his own divine power, or (2) the divine resources of the Father and the Holy Spirit. Three logical positions are possible along this spectrum:

(1) *Occasionally Dependent.* At times, Jesus used his own divine power, while at other times he relied on the divine resources of the Father and the Holy Spirit. John Walvoord seems to hold this view:

> On two specific occasions Christ is revealed to have performed His miracles in the power of the Holy Spirit (Matt 12:28; Luke 4:14–18). In these instances Christ chose voluntarily to be dependent upon the power of the Father and the Holy Spirit to perform His miracles. In view of the fact that this is mentioned only twice and hundreds of miracles were performed, it would seem clear that Christ exercised His own [divine] power when He chose to do so as, for instance, when He commanded the waves to be still and caused Lazarus to come forth from the tomb at His command. The anointing of the Holy Spirit (cp. Lk 4:18) would support the conclusion that many of Christ's miracles were performed in the power of the Holy Spirit, but his deity still included omnipotence which was not surrendered in the kenosis.[34]

(2) *Predominantly Dependent.* Jesus lived normally within his own human power, relying predominantly on the divine resources of the Father and the Holy Spirit, while using his own divine power infrequently, if at all. Paul Feinberg notes, "The kenosis required that Jesus depend on the Holy Spirit. This is simply the other side of his voluntary setting aside

---

[34] John Walvoord, *Jesus Christ Our Lord* (Chicago: Moody, 1969), 144. This argument from silence can swing either way. Jesus explicitly claims that he casts out demons by the Spirit's power in Matt 12:28, yet Scripture never records any cases when Jesus himself actually invokes the Spirit's name before casting out a demon. Would not Jesus' explicit claim hold more weight than Walvoord's argument from silence?

of his position. As true man, he walked in dependence on the Spirit (e.g., Matt 12:28, Luke 4:14–18)."[35]

(3.) *Exclusively Dependent.* Jesus lived exclusively within his own human power without any recourse to his own divine power, but relied exclusively on the divine resources of the Father and the Holy Spirit. Gerald Hawthorne, who seems to hold this view, explains that "without denying the reality of the incarnation, or that God became a man, it is the purpose of this book, nevertheless, to argue for the reality of Jesus' humanness and that as such he was not aided to rise above and conquer temptations *as God*, but rather as a man whose will was set to do the will of God. His sinlessness was nothing other than the continued obedience to the Father and to the Father's will."[36]

Some might wonder, Why worry about the source of Jesus' supernatural power? Does it really matter? If we hold to supernatural theism, then Jesus' supernatural life and his ministry of miracles actually occurred and touched the lives of many in his day, whether he used his own divine power or relied on the supernatural power of the Father and the Holy Spirit. Yet the critical issue raised in this chapter is whether Jesus can be our example in his supernaturally oriented lifestyle. Christians cannot emulate his example if he relied on his own divine power to live and minister to others. As William Barry argues, "If Jesus is superhuman, then I can admire him, but I do not have to take seriously his call to emulate him. I can never be a superhuman being."[37] To the extent Jesus lived within his humanity and relied on the divine power of the Father and the Son, to that extent, Jesus can genuinely be an example we can emulate.[38]

[35] Paul Feinberg, "The Kenosis and Christology: An Exegetical-Theological Analysis of Phil 2:6–11," *TJ* 1 NS (1980): 46. In stating options 1 and 2, I assume there is no need for Jesus to rely on the Holy Spirit's divine power while at the same time he is *himself* using his own divine power, as implied in the mutually exclusive option 1 from Walvoord above.

[36] Gerald Hawthorne, *The Presence and the Power: The Significance of the Holy Spirit in the Life and Ministry of Jesus* (Dallas: Word, 1991; repr., Eugene, OR: Wipf & Stock 2003), 96, n. 94. Hawthorne's book is the sole academic monograph given wholly to discussing the relationship of the Spirit in the life of Jesus, while others devote only a portion of their book on this topic (e.g., James Dunn, *Jesus and the Spirit* [Grand Rapids: Eerdmans, 1975]).

[37] William Barry, *Letting God Come Close* (Chicago: Loyal, 2001), 111.

[38] What of the expectation for believers to emulate God? We are not expected to be like God in every way, but only in specific ways that are possible for us to emulate, being created in

This study will argue for option 2, against option 1, that rather than occasional dependence, Jesus predominantly depended on the Father and the Holy Spirit for his life and ministry on earth.[39] Defending the thesis that Jesus was predominantly dependent on the Father and Spirit requires some sort of accounting for the occasions on which Jesus apparently did make use of his own divine power. These occasions are infrequent but are part of the evidence pool and cannot be simply disregarded. Advocates of exclusive dependence on the Father and Spirit (option 3) would have to explain these divine manifestations as the Father's or the Spirit's action through the humanity of Jesus. But my claim is that Jesus was predominantly, though not exclusively, dependent on the Father and Spirit. Therefore, the following special cases can be acknowledged:

1. Jesus forgave sins. Exclusivists argue that he was declaring God's forgiveness as God's agent and representative.
2. Jesus was transfigured. Exclusivists argue that this was the display of his messianic, not divine, glory.
3. Jesus displayed his glory at his first miracle at Cana (John 2:11). Exclusivists claim this too as a display of messianic glory.
4. Jesus responded to the soldiers' question with "I am" and they fell down (John 18:6; Beasley-Murray argues that this reflects their shock at Jesus' direct self-disclosure and claim to be God[40]).
5. Jesus yearned for his preexistent glory with the Father (John 17:5). Exclusivists could view this as a prayer based on inference, not necessarily his current experience.

If these are genuine cases of Jesus' using his own divine powers, the proposal I am defending in this chapter (option 2) permits this. In my view,

---

God's image and now being conformed to the image of his Son (Rom 8:29); for example: (1) holiness and righteousness (Lev 19:2; Eph 4:24; 1 Pet 1:15–16), (2) love (Matt 5:43–48; Eph 5:1), and (3) being merciful (Luke 6:36). Similarly, we are not expected to emulate Jesus in every way, but in ways that regenerated humans can become more Christlike, the manner of his lifestyle, which we will manifest perfectly as glorified Christians (e.g., Rev 21:4,27).

[39] The preponderance of evidence supports my proposal as one legitimate option, compatible with orthodox Christianity. Those I cite in this section are included to indicate the plausibility of these points (when I cite a scholar, it does not necessarily indicate his or her agreement with the larger proposal, only for that specific point). Although I may be wrong on a point here or there, the proposal does not fail if one point must be conceded.

[40] George Beasley-Murray, *John* (Nashville: Thomas Nelson, 1999), 322.

Jesus' normal course of action was to depend on the Father and Spirit working through his humanity, but this does not exclude exceptional manifestations of the divine nature which, after all, orthodox Christology affirms him to possess.

The argument is developed along two broad themes, presenting evidence for Jesus' dependence on the Father and on the Holy Spirit. Further, his dependence on the Father can be subdivided into his explicit dependence and his implicit dependence (especially seen in his personal faith).

Jesus' Dependence on the Father's Resources

Jesus depended explicity on the Father. There are multiple occurrences of Jesus' own declaration of his complete dependence on the Father in the Gospel of John. "Very truly, I tell you, the Son can do nothing on his own, but only what he sees the Father doing; for whatever the Father does, the Son does likewise" (John 5:19). Similar declarations appear also in John 5:30; 7:28–29; 8:28–29,42; 12:49–50; 14:10,26,31; 15:9–10,15; 16:32; and 17:8,18.

Later in John's Gospel, Jesus develops a parallel between his dependency on the Father as the analogy for how his disciples will depend on him. For example we can compare John 5:19, quoted above with John 15:5: "I am the vine, you are the branches. Those who abide in me and I in them bear much fruit, because apart from me you can do nothing." Jesus offers himself as an example of dependency for believers.[41]

Jesus depended implicitly on the Father. Evidence of his faith in God the Father is found in (1) a study of Hebrews 12:2, (2) his claims about having faith, and (3) the phrase *"pistis Christou."* That Jesus himself expressed faith during his earthly sojourn did not cross the minds of some translators of Hebrews 12:2, so they inserted an "our" in the text, making it read "looking to Jesus the pioneer and perfecter of our faith" (NRSV; so also, KJV, NIV, and NET Bible). We can trace that view at least as far back as Aquinas, who believed Jesus had the full beatific vision of God in the cradle as a new infant, eliminating any need for faith in God.

---

[41] Believers are to abide *in* Christ as subsequent New Testament teaching emphasizes (e.g., Col 3:15–17). Yet we still direct our prayer requests to the Father in the name of Jesus (e.g., John 14:14; 15:7,16; 16:23; Matt 6:9; Eph 3:14).

Gerald O'Collins notes: "Aquinas and the subsequent Catholic theological tradition held that in his human mind Jesus enjoyed the beatific vision and hence lived by sight, not by faith. Aquinas expressed classically this thesis: 'When the divine reality is not hidden from sight, there is no point in faith. From the first moment of his conception Christ had the full vision of God in his essence . . . Therefore he could not have had faith' (*Summa theologiae*, 3a. 7. 3 *resp.*)."[42]

The New American Standard Bible translates Hebrews 12:2 "Fixing our eyes on Jesus, the author and perfecter of faith." Many recent commentators take this approach. Lane explains: "The poignant description as a whole points to Jesus as the perfect embodiment of faith, who exercised faith heroically. By bringing faith to complete expression, he enabled others to follow his example. The phrase reiterates and makes explicit what was affirmed with a quotation from Scripture in [Hebrews] 2:13, that Jesus in his earthly life was the perfect exemplar of trust in God."[43]

Donald Hagner adds, "[Jesus] is not only the basis, means, and fulfillment of faith, but in his life he also exemplifies the same principle of faith that we saw in the paragons of [Hebrews] chapter 11."[44]

The writer to the Hebrews twice uses the distinctive term *archēgos* for Jesus (Heb 2:8; 12:2, [cf. Acts 3:15], translated by NRSV and NIV as "pioneer" and by NASB as "author;" or could also be translated as "initiator" or "forerunner"). In light of the athletic imagery, Lane suggests the use of "champion" as appropriate, with some connection to the Greek tradition of Hercules: Jesus is "the champion in the exercise of faith and the one who brought faith to complete expression."[45] Harold Attridge notes: "Of equal importance is the fact that [Jesus] provides a perfectly adequate model of what life under that covenant involves. Thus the 'faith' (*pisteōs*) that Christ inaugurates and brings to perfect expression is not the content of Christian belief, but the fidelity and trust that he himself exhibited in a fully adequate way and that his followers are called upon to share . . . It is precisely as the one who perfectly embodies

---

[42] Gerald O'Collins, *Christology* (Oxford: Oxford University Press, 1995), 254–55.
[43] William L. Lane, *Hebrews 9–13*, WBC 47B. (Dallas: Word, 1991), 412.
[44] Donald Hagner, *Hebrews*, NIBC (Peabody, MA: Hendrickson, 1990), 212.
[45] Lane, *Hebrews 9–13*, 397.

faith that he serves as the ground of its possibility in others (*archēgos-aitios* ["source"]) and the model they are to follow (*archēgos-prodromos* ["forerunner," Heb 6:20])."[46]

Furthermore, in the Gospel account of the healing of the demonized son, some commentators suggest that Jesus' reply to the father's request in Mark 9:23 is both a challenge to the father, and also a testimony of his own life of faith, "And Jesus said to him, "'If You can!' All things are possible to him who believes'" (NASB). Sharyn Dowd explains, "Jesus is not merely an example to be imitated, but a leader to be followed. It is likely, then, that 'the one who believes' in 9:23 is deliberately ambiguous. Jesus has faith and he calls the father to have faith."[47] Ian Wallis notes, "The disciples may have been ineffectual . . . owing to their *oligopistia* ['little faith'], but Jesus was successful because he demonstrated that faith . . . a faith which all who intend to fulfill Christ's commission must demonstrate."[48] O'Collins agrees, "[Jesus] speaks about faith as an insider, one who knows personally what the life of faith is and wants to share it with others (see 2 Cor 4:13)."[49] If Jesus was such an insider as a man of faith himself, then when he criticizes the disciples for their lack of faith (e.g., Matt 6:30; 8:26; 16:8 *oligopistoi,* "little faiths"), he speaks as one who experientially knows what he is talking about.

Finally, support for Jesus' faith also comes from reconsidering the Greek phrase *pistis Christou,* which appears in seven verses of Paul (Rom 3:22,26; Gal 2:16 [twice]; 2:20; 3:22; Eph 3:12; Phil 3:9) as well as in Acts 3:16 and Revelation 14:12. The traditional translation has been as an objective genitive ("faith *in* Christ"). There is general agreement that believers must place their faith *in* Jesus, as taught in other New

---

[46] Harold Attridge, *Hebrews,* Hermeneia (Philadelphia: Fortress, 1989), 357–58.

[47] Sharyn Dowd, *Prayer, Power, and the Problem of Suffering: Mark 11:22–25 in the Context of Markan Theology,* SBLDS 105 (Atlanta, GA: Scholars' Press, 1986), 111.

[48] Ian Wallis, *The Faith of Jesus Christ in Early Christian Traditions,* SNTSMS 84 (Cambridge: Cambridge University Press, 1995), 36. Wallis concludes, "It is the conviction of the present author that interest in Jesus' faith was an unfortunate and unnecessary casualty of early Christological controversy, in which its significance was determined more in terms of what it conceded to rival positions rather than of what it contributed to our knowledge of God and humanity of Jesus Christ . . . Certainly, Jesus' faith does seem to provide a point of departure for Christology which is rooted in common human experience and which explores his theological significance through reflection upon his human being in relation to God" (221).

[49] O'Collins, *Christology,* 261.

Testament passages (e.g., John 3:16; Acts 20:21; Col 1:4; 1 John 3:23). The debate concerns whether the genitive noun (Jesus, or Son of God) is either objective or subjective. More commentators are recognizing the phrase as a subjective genitive, that is, "faith [or faithfulness] *of* Jesus," that Jesus himself experienced faith in God.[50] Thus, that Jesus depended on the Father is both explicitly and implicitly evident in Scripture.

Jesus' Dependence on the Divine Resources of the Holy Spirit

Is the role of the Spirit superfluous or necessary in Jesus' life and ministry? As the Anointed One, Jesus was the unique bearer of the Spirit (Luke 4:16–21) given without measure (John 3:34). Old Testament prophecies[51] and the Gospels portray the Holy Spirit as being associated with the Messiah. Jesus was conceived by the Holy Spirit (Matt 1:20; Luke 1:35); was full of the Spirit and led by the Holy Spirit (e.g., Luke 4:1); was empowered by the Spirit (e.g., Luke 4:16); cast out demons by the Holy Spirit (Matt 12:28 = Luke 11:20); and gave instructions by the Holy Spirit (Acts 1:2).

Although the quantity of Gospel passages mentioning the Spirit is less than what might be expected,[52] the Gospels do give important emphasis to the role of the Spirit in the life of Jesus. G. R. Beasley-Murray explains, "Prominence is given to narratives associated with the Spirit's action in the life of Jesus through occurring at a prominent point in the Gospels, namely at their beginning."[53] In Mark 1:8–13 the Spirit is mentioned three times in relation to Jesus' baptism and temptation.[54]

---

[50] Daniel Wallace summarizes the grammatical options in *An Exegetical Syntax of the New Testament* (Grand Rapids: Zondervan, 1996), 115–16. For further treatment on this important issue, see Richard B. Hays, *The Faith of Jesus*, 2nd ed. (Grand Rapids: Eerdmans, 2001). Compare the discussion of Romans 3:22–26 by Douglas Moo, who opts for the objective genitive view ("in Christ") (*The Epistle to the Romans* [Grand Rapids: Eerdmans, 1996], 224–43), and Richard Hays, who opts for the subjective genitive view ("of Christ") (*"Pistis* in Romans 3.25: Neglected Evidence for the 'Faithfulness of Christ?'" *NTS* 39 [1993]: 22–26).

[51] Various passages in Isaiah note the role of the Spirit in Messiah's life and ministry (e.g., 11:1–2; 42:1; and 61:1–3).

[52] Quantity of references is not always a decisive criterion. For instance, the doctrine of Jesus' virgin birth (or rather, virgin conception) is based solely on two passages, Matthew 1:18–25 and Luke 1:36–38.

[53] G. R. Beasley-Murray, "Jesus and the Spirit," in *Melanges Bibliques en homage au R. P. Beda Rigaux*, ed. A. Deschamps and A. de Halleux (Gembloux: Duculot, 1970), 463.

[54] Craig Keener explains, "The Holy Spirit appears rarely in Mark's Gospel, primarily in the introduction (1:8,10,12) and in references to power for exorcism (3:29) and prophetic

Matthew indicates the Spirit's involvement six times, the first three in the announcement related to Jesus' conception (1:18,20 twice), and the other three in relating his baptism and temptation (3:1,16; 4:1). The Spirit is mentioned twelve times in Luke chapters 1–4; three times in John 1, and three more times in John 3. Thus, regarding prominence at the beginning of their narratives, all four gospels emphasize the role of the Holy Spirit in Jesus' life.

Regarding Jesus' teaching on the Spirit, Beasley-Murray explains, "Inasmuch as he rarely made his vocation [as bearer of the Spirit] a subject of his instruction, there is as much instruction on the Spirit in the recorded teaching of Jesus as the situation warranted."[55] Furthermore, the disciples as convinced Jewish monotheists (Deut 6:4) perhaps were not ready to receive instruction on the third person of the Trinity. For in his teaching, Jesus—in the progress of revelation—offers the clearest presentation to date that God is a trinitarian Being. Must not Jesus then teach the concept to his disciples in a careful and progressive manner, first distinguishing the Father from the Son, and then at some later point teaching about the third person, the Holy Spirit? Gregory of Nazianzus clarifies: "For the matter stands thus: the Old Testament proclaimed the Father openly, and the Son more obscurely. The New manifested the Son, and suggested the deity of the Spirit. Now the Spirit himself dwells among us, and supplies us with a clearer demonstration of himself. For it was not safe, when the Godhead of the Father was not yet acknowledged, plainly to proclaim the Son: nor when that of the Son was not yet received, to burden us further (if I may use so bold an expression) with the Holy Spirit."[56]

---

inspiration, both in the Old Testament (12:36) and among disciples (13:11). This suggests two important points for the interpreter: Mark views the Spirit as the source of empowerment for the church's mission, and Mark gives his primary lesson on pneumatology up front, in the introduction, one of the most critical sections of his Gospel. Because a proem typically introduced a writer's main themes, and because Mark has tightened the tradition we have from Q into a concise summary of John's [the Baptist] announcement and Jesus' baptism and testing, the Spirit plays a far greater role in Mark's Gospel than a mere concordance survey might suggest." *The Spirit in the Gospels and Acts* (Peabody, MA: Hendrickson, 1997), 50.

[55] Beasley-Murray, "Jesus and the Spirit," 476.

[56] Gregory of Nazianzus, *Orations* 5.26, cited by Gary Badcock, *Light of Truth and Fire of Love: A Theology of the Holy Spirit* (Grand Rapids: Eerdmans, 1997), 58. Another reason might be that, as the divine author of Scripture, the "shy" and humble Spirit, who points to Christ, is reluctant to mention his own name in the scriptural text very often.

During the upper room discourse, Jesus presented more systematic teaching about the Spirit, yet the disciples, who did not comprehend that Jesus would be leaving them shortly to return to the Father, did not seem to pay much attention. No follow-up questions about the Spirit are recorded (as sometimes occurred with other teachings that puzzled them, e.g., Matt 13:36; 17:19).

Table 6.2 lists the main references to the Spirit's participation in Jesus' life in the Gospels (passages marked with * will receive further comment below).

Table 6.2 Jesus and the Spirit in the Gospels

Explicit:	
Spirit without measure— John 3:34	Rejoice in the Spirit— Luke 10:21
Baptism—Matt 3:16, Mark 1:10, Luke 3:22	*Spirit is willing—Matt 26:41, Mark 14:38
Temptation—Matt 4:1, Mark 1:12, Luke 4:1	Give commands through the Spirit Acts 1:2
*Exorcism—Matt 12:28, Luke 11:20	*[Offered through the eternal Spirit—Heb 9:14]
Implicit:	
*Power to heal—Luke 5:17b, Mark 5:30	

Matthew 12:28 attributes Jesus' exorcisms to the divine resources of the Holy Spirit: "But if it is by the Spirit of God that I cast out demons, then the kingdom of God has come to you" (Matt 12:28; "finger of God" Luke 11:20[57]). Beasley-Murray notes that this saying "gives Jesus' own explanation of his exorcisms: they are performed not by his own power but by the power of God, i.e., by the Spirit of God, and since the defeat of the evil power is a feature of the end time, they show that the kingdom of God has appeared in his activity."[58] Furthermore Jesus' follow-up reference to the blasphemy of the Holy Spirit (Matt 12:32) also

---

[57] D. A. Carson states, "Luke 11:20 has 'the finger of God' instead of 'the Spirit of God.' Possibly the latter is original . . . , but the matter is of little consequence since they both refer to the same thing (cf. Exod 8:19; Deut 9:10; Ps 8:3)." *Matthew, EBC* 9 (Grand Rapids: Zondervan, 1981), 289.

[58] G. R. Beasley-Murray, "Jesus and the Spirit," 471.

indicates how important Jesus viewed the ministry of the Holy Spirit as being. Donald Hagner explains:

> Given Matthew's Christological interests and the unique and central position held by Jesus throughout the Gospel, one may understandably be surprised that Matthew has not said the reverse of what stands in the text, i.e., that blasphemy against the Spirit is forgivable but not that against the Son of Man. The gravity of the blasphemy against the Spirit, however, depends upon the Holy Spirit as the fundamental dynamic that stands behind and makes possible the entire messianic ministry of Jesus itself. . . . The failure to understand Jesus is yet forgivable but not the outright rejection of the saving power of God through the Spirit exhibited in the direct overthrow of the kingdom of Satan.[59]

Luke 5:17b and Mark 5:30, two implicit references, indicate Jesus as an agent of the Father's power. According to Luke 5:17b, "the power of the Lord was with him to heal." Nolland explains, "The reference to 'power' (*dynamis*) links back to [Luke] 4:14 and prepares the way for the coming references to tangible power proceeding from Jesus (6:19, 8:44): the power that flows out of Jesus and brings healing is the power of God himself . . . It is more likely that Luke is continuing to clarify what it means for Jesus to have become through the descent of the Spirit the repository of the power of God (3:22; 4:1,14,18–19; 6:19; 8:44)."[60]

According to Mark 5:30, "Immediately aware that power had gone forth from him, Jesus turned about in the crowd and said, 'Who touched my clothes?'" Lane notes: "Jesus possesses the power of God as the representative of the Father. Nevertheless, the Father remains in control of his own power. The healing of the woman occurred through God's free and gracious decision to bestow upon her the power which was active in Jesus. By an act of sovereign will God determined to honor the woman's faith in spite of the fact that it was tinged with ideas which bordered on magic."[61]

---

[59] Donald Hagner, *Matthew 1–13*, WBC 33A (Dallas: Word, 1993), 348.
[60] John Nolland, *Luke 9:21–18:34*, WBC (Nashville: Thomas Nelson, 1993), 234.
[61] William Lane, *The Gospel of Mark*, NICNT (Grand Rapids: Eerdmans, 1974), 192–93.

Hebrews 9:14 offers a distinctive comment regarding Jesus' experience of the passion and his death: "How much more will the blood of Christ, who through the eternal Spirit offered himself without blemish to God, purify our conscience." Lane explains, "The fact that his offering was made *dia pneumatos aiōniou*, 'through the eternal Spirit,' implies that he had been divinely empowered and sustained in his office. The formulation does not occur elsewhere in the New Testament or early Christian literature, but it may be understood as a designation for the Holy Spirit. A reference to the Spirit is appropriate in a section under the influence of Isaiah, where the Servant of the Lord is qualified for his task by the Spirit of God (Isa 42:1; 61:1)."[62]

Finally, Jesus taught that "the Spirit indeed is willing, but the flesh is weak" (Matt 26:41; Mark 14:38). The common view of Jesus' statement to the three sleeping disciples in Gethsemane is that it refers to the continuing internal struggle within human nature between the human spirit against the weak physical body. If this were so, Jesus' preceding words ("Stay awake and pray that you may not come into the time of trial") would then be a challenge to muster more human effort to override their bodily weakness so they could pray. Another interpretation considers the contrast as one between relying on divine power of the Holy "Spirit," rather than solely relying on human resources ("flesh"), which can never stand alone against the assaults of Satan. Jesus made similar contrasts between the divine sphere and human sphere elsewhere (John 3:6; 6:63), which have Old Testament precedent in Isaiah 31:1, contrasting an Egyptian alliance ("flesh") against relying on the Lord God ("spirit"; see also Ps 51:11–12). Is not Jesus giving the three disciples the secret to his own victory in the garden? William Lane comments on Mark 14:38, "Spiritual wakefulness and prayer in full dependence upon divine help provide the only adequate preparation for crisis . . . Jesus prepared for his own intense trial through vigilance and prayer, and thus gave to the disciples and to the Church the model for the proper resistance of eschatological temptation."[63] Jesus' comment then furnishes the most explicit reference to his own dependence

---

[62] Lane, *Hebrews 9–13*, 240.
[63] Lane, *Mark*, 520–21.

on the Holy Spirit and its implications as a teaching for all believers for all times.

Any understanding of Jesus' earthly pilgrimage must account for the numerous references to the Holy Spirit regarding Jesus' life and ministry.[64] If he planned to live as a human just like us then, once the Son voluntarily decided to add on human nature, he would need to veil his divine glory and predominantly rely on divine resources outside of his own divine power. Scripture gives sufficient evidence to affirm that, without the filling and empowering ministry of the Spirit in Jesus' life, Jesus would not have lived an exemplary human life nor accomplished his messianic mission.

In sum, the pervasiveness of the scriptural evidence presented above—of dependence on the Father, of expressing his own faith in God, and of dependence on the Holy Spirit—supports a lifestyle for Jesus as *predominantly* dependent on the divine resources of the Father and the Spirit (option 2) rather than only occasional dependence (option 1).[65]

Differences Between Jesus and Us and Potential Objections

Jesus shares a common humanity since believers, having been regenerated, now share the same human nature as Jesus does and as Adam and Eve did at creation. Also, believers have access to the same divine resources that Jesus did. Let us consider differences.

Uniqueness of Jesus and the Spirit. Is the Holy Spirit's ministry unique

---

[64] Hawthorne groups a number of implicit references to Jesus and the Spirit around four particular themes; (1) acting with authority (*exousia*): Mark 1:22/Matt 7:29/Luke 4:32; Mark 1:27/Luke 4:36; Mark 2:10/Matt 9:6/Luke 4:36; Mark 2:12/Matt 9:6/Luke 5:24; Mark 11:28–29,33/Matt 21:23–34,27/Luke 20:2,8; (2) performing his miracles with power (*dynameis, dynamei*): Mark 5:30/Luke 8:46; Mark 6:2/Matt 13:54; Matt 11:20–22; 14:2; Luke 4:14,36; 5:17; (3) being perceived by the people as a prophet: Mark 6:15–16/Luke 9:8–9; Mark 8:28/Matt 16:14/Luke 9:19; Mark 14:65/Matt 26:68; see also Matt 21:11,46; Luke 7:16,39; 24:19; (4) perceiving himself as a prophet [and also more than a prophet]: Mark 6:4/Matt 13:57/Luke 4:24; 13:33; cf. Matt 23:31–38; Luke 11:47–51 (*The Presence*, 115).

[65] John McKinley explores the role of the Spirit in the life and ministry of Jesus, evaluating five proposals: Gerald Hawthorne (American Evangelical), James Dunn (British Evangelical), Roger Stronstad and Robert Menzies (Pentecostal), Max Turner (Charismatic), and Ralph Del Colle (Catholic). McKinley then offers his own proposal in an unpublished manuscript (2003), "Why Did Jesus Have the Holy Spirit When He Was Already Divine?"

to Jesus as the Anointed One/Messiah, or does the Holy Spirit empower Jesus to live his earthly life in a manner similar to how the Spirit works with believers? One consequence of Jesus' departure to the Father is that it would permit the Spirit to come (John 7:39; 16:7). Believers have been designed to be indwelt by the Spirit forever (John 14:16). That is, God has so fashioned humankind that both a human person and a divine person can occupy together the cockpit of one's life in which the believer can be formed, informed, empowered by the Spirit, in a fashion similar to Jesus. Jesus showcases the possibilities of a human life completely filled by the Spirit. One significant implication for Christian living today becomes very clear: Jesus walked by the Spirit, and so it is possible for us to do so as we yield in dependence on God.

Although the same Spirit that indwelt Jesus indwells all believers, John 3:34 indicates that Jesus had a greater measure of the Spirit. This may have been due to Jesus' unique role as the divine-human messiah (level 2 in Table 6.1) which required the full measure of the Spirit's ministry (John 3:36). Or this greater measure may also have been the consequence of Jesus' complete dependence on the Father and his life of holiness, which permitted a full measure of the Spirit in Jesus' life and ministry. Sadly, our faith and life in holiness are limited, being hindered by doubt and unbelief as we are still in the process of being conformed to the image of the Son. Our honest prayer can be that of the man in Mark 9: "I do believe; help me overcome my unbelief!" (Mark 9:24). Jesus teaches that it is possible to grow in greater dependence on God so we can emulate more and more of his life and ministry (e.g., Mark 11:22–25; John 13:12–17; 14:12–14).

Supernatural Elements in Jesus' Life. If Jesus did not predominantly use his own divine powers, then how can one give an account for the various supernaturally oriented aspects of Jesus' life that go beyond the limits of human powers? Note that most of the supernaturally oriented activities of Jesus were not unique to him alone but are also performed by "mere" humans, which supplies additional evidence for the dependency proposal.

1. *Miracles.* Both the Old Testament and New Testament record miracles done by mere humans—not in their own human power, but sourced

in the power of God—that were similar to those Jesus performed; for example: (1) raising the dead (2 Kings 4:8–37; Acts 9:36–42); (2) curing a leper (2 Kings 5:1–15); (3) healing the lame (Acts 3:1–10); (4) making an ax head float on water (2 Kings 6:4–7); (5) multiplying food (2 Kings 4:42–44); (6) walking on water for a brief time (Matt 14:28–30); and (7) healing the sick and casting out demons by means of Paul's handkerchief and clothes (cp. Acts 19:11–12).[66]

2. *Jesus' knowledge.* This includes his knowledge of God's authoritative message and Jesus' knowledge of the thoughts of others (e.g., Matt 12:25; Luke 11:17). Daniel reported and interpreted the dream of King Nebuchadnezzar (Dan 2:1–49), and Peter knew the secret sin of Ananias and Sapphira (Acts 5:1–11).

3. *Jesus' temptability and impeccability.* Jesus is human, but also uniquely divine. Scripture explicitly teaches that Jesus was tempted (didactic material, e.g., Heb 2:18; 4:15; life examples narrated in the Gospels, e.g., Matt 4:1–11; 16:23; 26:38–46). Yet James teaches that God cannot be tempted by evil (Jas 1:13). The teaching about Jesus' impeccability claims that either he *could* not sin or that he *would* not sin (Scripture only explicitly teaches that Jesus *did* not sin).

No matter which incarnational model one holds, all must address this seeming paradox. That Jesus fought against temptation is obvious, particularly in Gethsemane (even sweating blood, Luke 22:44; Heb 12:4). We infer that Jesus thought it was possible for him to sin, and thus he struggled to resist; otherwise we must interpret Jesus' dramatic performance as an actor to be worthy of an Academy Award. Resolving the temptability issue requires more space than can be allotted here, but suffice it to suggest one possible resolution, as O'Collins notes: "Jesus

---

[66] If option 2 is affirmed, what evidence in the Gospels can be marshaled to support Jesus' deity? Although the proposal affirms that each miracle is done by the power of the Spirit, the cumulative effect of the miracles, in combination with the other evidences, still point to Jesus' deity as well as his unique and distinctive Messianic mission (e.g., Matt 11:3–5). Various standard evidences can be cited for his deity, as mentioned at the beginning of the chapter: Jesus received worship (e.g., Matt 28:9,16; John 20:28); his self-claims (e.g., Matt 22:42–45; John 8:58–59); use of *Lord* (e.g., Luke 2:11; John 20:28); and the testimony of Gospel writers (John 1:1,18). Also, evidence of Jesus' messianic mission as the Christ proves that Jesus is more than just a prophet (e.g., Luke 4:16–21; Matt 16:16; Mark 10:45; Luke 4:41). Thus, despite the veiling of Jesus' deity during the incarnation, there is sufficient manifestation of his divine person that still shines through clearly; for, as Jesus teaches, "Whoever has seen me has seen the Father" (John 14:9).

could be truly tempted and tested, provided that he did not know that he could not sin. If he had known that he could not sin, it would be difficult, if not impossible, to make sense of genuine temptations; they would be reduced to make-believe, a performance put on for the edification of others. It was quite a different situation to be incapable of sin but not to know that."[67]

We can affirm that Jesus could not actually sin—that it was not a *metaphysical* possibility—if we also can affirm that it was an *epistemic* possibility.[68] That is, within Jesus' own understanding and perception of reality during his state of humiliation, he *thought* it was possible that he could still sin. Furthermore, due to his formed heart of holiness, Jesus was much more painfully aware of the evil attacking him than we are. And he resisted every temptation, requiring greater intentionality in effort and reliance on divine help; believers are usually more clueless and less intentional (e.g., Heb 12:3–4).

4. *Jesus' sinless life.* Was this *solely* the result of his deity, or is it possible for a human person to live without sinning? First, human nature is not essentially corrupt or sinful (e.g., Gen 1:31). Sinful propensities are a feature added on since the fall. For a brief period of time Adam and Eve lived without sinning. Also, the Bible promises that all believers in the future eternal state, although still being human, will live continuously without sin (Rom 8:17,28–30; 1 Cor 15:50–57; Rev 21:4,27), sustained by the Spirit who indwells us forever (John 14:16). Being regenerated, believers now have a new heart (Ezek 36:25–27) and have been freed from the power of sin (Rom 6:6–7,11–12,18). Yet believers take with them into their new life in God's family all of their sinful habits and propensities, and sadly we may continue to maintain and learn new sin

---

[67] O'Collins, *Christology*, 271. One practical implication is worthy of note. By walking in the power of the Spirit, we do not need to yield to any temptation. In fact, 1 Corinthians 10:13 offers the promise that there is always a sinless way out of each temptation. In other words, at any given moment, a believer *need not sin*. More to the point, in light of the promise of 1 Corinthians 10:13, can it be proposed that Jesus, in living a sinless life, is the first human being ever who fully actualized the theoretical possibility of 1 Corinthians 10:13 throughout his whole life—that there is always a sinless way out of temptation?

[68] Thomas Morris notes, "We have said that it seems to be a conceptual truth that, in some sense, temptation requires the possibility of sinning. On reflection, we can see that it is the *epistemic* possibility of sinning rather than a broadly logical, or metaphysical, or even physical possibility that is conceptually linked to temptation . . . Jesus could be tempted to sin just in case it was epistemically possible for him that he sin," *Logic*, 147–48.

patterns even as Christians. But we are commanded to walk in Christlike ways through the power of God's grace working in us—ought implies *can* in God's grace. Jesus demonstrated the possibility for regenerated humans to live sinlessly, becoming another "Adam" of a new God-oriented human race (1 Cor 15:45–49). Jesus' life makes the point that living sinlessly is theoretically possible for humans through God's power (e.g., Gal 5:16; 1 Cor 10:13).[69]

Role of the Spirit in Jesus' Childhood

Some theories about the incarnation seem to imply that Jesus was basically on his own during his childhood and young adult years prior to his public ministry, yet two lines of evidence suggest otherwise.

Parallels between the Forerunner and the Messiah

If the forerunner of Messiah was filled with the Spirit while in the womb (Luke 1:15,17), would not the Messiah himself be also (Matt 1:20; Luke 1:35)? Luke moves back and forth between the accounts of the birth and childhood of John the Baptist on the one hand and Jesus on the other, indicating the close association between the two, although

---

[69] Regarding the common notion that believers have a "sin nature" and Jesus did not, although a full discussion is beyond the scope of the chapter, a brief comment is needed. First, the term "sin nature" is problematic. We always will only have one nature; we have a human nature (see Garrett J. DeWeese's chapter 4 for clarification); the NIV adds to the confusion by usually translating the Greek word "flesh" [*sarx*] as "sin nature." "Sinful propensity" is a preferable term. Second, often Romans 7:14–25 is used as evidence for indwelling sin in the believer. Yet some New Testament scholars, and I am in agreement, understand Paul's argument in Romans 7 as rendering 7:14–25 irrelevant to the topic of a believer's sinful propensity (see Douglas Moo, *The Epistles to the Romans* [Grand Rapids: Eerdmans,1996], 442–51 for a discussion of the issues involved and his reasons for this interpretation). Two biblical teachings need to be kept in mind. First, because of regeneration, believers are free from the power of sin, so that sinning is never a necessity (e.g., Rom 6:6,10–12,18; 1 Cor 10:13; Gal 5:16). Second, this side of heaven, living completely sinlessly is not actually possible in this life (e.g., 1 John 1:8–9), due to the depth of our sinful compulsions acquired since birth, with the constant pressure of living in a world system antagonistic to God (1 John 2:15–17) that is constantly assaulted by Satanic forces (Eph 6:12). What we hold in common with Jesus is that we never need to sin. Furthermore, facing temptations for Jesus was much more difficult than what we experience. Jesus always felt the full brunt of the temptation and suffering he faced as a sinless person, yet without yielding, struggling once to the point of sweating profusely (Luke 22:44; cf. Heb 12:3–4).

each had distinctly different origins and roles (on John the Baptist: Luke 1:5–25,57–80; on Jesus: Luke 1:26–56; 2:1–52).

An implied parallel is made between John's growth (Luke 1:80) and Jesus' growth (Luke 2:40) in that both verses begin the same way: "The child grew and became strong . . ." (cp. Samuel as a child, 1 Sam 2:26). Bock notes, "The verse parallels what was said of John the Baptist (1:80), but what is said about Jesus is more extensive. John is said simply to grow in his human spirit, but Jesus grows in the wisdom of God."[70] There is a connection between Isaiah 11:2 ("The Spirit of the LORD will rest on him, The spirit of wisdom and understanding [LXX *pneuma sophias kai suneseōs*], The spirit of counsel and strength, The spirit of knowledge and the fear of the LORD.") with Luke 2:40 ("increasing in wisdom" [*plēroumenon sophia*] and "the favor of God was upon him;" cp. Acts 4:33). Dunn comments, "It is quite probable, though not certain, that Luke means us to understand that Jesus was every bit as full of the Holy Spirit as John was (1:15), and that Jesus' growth in wisdom and grace was due to his possession of the Spirit (2:40,52); the link between the Spirit and divine sonship (and filial consciousness) would also be a pointer in this direction (1:35; 2:49; 3:22; cp. Rom. 8:15–16; Gal. 4:6)."[71]

Twelve-Year-Old Temple Visit

Regarding the matter of wisdom, Jesus' encounter at age twelve with the religious teachers offers evidence of unusual wisdom at a young age (Luke 2:46–47). Earle Ellis notes that Luke 2:47, in which the teachers "were amazed at his understanding (*synesis*) and his answers" is not intended "just as a tribute to Jesus' intelligence but as a witness to his relationship to God . . . The same 'Holy Spirit' power, later to be manifested in Jesus' ministry, even now is at work. Jesus interprets the Scripture not

---

[70] Darrell L. Bock, *Luke 1:1–9:50* BEC (Grand Rapids: Baker, 1994), 254. Bock continues, "The extent of this growth, especially in respect to wisdom, will be demonstrated by Jesus' wise perception in 2:41–52."

[71] James D. G. Dunn, *Baptism in the Spirit* (London: SCM, 1970), 24. Max Turner observes, "If the Baptist's own experience of the Spirit was itself an eschatological novum, Jesus' surpasses it. Gerd Schneider explains: 'Jesus is not merely filled with the Spirit, like John, rather his very being is attributed to the Spirit'" (Max Turner, *The Holy Spirit and Spiritual Gifts in the New Testament and Church Today* [Peabody, MA: Hendrikson, 1996], 25).

from the knowledge gained in rabbinic training but from the 'wisdom' given by God."[72]

Gerald Hawthorne explains, "Here is a glimpse into what Jesus would be like in years to come, about whom it could well be said, 'The Spirit of the Lord shall rest upon him, the spirit of wisdom [*sophia*] and under-standing [*synesis*]' (Isa 11:2 [LXX]; cp. Isa 42:1; Luke 4:18; 11:31)."[73] Note Luke's use of the phrase in Luke 2:40 ("the favor of God was upon him") along with Acts 4:33 ("and with great power the apostles gave their testimony to the resurrection of the Lord Jesus, and great grace was upon them all").

Regarding this temple visit in Luke 2:41–51, Bock notes, "This is the only account in Luke where Jesus takes instruction from Jewish teach-ers."[74] Hawthorne adds, "On special occasions, such as the seven-day feast of Passover, the Temple Sanhedrin sat in the Temple area and infor-mally received questions and stated their traditions (Sanh. 88b) . . . [On this first temple visit] possibly numbered among [the Jewish teachers] were Symeon, Gamaliel (cp. Acts 22:3), Annas, Caiaphas, Nicodemus, Joseph of Arimathea . . ."[75] Perhaps this kind of special learning experi-ence for Jesus was the first of many such encounters to which he looked forward during his subsequent annual temple visits to learn from these Jewish teachers, until he left home around age thirty.[76]

Though these verses are few, it is possible to infer the active role of the Spirit in Jesus' early years. Sinclair Ferguson explains: "There is a continuing ministry of the Spirit in the life of Jesus ('filled,' *plēroumenon*, in Luke 2:40 indicates experience which was progressive

---

[72] E. Earle Ellis, *The Gospel of Luke* (London: Marshall, Morgan & Scott, 1966), 85; cf. Jas 3:15,17 (cited in Hawthorne, *The Presence*, 108).

[73] Ibid., 107. Regarding Jesus' early schooling Hawthorne suggests that "Jesus remains in the circle of his Galilean family. This would appear to suggest that the Holy Spirit, in filling Jesus with wisdom, did not work in this instance independently of social structures but through them. That is to say, the Holy Spirit took advantage of every educational instrument that was thus readily available–home, parents, school, Scriptures, life and worship of the synagogue, and so on–to mold the intellectual and spiritual dimensions of this developing personality" (100–1).

[74] Bock, *Luke 1:1–9:50*, 267; cf. Ellis, *Luke*, 85.

[75] Hawthorne, *The Presence*, 104.

[76] Some understand the phrase by John the Baptist "come/follow after" (John 1:15,27,30; Matt 3:11, and Mark 1:7) as the technical term used to designate a follower or disciple, thus John would be identifying the future Messiah as a current disciple of John's (Lane, *Mark*, 52; Kendrick Grobel, "He That Cometh After Me," *JBL* 60 [1941]: 397–401).

as well as passive). We may assume, from Luke's comment that Jesus 'increased in wisdom and in stature, and in favor with God and man' (Luke 2:52, RSV), that he gave expression to the appropriate fruit of the Spirit at each period of his human development."[77]

Implications of Jesus' Limited Knowledge during His Childhood

Assuming the proposal argued above is compatible with Scripture, what implications can be drawn regarding Jesus' childhood? Would it not be the case that Jesus' teaching, "Truly I tell you, whoever does not receive the kingdom of God as a little child will never enter it" (Luke 18:17), is based on his reflections of being a child himself? Jesus could have made his initial appearance on Earth as an adult, as Adam and Eve were created. By being born as a baby, Jesus affirms the human development process from birth onward. Biblical evidence about Jesus' childhood is limited, but Scripture teaches that Jesus grew as a normal human person (e.g., Luke 2:40,52). Can we not infer that his adult character is in some way connected with a normal human development process, as it is for all humans (though not limited to it)?

Furthermore, if we affirm a full experience of normal child development for Jesus (e.g., Luke 2:40,52), we must assert that, although Jesus was fully God, during his early years on this earth Jesus was not fully aware of all the knowledge he has during adult public ministry. That is, at one month old, the baby Jesus would have been ignorant of his deity. Yet it seems reasonable to conclude that Jesus' conceptual understanding of his identity, mission, and teaching, and his virtuous character were all mainly formed during his obscure years prior to beginning his public ministry.

Accordingly, not only did the Spirit participate in the conception and birth of Jesus, but he would also be involved in the drastic limitation of the Son's preexistent conscious life to that of a baby boy.[78] Since Jesus

---

[77] Sinclair B. Ferguson, *The Holy Spirit* (Downers Grove, IL: InterVarsity, 1996), 44. In his discussion Ferguson includes references to Isaiah 11:1–3 and 42:1 and 50:4–5 as offering hints regarding how the Spirit might have worked with Jesus during his growing years.

[78] Donald Macleod complains that this is an unbelievable "degree of amnesia to which there can be no parallel" (*The Person of Christ* [Downers Grove, IL: InterVarsity, 1998], 210). Of course, the whole matter of the incarnation itself is vastly incredible and mysterious from a human point of view—of joining finite human nature to infinite divine nature—so it

continues to be divine during his temporal humiliation, he retains his omniscience and remains sinless. Yet how can this be reconciled with the normal human development process of learning?

Perhaps the Holy Spirit who indwelled and filled Jesus provided some kind of "fire wall" to Jesus' divine mind, or otherwise enabled his divine knowledge and abilities to remain in his subconscious mind.[79] Accordingly, the Spirit would then permit Jesus' increasing awareness within his limited human consciousness in a way that would be appropriate at each stage of Jesus' growing years. Just as the Spirit walked with the child Samuel in the Old Testament (1 Sam 3:1–21), so the Spirit walked with the child Jesus to be his inner divine tutor, helping him avoid the development of fallible beliefs in literary and historical matters as well as spiritual and moral matters.[80]

Furthermore, Jesus could fully sympathize and identify with infants and children through his own experience as the sympathetic high priest for all humans, regardless of their developmental stage (Heb 4:15). Once Jesus developed his adult abilities of reflection, the Spirit could then bring to Jesus' mature consciousness his own experience of being an infant.[81] Yet, even during those early years, Jesus would have had a

---

would follow that certain facets of the incarnation would also be incredible, but when God is involved, the seemingly impossible can become possible (Mark 10:27).

[79] Discussion of Jesus' consciousness is beyond the scope of this chapter. Regardless of which view one takes, a similar functional outcome results.

[80] That Jesus would not develop fallible beliefs in these important matters is crucial for maintaining his sinlessness. Philosopher Dallas Willard explains, "We always live up to our beliefs—or down to them, as the case may be" (*The Divine Conspiracy* [San Francisco: HarperSanFrancisco, 1998], 307). Due to the nature of beliefs, the Spirit would need to guide the child Jesus into true beliefs about these important aspects of reality. Perhaps the teaching about an age of accountability would also apply in Jesus' case. For a defense of the age of accountability for children, see Klaus Issler, "Biblical Perspectives on Developmental Grace for Nurturing Children's Spirituality," in *Children's Spirituality: Christian Perspectives, Research, and Application*, ed. Donald Ratcliff (Eugene, OR: Cascade/Wipf & Stock, 2004), chap. 4.

[81] This suggestion of the Spirit's bringing to mind Jesus' experience of childhood responds to A. B. Bruce's critique that though Jesus had been a child, he would not have remembered those early years: "A mighty impulse of free self-conscious love constrained the eternal Son to descend into humanity, and in the descent that love lost itself for years; till at length the man Jesus found out the secret of His birth . . . [Yet] on this view, the Logos had no acquaintance with some of the most interesting stages in the experience of Christ . . . Therefore with infants, children, and youths He has not learned to sympathise; only with full-grown tempted men has His experience fitted Him to have a fellow-feeling" (*The Humiliation of Christ* [1881; repr., Grand Rapids: Eerdmans, 1995], 175–76).

heightened consciousness, beyond what we typically have as children, in that the Spirit was his divine tutor, his inner teacher.[82] Millard Erickson, though focusing on Jesus' dependence on the Father, makes the same point: "The infinite knowledge possessed by [Jesus'] deity was accessible to him, not when his divine nature permitted access, as [Thomas] Morris suggests, but when the Father permitted access. The Son had chosen to live in dependence or subordination. Presumably the access the Father allowed was selective; that is to say, the whole divine knowledge did not come pouring in during moments of illumination. This particular model has the advantage of tying the persons of the Trinity together more closely than do some other views."[83]

Scripture affirms the Spirit's role of supervision and supervenience not only in Jesus' adult life and ministry, but also during his childhood. Jesus was formed and informed by the Spirit throughout his development as a child and young adult to prepare him for his future ministry, relying on the Spirit as his private tutor and source of power so that he could transcend average human limitations.[84]

Conclusion: Jesus, Our Genuine Example

In this chapter a case has been made that our Lord Jesus Christ, in his common life with us, gave to believers of all time a *genuine model* for how to live beyond the limitations of an average human life. Contemporary Christians tend to give greater attention to Jesus' deity than his full humanity, thus tending toward a functionally docetic Christology. Without an appreciation of the predominant role of the Father and the Holy Spirit in Jesus' life, it is impossible to make sense of how Jesus can be our genuine example.

Specifically, I defended the view (called option 2 above) that Jesus predominantly depended on divine resources other than his own. Prior to his incarnation, Jesus voluntarily agreed to conceal to a great extent his

---

[82] Early in his life, Jesus developed a conversational relationship with the Spirit. For further guidance on what this can look like, see Klaus Issler, *Wasting Time with God: A Christian Spirituality of Friendship with God* (Downers Grove, IL: InterVarsity, 2001), chap. 6.

[83] Erickson, *The Word*, 559.

[84] As has been proposed, both the Father and the Spirit are involved in Jesus' life, yet in a unique role, the Holy Spirit working as the agent of the Father.

divine nature and powers to live mainly within his human powers and to rely predominantly on the tutelage and power of the Father and the Holy Spirit. Jesus was indwelt by and filled with the Spirit from his conception and birth onward, not just from his baptism.

The work of the Holy Spirit in Jesus' birth, growth, life, ministry, and death was significant, without which Jesus would not have succeeded and accomplished his mission. At the beginning of his sojourn Jesus, as a human infant, was unaware of his divine nature, as the consciousness of it was locked up in his divine mind or subconscious. He grew and learned as would any human of that day. Yet Jesus was formed and informed by the Father and the Spirit throughout his growth as a child and as a young adult in order to prepare him for his future ministry. Jesus relied on the Father and the Spirit as his private tutor and source of power in order to exceed average human limitations. Guided by the Father and the Spirit from his birth onward, during his childhood and young adult years and prior to his baptism Jesus became fully aware of his identity, unique Sonship with the Father, and his messianic mission. During Jesus' public ministry, he depended on the Father through the agency of the Holy Spirit and exercised a delegated authority from him for word and deed in his life and ministry.

Jesus lived within his humanity, remaining sinless, thereby qualifying himself to be our atoning sacrifice, and our sympathetic high priest. He performed miracles, knew the thoughts of others, and lived a sinless life by the power of the Holy Spirit. In a sermon to the Gentile Cornelius and his household, the apostle Peter offered a summary statement of the ministry of Jesus: "how God anointed Jesus of Nazareth with the Holy Spirit and with power; how he went about doing good and healing all who were oppressed by the devil, for God was with him" (Acts 10:38).

More work is required to tackle various remaining issues, yet the hope is that, if sufficient evidence has been marshaled to offer legitimacy to the proposal, it will serve as a catalyst for further discussion of these important matters, both for greater theological clarity and for greater empowerment in the church's life and ministry.[85] For, if Jesus is

---

[85] Shuster comments, "It will probably be evident that I do not hold anything resembling a thoroughly kenotic Christology. Obviously, the degree to which one does hold such a Christology will bear upon the extent to which one can reasonably take Jesus as a model.

our genuine example, then we are not limited to the current quality of our life and ministry—much more is possible! "This is how we know we are in him: Whoever claims to live in [God] must walk as Jesus did" (1 John 2:5b–6, NIV).[86]

For Further Reading

The following two studies provide a helpful introduction to the theme of the imitation of Christ. Tinsley offers a book-length treatment and is positively sympathetic to the subject. Also sympathetic, Hawthorne presents an analysis based on Philippians 2. Shuster's study offers a good overview of key issues, though is more cautious about the subject.

Tinsley, E. J. *The Imitation of God in Christ: An Essay on the Biblical Basis of Christian Spirituality*. Philadelphia: Westminster, 1960.

Hawthorne, Gerald. "The Imitation of Christ: Discipleship in Philippians." In *Patterns of Discipleship in the New Testament*, ed. Richard Longenecker. Grand Rapids: Eerdmans, 1996.

Shuster, Marguerite. "The Use and Misuse of the Idea of the Imitation of Christ." *Ex Auditu* 14 (1998): 70–81.

The following studies focus primarily on the human experience of Jesus himself. Ramsay's scope is the broadest, arguing that Jesus' own experience is the key to his teachings. Hawthorne and Smail look at Jesus' dependence on the Spirit. Wallis addresses Jesus' own experience of faith from the Gospels and includes a lengthy discussion of Paul's term *pistis Christou*.

Michaels, J. Ramsay. *Servant and Son: Jesus in Parable and Gospel*. Atlanta: John Knox, 1981.

But so will how one construes the relationship between the divine and the human in the incarnate Lord, including views of his sinlessness, divine consciousness, subjective experience of temptation, emotional life, and so on" (Shuster, "Use and Misuse," 80, n. 11). Because these matters are foundational to the concept of Jesus as our example, it is precisely these topics that need to be addressed, and a few have been treated in the present chapter.

[86] A preliminary study was presented at the 2003 annual meeting of the Evangelical Theological Society. I am grateful for comments in preparing that presentation and for those received in preparing this chapter.

Hawthorne, Gerald. *The Presence and the Power: The Significance of the Holy Spirit in the Life and Ministry of Jesus.* Dallas: Word, 1991; reprint, Eugene, OR: Wipf and Stock, 2003.

Smail, Thomas. *Reflected Glory: The Spirit in Christ and Christians.* Grand Rapids: Eerdmans, 1975.

Wallis, Ian. *The Faith of Jesus Christ in Early Christian Traditions*, SNTS 84. Cambridge: Cambridge University Press, 1995.

Study Questions

1. What biblical evidence is offered to support
   a. Jesus' full humanity?
   b. Jesus' full deity?
   c. Jesus is the Christian's example?
   d. Jesus' uniqueness from Christians, and Jesus' commonality with Christians?
2. How does the author resolve the tension expressed in "emptied himself"?
3. What are the major options for explaining Jesus' dependent lifestyle? What is the evidence for each view? What are the main objections for each view?
4. Summarize the argument and evidence for the author's claim that Jesus lived a predominantly dependent life on earth.

AXIOMS FOR CHRISTOLOGICAL STUDY

Chapter One (Sanders):

1. Christology is an interdisciplinary theological project requiring insight from biblical, historical, philosophical, practical, and systematic theologians.

2. To think rightly about the Trinity, the incarnation, or the atonement, the theologian must think about them all at once, in relation to each other.

3. The good news of Jesus the Savior presupposes the long story of the eternal Son of God's entering into human history, and the doctrinal categories provided by Chalcedon are a helpful conceptual resource for making sense of it.

Chapter Two (Horrell):

1. Speculations of trinitarian theology are not to supercede the metanarrative of divine revelation, particularly as revealed in Jesus Christ.

2. Ontological equality of the members of the Godhead and reciprocal indwelling of each in the other does not necessarily preclude eternal relational order among the Father, Son, and Holy Spirit.

3. Biblical revelation points beyond mere economy to transcendent relationality, such that a univocal correspondence of the economic and immanent Trinity cannot be affirmed.

Chapter Three (Fairbairn):

1. All doctrine should be intimately and clearly connected to soteriology.

2. Any Christology that purports to be biblical and consistent with the early Church must assert that the one person in Christ is God the Logos.

3. One must not treat a nature as if it were a person. Rather than stating that the human nature of Christ died on the cross, one must assert

that God the Son died on the cross through the human nature he had assumed into his own person.

Chapter Four (DeWeese):

1. Christ is one person with two natures; therefore, whatever goes with natures, Christ has two of, and whatever goes with persons, he has one of.
2. Attempts to explicate the Chalcedonian Definition do so from the standpoint of a particular metaphysics; the differences between medieval and contemporary metaphysics will result in different models of the incarnation.
3. Models of the incarnation are conceptual structures that aim at being faithful to biblical and orthodox theological claims and at rebutting of charges of incoherence or implausibility directed at the doctrine of the hypostatic union.

Chapter Five (Ware):

1. Jesus Christ cannot be understood in his person or his work without the Trinity. Without the Father and the Spirit, Jesus would not be who he is and could not have done what he did.
2. The person and work of Christ are based not merely on his being divine, but on his Sonship both in eternity and in history.
3. The identity of Jesus as Savior is inextricably tied to his being the Spirit-anointed Messiah, whose very Person requires the indwelling and empowering Spirit for him to be who he is and to accomplish what he has come to do.

Chapter Six (Issler):

1. Jesus is an example for all Christians.
2. What is unexemplified in Jesus' life cannot be an example for Christians.
3. Much of Jesus' mission on Earth was unique to him as the Messiah-King, yet what Christians can share in common with Jesus is the *manner* in which he lived and in which he carried out his mission.

ABBREVIATIONS

AB	Anchor Bible
ABR	*Australian Biblical Review*
ACO	*Acts conciliorum oecumenicorum.* Edited by Edward Schwartz. Berlin, 1914
BEC	Baker Exegetical Commentary
Brown.	4 vols. Grand Raids, 1975–1985.
CC	*Creeds of Christendom.* Edited by Phillip Schaff, 6th ed. 3 vols. New York, 1919. Repr., Grand Rapids, 1998
CCT	Contours of Christian Theology
Di	*Dialog: A Journal of Theology*
EBC	Expositor's Bible Commentary
ExA	*Ex Auditu*
FaCh	Fathers of the Church
FP	*Faith and Philosophy*
HeyJ	*Heythrop Journal*
HPQ	*History of Philosophy Quarterly*
IJST	*International Journal of Systematic Theology*
JBL	*Journal of Biblical Literature*
JEH	*Journal of Ecclesiastical History*
JETS	*Journal of the Evangelical Theological Society*
JTS	*Journal of Theological Studies*
LCC	Library of Christian Classics
LoF	Library of the Fathers of the Holy Catholic Church
LS	*Louvain Studies*
NAC	New American Commentary
NACSBT	NAC Studies in Bible and Theology
NCTS	New Century Theological Series
NIBC	New International Biblical Commentary
NICNT	New International Commentary on the New Testament
NIGTC	New International Greek Testament Commentary
NIVAC	NIV Application Commentary

NL	*Nicaea I to Lateran V*, vol. 1, *Decrees of the Ecumenical Councils*, ed. Norman P. Tanner. London: Sheed & Ward, 1990
NPNF¹	*Nicene and Post-Nicene Fathers, First Series*
NPNF²	*Nicene and Post-Nicene Fathers, Second Series*
NS	*The New Scholasticism*
NTS	*New Testament Studies*
OECS	Oxford Early Christian Studies
OECT	Oxford Early Christian Texts. Oxford, 1970–
PE	*Pro Ecclesia*
PG	Patrologia graeca
PRS	Perspectives in Religious Studies
RS	*Religious Studies*
RTR	*Reformed Theological Review*
SBLDS	Society of Biblical Literature Dissertation Series
SC	Sources Chrétiennes. Paris: Cerf, 1943–
SJT	*Scottish Journal of Theology*
SNTSMS	Society of New Testament Studies Monograph Series
SP	*Studia Patristica*
SVC	Supplements to Vigiliae Christianae
TDNT	*Theological Dictionary of the New Testament*. Edited by G. Kittel and G. Friedrich. Translated by G. W. Bromiley. 10 vols. Grand Rapids, 1964–1976
TJ	*Trinity Journal*
TS	*Theological Studies*
WBC	Word Biblical Commentary
WTJ	*Westminster Theological Journal*

CONTRIBUTORS

Fred Sanders (Ph.D., Graduate Theological Union, Berkeley, CA) is Assistant Professor of Theology in the Torrey Honors Institute at Biola University in La Mirada, California. He is the author of *The Image of the Immanent Trinity: Rahner's Rule and the Theological Interpretation of Scripture* (Peter Lang, 2005) and *Dr. Doctrine's Christian Comics* (InterVarsity, 1999).

Donald Fairbairn (Ph.D., University of Cambridge) is Professor of Historical Theology at Erskine Theological Seminary in Due West, South Carolina. He is the author of *Grace and Christology in the Early Church* (Oxford, 2003) and *Eastern Orthodoxy through Western Eyes* (Westminster John Knox, 2002).

Garrett J. DeWeese (Ph.D., University of Colorado) is Professor of Philosophy and Philosophical Theology at Talbot School of Theology in La Mirada, California. He is the author of *God and the Nature of Time* (Ashgate, 2003).

J. Scott Horrell (Th.D., Dallas Theological Seminary) is Professor of Systematic Theology at Dallas Theological Seminary. He is author of *From the Ground Up: New Testament Foundations for the 21st Century Church* (Kregel, 2005).

Bruce A. Ware (Ph.D., Fuller Theological Seminary) is Professor of Systematic Theology at Southern Baptist Theological Seminary in Louisville, Kentucky. He is author of *Father, Son, and Holy Spirit: Relationships, Roles, and Relevance* (Crossway, 2005), and *God's Greater Glory: The Exalted God of Scripture and the Christian Faith* (Crossway, 2004).

Klaus Issler (Ph.D. Michigan State Univerity) is Professor of Christian Education and Theology at Talbot School of Theology in La Mirada, California. He is the author of *Wasting Time with God: A Christian Spirituality of Friendship with God* (InterVarsity, 2001).

NAME INDEX

A

Acacius of Melitene 98
Adams, Marilyn 125
Agatho 149
Allison, C. FitzSimon 22, 23
Alston, William 120
Anselm 156, 157, 158, 201
Apollinarius of Laodicea 19, 147
Aquinas. *See* Thomas Aquinas
Aristotle 50, 120, 126
Athanasius 153
Attridge, Harold 206, 207
Augustine 51, 52, 61, 67, 69, 71,
 112, 168, 169, 170
Ayres, Lewis 19

B

Badcock, Gary 209
Balthasar, Hans Urs von 68, 73, 190
Barbour, Ian 117
Barry, William 203
Bartel, T. W. 55
Barth, Karl 30, 34, 54, 59, 61, 67
Basil of Caesarea 50, 60, 71
Beasley-Murray, George R. 204, 208,
 209, 210
Behr, John 19
Beilby, James K. 177
Benedict XVI 51
Betz, H. D. 196
Bobrinskoy, Boris 173
Bock, Darrell 218, 219
Boethius 125
Boff, Leonardo 54
Bowden, John 54
Bray, Gerald 18, 41
Bromiley, Geoffrey W. 54, 62, 230
Bruce, A. B. 188, 221
Buswell, J. Oliver 62, 136

C

Calvin, John 56, 200
Carson, D. A. 210
Chrysostom, John 87, 89, 90, 91, 93
Ciocchi 143
Coakley, Sarah 55, 121, 137
Colle, Ralph Del 213
Constans II 123
Constantine IV 123
Constantinople II 26
Cowan, Christopher 164
Craig, William Lane 59, 62, 68, 128,
 130, 137, 145, 146, 147, 151,
 152, 200, 208
Cross, Richard 55, 125, 153
Cyril of Alexandria 2, 21, 28, 37,
 51, 80, 82, 87, 90, 93, 94, 96, 97,
 98, 100, 101, 103, 106, 107, 112,
 113, 120, 148

D

D'Costa, Gavin 68
Daley, Brian 26, 27, 29, 124
Daley, Brian E. 30
Davidson, Ivor 35
Davis, Leo Donald 17, 18, 40, 78,
 121, 124, 126, 153
Davis, Stephen T. 55, 120, 137, 194
Demarest, Bruce A. 136
DeWeese, Garrett J. 217
Dibelius, Martin 196
Diodore of Tarsus 87, 91
Dowd, Sharyn 207
Due, William J. La 54
Dulles, Avery Cardinal 61
Dunn, James D. G. 203, 213, 218

E

Ebrard 145
Eddy, Paul R. 177
Edgar, Brian 49

Ellis, Earl E. 219
Erickson, Millard J. 48, 54, 61, 62, 128, 129, 137, 145, 153, 192, 194, 200, 222
Eustathius of Antioch 87, 88

F

Fairbairn, Donald 93, 111, 141
Farley, Edward 9
Farrow, Douglas 35
Feinberg, John 48, 62
Feinberg, Paul 202, 203
Ferguson, Sinclair B. 220
Ferrara, Dennis M. 30, 32, 33
Fish, John H. III 49
Flint, Thomas P. 126, 128
Forsyth 145
Forte, Bruno 63
Frame, John M. 117
France, R. T. 195
Frank, G. L. C. 28
Freddoso, Alfred J. 120, 126, 128, 129, 130

G

Gathercole, Simon J. 165, 166
Gavrilyuk, Paul 107, 111
Gess, W. F. 201
Giles, Kevin 61, 68, 70, 72, 169, 170, 195, 196
Gomes, Alan 147, 152
Gregory of Nazianzus 20, 50, 58, 60, 71, 124, 133, 148, 153, 209
Gregory of Nyssa 50, 51, 71, 153
Gregory the Great 17
Grenz, Stanley J. 54, 55, 74, 78, 147, 163
Grillmeier, Aloys 40
Grobel, Kendrick 219
Grudem, Wayne 68, 163, 169, 194, 200
Gruenler, Gordon 48
Gunton, Colin E. 52, 54, 170

H

Haberman, David L. 143
Hagner, Donald 206, 211
Hamilton, James M. 173, 187
Hanson, A. T. 132
Hanson, R. P. C. 133
Hardy, Edward R. 20, 124, 153
Harnack, Adolf von 5, 122
Harrison, Verna 59
Hawthorne, Gerald F. 173, 185, 187, 195, 198, 203, 213, 219, 224, 225
Hay, Camillus 90
Hays, Richard 194, 208
Hellerman, Joseph 198, 199
Heraclitus, Emperor 123
Hick, John 7, 116
Hilary of Poitiers 167, 168
Hipp, Stephen A. 52
Hodgson, Leonard 54
Hoffman, Joshua 119, 143
Honorius I 123
Hooker, Morna 198
Hopko, Thomas 50
Hughes, Christopher 128
Humphreys, Fisher 55

I

Ice, Laura M. 48
Issler, Klaus 152, 179, 221, 222

J

Jenson, Robert W. 54, 55, 61, 63, 71, 74, 166
John of Antioch 87, 89, 90, 91, 93, 98
John of Damascus 30, 31, 58, 59, 124
John Paul II 51
Johnson, Elizabeth A. 68
Johnson, Luke T. 194
Jüngel, Eberhard 63
Justinian 27

K

Kasper, Walter 34
Keener, Craig S. 68, 208

Kempis, Thomas à 194
Kendall, Daniel 78, 120, 153, 194
Knight, George A. F. 48
Kohl, Margaret 52

L

L'Huillier, Peter 18
LaCugna, Catherine 54
Lage, Dietmar 197
Lane, William L. 206, 211, 212, 219
Lang, U. M. 30
Leftow, Brian 55
Leontius of Byzantium 30, 149
Leontius of Jerusalem 30, 33
Leo the Great 105
Letham, Robert 49, 72, 73, 78
Lewis, Gordon 136
Lombard, Peter 61
Longenecker, Richard 195
Lossky, Vladimir 53
Loux, Michael J. 120
Luther, Martin 196, 197

M

Mackintosh, H. R. 34
Macleod, Donald 134, 147, 200, 220
Macmurray, John 54
Macquarrie, John 121, 132
Marenbon, John 119
Marshall, I. Howard 201
Martin, Ralph 198
Masaccio 77
Maximus the Confessor 58, 123
McCormack, Bruce 34
McCready, Douglas 35
McGrath, Alister 107, 108, 197
McKinley, John 150, 213
Menzies, Robert 213
Merricks, Trenton 132
Meyendorff, John 40, 112, 124
Michaelis, Wilhelm 196
Michaels, J. Ramsey 224
Molnar, Paul 163
Moltmann, Jürgen 52, 54, 58, 63, 77, 79

Moo, Douglas 208, 217
Moreland, J. P. 59, 62, 137, 139, 141, 143, 145, 151, 152
Morris, Leon 199, 200
Morris, Thomas 131, 132, 135, 142, 143, 145, 146, 201, 216, 222
Müller, Richard 137

N

Nachef, Antoine E. 51
Nazianzen, Gregory 50
Nestorius 87, 89, 90, 91, 92, 96, 101, 106
Newman, John Henry 6
Nolland, John 211
Norris, Richard A. 121

O

O'Carroll, Michael 59, 77, 78
O'Collins, Gerald 48, 55, 71, 72, 78, 120, 131, 137, 153, 194, 206, 207, 215, 216
O'Keefe, John J. 112
Oden, Thomas 191
Olson, Robert 86, 87
Origen 50, 88
Ouellet, Marc Cardinal 55
Owen, John 61

P

Packer, J. I. 6
Pannenberg, Wolfhart 54, 62, 63, 66, 74
Pasnau, Robert 143
Peters, Ted 54, 63, 74
Pfleiderer, Georg 158
Photinus 168
Plantinga, Cornelius Jr. 54
Pope John Paul II 51
Pyrrhus 123

R

Rahner, Karl 48, 49, 59, 72, 74, 133, 134, 163, 231
Ramm, Bernard 192
Ratcliff, Donald 221

Rosenkrantz, Gary 119, 143
Rublev, Andrei 77

S

Sabellius 168
Sanders, Fred vi, 1, 48, 54, 63, 116, 117, 152, 163, 226, 231
Saucy, Robert 141, 147, 149, 152
Schleiermacher, Friedrich 54
Schneider, Gerd 218
Schreiner, Thomas R. 166, 177
Schulz, A. 196
Schwöbel, Christoph 26
Scotus, John Duns 126, 128, 129, 153
Seamands, Stephen 55
Sellers, Richard V. 87
Senor, Thomas 135
Sergius of Constantinople 123
Sheldon, Charles 194
Sherman, Robert 158
Shults, F. LeRon 30, 55
Shuster, Marguerite 195, 197, 223, 224
Smail, Tom 55, 224, 225
Stevenson, Leslie 143
Stott, John R. W. 187
Strong, A. H. 135, 136, 144, 201
Stronstad, Roger 213
Stump, Eleonore 126, 135
Sturch, Richard 132, 137, 143, 145, 146, 147
Swinburne, Richard 54, 60, 118, 119, 132, 133, 135, 138, 141

T

Tanner, Norman P. 28, 29, 34
Tertullian 52
Theodore of Mopsuestia 27, 87, 88, 89, 90, 91, 93, 93–94, 96, 103

Theodoret of Cyrus 87, 88, 89, 90, 91, 107
Theodosius 19
Thiemann, Ronald F. 158
Thomas Aquinas 51, 52, 71, 125, 126, 128, 129, 135, 143, 153, 205, 206
Thomasius, Gottfried 145, 201
Thompson, John 161
Tinsley, E. J. 195, 197, 224
Toon, Peter 18, 41, 48
Torrance, Thomas F. 112
Torrey, R. A. 191, 231
Turner, Max 213, 218

V

van Inwagen, Peter 135
Volf, Miroslav 46, 54, 55, 78, 158

W

Wainwright, Arthur W. 48
Wainwright, Geoffrey 159, 160
Wallace, Daniel 208
Wallis, Ian 207, 225
Walvoord, John 202
Ware, Bruce A. 49, 55, 152, 188
Welker, Michael 46, 55, 78, 158
Wendebourg, Dorothea 22
Wesley, Charles 14, 15, 16
Wickham, Lionel 82, 97, 101, 112
Wierenga, Edward R. 143
Willard, Dallas 195, 221
William of Ockham 119, 126, 128
Witherington, Ben III 48, 200, 201

Y

Young, Frances M. 88

Z

Zagzebski, Linda 194
Zizioulas, John D. 54, 60

SUBJECT INDEX

A

Adam and Christ 192
akoloutheo 196
Alexandria, school of 82, 86–88,
　94–106
analytic philosophy of religion 38
anathema 18, 20, 22, 34
anhypostatic/enhypostatic 31, 35
Antioch, school of 81, 86–92
Apollinarianism 18, 19–20, 34, 146
archeµgos 207
Arianism 18, 18–20
Athanasian Creed ix
atonement 106–110, 157–188

B

begottenness 62, 64, 66, 71
belief 139

C

Cappadocians 52, 61, 112
Chalcedon. *See* Council of Chalcedon
Chalcedonian Definition 4, 192
and the Bible 25, 83
categories of 13–35
and contemporary theology 84
Cyril on 104–106
and Later Christology 13–35
text of 104–105
childhood of Jesus 217–222
Christology
task of 13–22
Christotokos 21, 97
conformitas Christi 196
consciousness 138
Constantinople. *See* Council of Con-
　stantinople
Council of Chalcedon 22–24,
　123–124
Council of Chalcedon III
and Ephesus 32

Council of Constantinople 1 19–21
Council of Constantinople II 7, 26,
　33
Council of Constantinople III 27–34,
　131, 135, 135–137
Council of Ephesus 21–22
Council of Nicaea I 18
Council of Nicaea II 3
Creator, Christ as agent of 167
Cyrillian Chalcedonianism 28
Cyrillian Christology 94–106

D

desire 139
dyophysites/diphysitism 28
dyothelite model 12, 123–135, 146,
　149–150

E

egalitarian trinitarianism 62, 70–73
enhypostatic 31
epistemic possibility 216
Eutychianism 18, 22
example
Jesus as 191, 195–199, 222–224
exorcism 210–211

F

Father 160–161
fons divinitatis 65

G

generation 61

H

Holy Spirit
and atonement 179–186
and conversion 185–186
and the identity of Jesus 171–174
Jesus' dependence on 201, 208–213,
　213–222, 220–222
procession of 61, 64

237

homoousios 18, 49
honor 198
Hooker, Morna 198
humanity of Jesus 213–222
humiliation, state of 200
humility 197, 198
hypostasis 12, 19, 31, 47, 52–53, 103
hypostatic union 22, 32

I

image of God 192
imitatio Christi 194–199, 196
imitation. *See imitatio Christi*
impeccability 179, 215–217
incarnation
omniscience and 213
indwelling 214

J

John the Baptist 217–218

K

kenosis 183–184, 198–208, 200
kenoticism, radical 146–147

L

levels of analysis in Christology 193
Logos 18, 21, 50, 101–103, 144
lordship 66
Lutheran scholastics 119

M

Mary, the virgin 23
mediator 193
metanarrative 68
metaphysical models 116
metaphysical possibility 216
mimeomai 196
mind 117
miracles of Jesus 214
modalism 59
model. *See* example
monarchia 69
monohpysitism 123–124
monothelite Christology 144

N

nature 49–52, 52–53, 74, 81, 117,
141–144. *See also* two natures
neomonothelite Christology 144
Neoplatonism 121–122
Nestorianism 18, 21, 22–23, 27, 93,
96
Nicaea. *See* Council of Nicaea
Nicene Creed 4, 19, 46
Niceno-Constantinopolitan Creed 47

O

obedience 194
omnipotence and the incarnation
201–205, 202
omniscience and the incarnation 183,
199
ontology 48, 61
origin 60, 71
ousia 19, 47, 52, 71, 120

P

penal substitution 177
perichoresis 45, 51, 53, 58, 59, 60
person 12, 29, 32, 52–53, 74, 81,
83–84, 117, 138–141. *See
also* persona, prosopon
persona 47, 52–53
physis 120
pistis Christou 205–208
procession 61, 62, 64, 71, 168
properties 142
prosopon 83, 104, 105, 106, 118, 137
psyche 118

Q

Quicunque vult ix

R

reduplicative strategy 201
relationality 139

S

sanctification 192
satisfaction 177

Subject Index

Second Adam 193, 217
self-awareness of Jesus 199–200
self-consciousness 139
sensation 138
sinlessness. *See* impeccability
sin nature 217
social trinitarianism 53–59
soul 121
source 51–52, 65
spirit 121
subordination 61, 167–171
subordinationism 72–73
substance 119–120
substantia 47

T

taxis 37, 61, 62, 67, 166, 169–171, 170
temptations of Jesus 215–216
theology
disciplines of 9–13
task of 6
Theotokos 21, 97, 98
Thirty-nine Articles of Religion 17

thought 138
Three Chapters 27
Trinity
and atonement 158
becoming in time 62–63
and Christology 6–8
economic 47, 163
eternal order within 60–75
gender and 68, 69–70, 160–161
immanent 47, 62, 163
intratrinitarian relationships 57
polemics and 70–73
social model of 47
tritheism 59
two natures 20, 20–35, 22, 99, 117
and reduplicative strategy 201

V

vocabulary 118–121, 137–144
vocation of Jesus 198, 209
volition 139

W

will 118

SCRIPTURE INDEX

Genesis
1   167
1:31   216

Exodus
8:19   210
15:9   141

Leviticus
19:2   204

Deuteronomy
6:4   209
9:10   210
18:15   193
23:24   141

1 Samuel
2:26   218
3:1–21   221
28   88

2 Kings
4:8–37   215
4:42–44   215
5:1–15   215
6:4–7   215

Psalms
2   161, 162
2:2   161
2:4   161
2:5–6   161
2:6–9   160
2:7   64, 162
2:7–9   162
8:3 210
17:9   141
22:1   178
22:19–31   178
33:6   67
42:1,2   141

51:11–12   212
63:1   141
119:20   141

Proverbs
21:10   141
25:25   141

Isaiah
11:1–2   179, 180,
    208
11:1–3   220
11:1–9   173
11:2   180, 218, 219
31:1   212
42:1   208, 212, 219,
    220
42:1–9   173
43:10c–11   56
50:4–5   220
53:10   175
61:1   212
61:1–2   181
61:1–3   173, 208

Jeremiah
12:7   141
26 Ezek
36:25–27   216
36:26–27   185

Daniel
2:1–49   215
7:13–14   162

Malachi
1:6   160

Matthew
1:18–25   208
1:20   208, 217
3:11   219
3:16   210
3:17   64, 130

4:1   210
4:1–11   192, 215
4:2   192
5:43–48   204
6:9   205
6:30   207
7:29   213
8:26   207
9:6   63, 213
11:3–5   215
11:20–22   213
11:27   63, 165, 193
11:29   195
12:25   215
12:28   173, 202,
    203, 208, 210
12:31   56
12:32   210
13:36   210
13:54   213
13:57   213
14:2   213
14:28–30   215
16:8   207
16:13–17   171, 173
16:14   213
16:16   130, 215
16:23   215
17:5   64, 130
17:17   192
17:19   210
20:25–28   196
20:28   195
21:11,46   213
21:23–34,27   213
22:42–45   215
23:31–38   213
24:36   199
25:35   192
26:27–28   64
26:37   192

26:38–46   215
26:39   150, 153
26:39–40   63
26:41   210, 212
26:68   213
27:46   177, 178
28:9,16   215
28:18   63, 165
28:19   68, 165, 166,
    193
28:20   7

Mark
1:7   219
1:8–13   208
1:10   210
1:11   64
1:12   210
1:22   213
1:27   213
1:35   165
1:41   151
2:10   213
2:12   213
3:5   192
5:30   210, 211, 213
6:2   213
6:3 192
6:4   213
6:15–16   213
6:34   192
8:28   213
9   214
9:23   207
9:24   214
10:27   221
10:45   193, 195, 215
11:13   200
11:22–25   214
11:28–29,33   213
13:32   165, 183, 199
14:38   210, 212
14:65   213
15:21   199

Luke
1:5–25,57–80   218
1:15   218
1:15,17   217
1:26–56   218
1:30–35   172
1:31–33   63
1:33   66
1:35   173, 208, 217,
    218
1:36–38   208
1:80   218
1–4   209
2:1–52   218
2:11   215
2:40   218, 219
2:40,52   182, 220
2:41–51   219
2:46–47   218
2:47   218
2:49   218
2:52   220
3:22   64, 210, 211,
    218
4:1   208, 210
4:1,14   173
4:1,14,18–19   211
4:1–2   181
4:14   181, 191, 211
4:14,36   213
4:14–18   202, 203
4:16   208
4:16–21   172, 208,
    215
4:18   202, 219
4:18–19   181
4:21   181
4:24   213
4:32   213
4:36   213
4:41   215
5:17   210, 211, 213
5:24   213
6:19   211
6:36   204

7:8   166
7:16,39   213
8:44   211
8:46   213
9:8–9   213
9:19   213
9:35   64
10:21   64, 210
10:22   63, 165
11:13   64
11:17   215
11:20   208, 210
11:31   219
11:47–51   213
13:33   193, 213
18:17   220
19:41   192
20:2,8   213
22:27   196
22:44   215, 217
23:34   178
23:46   64, 179
24:19   213

John
1 167, 209
1:1   193
1:1,18   215
1:3 67, 167
1:13   95
1:14   193
1:15,27,30   219
1:18   57
1:29   175, 178
1:31–34   172
1:32–33   57
2:11   204
3   209
3:3–8   185
3:5–8   57
3:6   212
3:7–8   57
3:11,32   57
3:16   64, 74, 208
3:16–17   164

3:17   159
3:20–21   185
3:32,34   57
3:34   57, 208, 210, 214
3:35   63
3:36   214
3:55   57
4:6   192
4:10–14   58
4:25–26   193
5:17,22,26   57
5:18   68
5:19   205
5:19,29,37   57
5:19–20   57
5:20   57
5:23   58
5:23–24,37–38   64
5:26   63
5:30   58, 205
5:30,37   57
5:31   64
5:36   63
5:36–37   57
6:37–39   64
6:38   57, 160, 164
6:38–39   64
6:38–42,50–51   64
6:46   57
6:63   212
7:17   57
7:28–29   57, 205
7:28–33   64
7:37–39   58
7:39   57, 214
8:12   196
8:16–18   64
8:17   57
8:26   57
8:26–29   176
8:28–29.42   205
8:29   58
8:38   57
8:39,42   64

8:42   164
8:50,54   58
8:55   57
8:58   56
8:58–59   215
10:15   57
10:17–18   58
10:27   196
10:27–30   64
10:29   64
10:30   56
10:36   165
10:38   58
11:41   57
12:26   58
12:27–28   57
12:44–45,49   64
12:49   63
12:49–50   57, 205
13:3 63
13:6   151
13:12–17   214
13:14,15,34   195
13:15   194, 195, 196
13:31–32   58
13:32   58
14:3 57
14:8–10   193
14:8–12   58
14:9   215
14:10   57
14:10,26,31   205
14:10–11   191
14:12   58
14:12–14   214
14:14   205
14:14,16   64
14:16   56, 58, 214, 216
14:16,26   57
14:20   56, 58
14:26   57, 165
15:5   205
15:7,16   205
15:9   57

15:9–10,15   205
15:12   195
15:26   57, 165
15:27–30   64
16:5,7   64
16:7   57, 214
16:7–11,13   57
16:8–15   57
16:14   58, 64
16:23   205
16:32   205
17:1,4   58
17:1,5,22,24   58
17:1,22,24   58
17:2   63
17:4   56
17:5   65, 200, 204
17:6,26   57
17:6–12   64
17:8,18   205
17:11,21–23   58
17:11–12   63
17:14,16   196
17:18–19   94
17:21–25   64
17:22   64
17:23–26   57
17:24   64
17:25   57
18:6   204
18:9   64
18:11   64
18:33–37   193
18:37   57
18:38   64
19:7   100
19:17   199
19:30–34   192
20:21   64, 196
20:22   57, 58
20:28   215

Acts
1:2   208, 210
1:8   182

2:23   175
2:33   165
2:38   148
3:1–10   215
3:15   206
3:16   207
3:22   193
4:33   218, 219
5:1–11   215
9:5   56
9:31   56
9:36–42   215
10:20   56
10:36–38   173
10:38   173, 182, 190, 191, 223
13:2   56
13:33   64
13:34   63
19:11–12   215
20:21   208
20:28   14, 102
22:3 219
26:18   185
45 Rom
3:21–26   193
3:22,26   207
3:22–26   208
3:23–26   177
3:25   177
5:12–21   192
5:14   193
6:6,10–12,18   217
6:6–7,11–12,18   216
6:11   195
7:14–25   217
8:6–8   186
8:9   57
8:11,14–17   64
8:14   56, 190
8:15–16   218
8:17,28–30   216
8:17,29   196
8:29   204
8:32   175

8:34   193
15:3,7   195

1 Corinthians
2:10–13   57, 58
2:11–13   57
4:16   196
6:19   56
8:4–7   68
8:6   167
10:13   216, 217
11:1   196
11:3 68, 75, 163, 164
11:23–24   64
12:11   57
15   67
15:20–22   192
15:24   64
15:24–28   66
15:25–28   170
15:27–28   160
15:45   193
15:45–49   217
15:50–57   216

2 Corinthians
1:5   195
4:4   185, 186
4:6   185, 186
4:13   207
5:21   176, 177, 178
8:9   196, 200
10:1   196

Galatians
2:16   207
4:6   57, 218
5:16   217
5:22–23   180

Ephesians
1 175
1:3–14   68
1:4   174
1:5   174
1:6–8,12,14   175

1:7   175
1:9–12   175
2:1   185, 186
2:8–9   186
2:18   57
3:12   207
3:14   205
4:10   200
4:17–24   197
4:24   204
4:32   195
5:1   204
5:2,25,29   195
6:12   217

Philippians
2   198
2:4–11   195
2:5   146
2:5–11   89, 198, 199
2:6–8   100
2:7   200
2:8   176
2:9–11   63
2:12–13   197
3:9   207
3:10–11   196
3:17   196

Colossians
1:4   208
1:12   167
1:12–14   175
1:16   67, 175
1:20   175
1:24   196
3:13   195
3:15–17   205

1 Thessalonians
1:6   196

2 Thessalonians
3:7–9   196

1 Timothy
1:16   195, 196

2:5   193, 194

Hebrews
1:1–3   159
1:3 67, 76
1:5   64
2:8   206
2:10–17   193
2:11   193
2:12–18   151
2:13   206
2:14–15   193
2:14–17   191
2:17   201
2:18   199, 215
4:15   192, 195, 199,
    215, 221
4:15–16   193
4:16   151
5:5   64
5:7–9   200
5:8   184
5:8–10   193
5:9   184
6:20   207
7:17   193

8:6   193
9:14   184, 210, 212
12:1–6   195
12:2   184, 191, 205,
    206
12:2–3   151
12:3–4   216, 217
12:4   215

James
1:13   192, 215
1:17   63
3:15,17   219

1 Peter
1:15–16   204
1:20–21   166
2:21   193
2:21–22   182
2:21–23   195
4:1   195
5:3 196

2 Peter
1:17   56
1:17,18   64

1 John
1:7   196
1:8–9   217
2:5–6   224
2:6   195
2:15–17   217
3:3 196
3:3,16   195
3:23   208

Revelation
1:1   64
1:5–6   65
1:8   56
1:17   56
14:12   207
17:14   193
19   162
19:13   162
19:16   162
21:4,27   216
22:4–5   204
22:13,16   56
22:17   67

CPSIA information can be obtained
at www.ICGtesting.com
Printed in the USA
LVOW12s2226271017
553933LV00003B/21/P